The Trade and Culture Debate

The Trade and Culture Debate

Evidence from US Trade Agreements

Gilbert Gagné

Foreword by Christian Deblock

LEXINGTON BOOKS
Lanham • Boulder • New York • London

Published by Lexington Books
An imprint of The Rowman & Littlefield Publishing Group, Inc.
4501 Forbes Boulevard, Suite 200, Lanham, Maryland 20706
www.rowman.com

Unit A, Whitacre Mews, 26-34 Stannary Street, London SE11 4AB

British Library Cataloguing in Publication Information Available

Library of Congress Cataloging-in-Publication Data Available
ISBN: 978-1-4985-2190-1 (cloth : alk. paper)
ISBN: 978-1-4985-2191-8 (electronic)

∞™ The paper used in this publication meets the minimum requirements of American National Standard for Information Sciences Permanence of Paper for Printed Library Materials, ANSI/NISO Z39.48-1992.

Printed in the United States of America

To Rita, Gilles, Vickie, Maude, and Bruno

Contents

List of Tables

List of Abbreviations

APEC	Asia-Pacific Economic Cooperation
AU	Australia
BH	Bahrain
BIT	Bilateral investment treaty
CA	Canada
CAFTA	United States—Central America Free Trade Agreement
CAFTA-DR	Dominican Republic—Central America—United States Free Trade Agreement
CDCE	Convention on the Preservation and Promotion of the Diversity of Cultural Expressions
CEO	Chief executive officer
CETA	Comprehensive Economic and Trade Agreement
CL	Chile
CO	Colombia
CR	Costa Rica
CREATE	Culture Research Education and Training Enterprise
DBS	Direct broadcasting satellite
DMB	Digital multimedia broadcasting
DR	Dominican Republic
DRFTA	United States—Dominican Republic Free Trade Agreement
DTH	Direct-to-home
ES	El Salvador
EU	European Union
FCC	Federal Communications Commission
FDI	Foreign direct investment
FTA	Free trade agreement

FTAA	Free Trade Area of the Americas
GATS	General Agreement on Trade in Services
GATT	General Agreement on Tariffs and Trade
GDP	Gross domestic product
GU	Guatemala
HO	Honduras
ICANN	Internet Corporation for Assigned Names and Numbers
IFAC-3	Industry Functional Advisory Committee on Intellectual Property Rights for Trade Policy Matters
IFAC-4	Industry Functional Advisory Committee on Electronic Commerce
IIPA	International Intellectual Property Alliance
ISAC-13	Industry Sector Advisory Committee on Services for Trade Policy Matters
ISP	Internet service provider
ITAC-8	Industry Trade Advisory Committee for Information and Communications Technologies, Services and Electronic Commerce
ITAC-10	Industry Trade Advisory Committee on Services and Finance Industries
ITAC-15	Industry Trade Advisory Committee on Intellectual Property Rights
KR	Korea
MEFTA	Middle East Free Trade Area
MFN	Most-favored-nation
MO	Morocco
MPAA	Motion Picture Association of America
MX	Mexico
NAFTA	North American Free Trade Agreement
NI	Nicaragua
OM	Oman
PA	Panama
PE	Peru
PTA	Preferential trade agreement

SAGIT	Cultural Industries Sectoral Advisory Group on International Trade
SG	Singapore
TIFA	Trade and Investment Framework Agreement
TiSA	Trade in Services Agreement
TPA	Trade Promotion Authority
TPP	Trans-Pacific Partnership
TRIMs	Agreement on Trade-Related Investment Measures
TTIP	Transatlantic Trade and Investment Partnership
UN	United Nations
UN CPC	United Nations (Provisional) Central Product Classification
UNESCO	United Nations Educational, Scientific and Cultural Organization
US	United States
USTR	Office of the United States Trade Representative
US-Australia FTA	United States—Australia Free Trade Agreement
US-Bahrain FTA	United States—Bahrain Free Trade Agreement
US-Canada FTA	United States—Canada Free Trade Agreement
US-Chile FTA	United States—Chile Free Trade Agreement
US-Colombia FTA	United States—Colombia Trade Promotion Agreement
US-Israel FTA	United States—Israel Free Trade Agreement
US-Jordan FTA	United States—Jordan Free Trade Agreement
US-Korea FTA	United States—Korea Free Trade Agreement
US-Morocco FTA	United States—Morocco Free Trade Agreement
US-Oman FTA	United States—Oman Free Trade Agreement
US-Panama FTA	United States—Panama Trade Promotion Agreement
US-Peru FTA	United States—Peru Trade Promotion Agreement
US-Singapore FTA	United States—Singapore Free Trade Agreement
WTO	World Trade Organization

Acknowledgments

I wish to thank an anonymous reviewer for constructive comments and helpful suggestions on a previous draft of the manuscript. I am also grateful to the staff at Lexington Books, who have been very supportive of the project leading to the publication of this monograph.

Gilbert Gagné

Foreword

Christian Deblock

American trade policy is most of the time misunderstood. Few specialists exist and too often, analyses in this area navigate between easy shortcuts and conspiracy theories. This is especially true where contentious issues are concerned, such as intellectual property, investment, labor standards or the one making up the topic of this book, culture. Far from giving in to simplistic interpretations, Gilbert Gagné masterfully demonstrates that it is possible to carry out a meticulous analysis of American positions on the debate surrounding culture and provisions pertaining to cultural products contained in trade agreements. His critical perspective will appeal to specialists as well as to students or concerned citizens. Plainly put, the book he has crafted is not only the most complete to have been written on the subject: Its fluid style and clear, accessible exposition of the complex issues involved also make it a pleasure to read.

At least in principle, culture and trade refer to different fields. Nonetheless, they converge in what have come to be called "cultural products." Should these be treated like any other product, or must they be granted special treatment? The answer might be simple if the issues involved were not multiple and contradictory. First, there are economic issues. Culture is an extremely lucrative sector, which has undergone phenomenal development with the digital revolution and the upheaval of its methods of dissemination. There are also political issues. Although we may speak of cultural industries, culture will never really be a "product" like others. It touches upon too many areas of our collective existence to be reduced to a purely mercantile dimension. Finally, there are commercial issues. If special treatment is to be given to cultural products, to what extent can exceptions be made without calling into question the principle of non-discrimination that guides contemporary international trade, and without giving in to protectionism under pretext of defending national cultures? It is obvious that the stakes are many and high, fully justifying the great caution with which the UNESCO Convention on the Diversity of Cultural Expressions was negotiated. However, not all countries share this caution, nor do they wish to treat culture differently from other products. Amongst these countries, and not least, is the United States.

Little inclined towards compromises, especially with regard to opening markets and paving the way for others to follow, the United States has always held a somewhat radical position in the matter of culture. While the United States is admittedly the planet's largest producer and exporter of cultural goods, there is more to it than that. Culture is also an instrument of power. Difficult to grasp, "soft" according to some, it nonetheless raises the issue of the influence that certain media can exercise on our collective lives, even our private ones. Be it in cinema, radio, music, or yet, as in Canada, in the field of publicity, this debate appeared early on, and consequently, many states have developed instruments to defend their culture and their cultural industries. Cultural policy was long treated as a "natural" mission of the state, a stance which has never truly been contested. But with the general liberalization of trade beginning in the 1980s, the debate on culture took a completely different turn. Since then, the protection of culture is no longer treated as a matter of principle, but as a reasonable exception to the general principle of competition. Thus, the debate on the specific nature of cultural products and the extent to which they should be granted exceptions came out in the open, crystallizing positions in the multilateral negotiations on services, in particular when the time came to address the audiovisual domain. While this debate eventually came to a standstill, it remained open. Indeed, although the United States maintained its stand on free trade, turning down any idea of cultural exemption, the chosen method of negotiations on services allowed countries to limit their levels of engagement, to exclude sensitive topics from negotiation, and thus to keep the upper hand on the main instruments of their cultural policies. This resulted in much frustration on all sides. At the heart of the dispute: the very principle of exemption.

With trade negotiations now extending beyond services to encompass areas like intellectual property, investment, and even public markets, all areas that inevitably converge with cultural policy, how indeed should culture be defended? Also, how could it be seriously defended within trade negotiations once it was demoted to the status of mere exception? Thus, rather than allowing themselves to be confined in this manner, the defenders of cultural identity, led by Canada and France, turned towards UNESCO to promote a different concept: cultural diversity. Far more attractive than that of cultural exception or exemption, the concept of cultural diversity would rally countries more easily and, despite fierce opposition from the United States, lead to the adoption in 2005 of a new international legal instrument, the *Convention on the Protection and Promotion of the Diversity of Cultural Expressions*. All this would seriously annoy the United States. Admittedly, the Uruguay Round, protracted and painful, was finally concluded with a series of major agreements, including one on intellectual property and one on services, the *General Agreement on Trade in Services*. However, the more litigious issues, notably on investment, had been set aside, and negotiations on services, taking on a far different tone from the one used until then, were difficult, as is clearly reflected in the final text. There were many loopholes and, in the end, the final result fell far short of initial ambitions. As for the UNESCO Convention, it reaffirmed the importance attached to culture by the international community and brought new legitimacy to cultural policies. The United States would respond through bilateralism and trade agreements, an avenue that had served it well with the *North American Free Trade Agreement* (NAFTA) and which now gave it the possibility of circumventing the UNESCO Convention and opening markets more quickly and extensively than at the World Trade Organization (WTO).

For a time, all the parties were to find satisfaction in the directions taken. The United States, followed by many other countries, multiplied bilateral negotiations, whilst the defenders of cultural identity, supported by coalitions for cultural diversity, now had a legal instrument with which to uphold their cultural policies and justify their reservations in international trade agreements. Today, once again, the tides have shifted. New information and communication technologies have not only disrupted our consumption habits, they have radically transformed our relationship to culture and to cultural industries. Business models have also been affected, as is evident in the phenomenal expansion of electronic trade, or e-commerce, and in the appearance of new methods of organization, operating in ever more interconnected networks. In plain, with digital technology, nothing is as it was before. In these conditions, what about the Convention on Cultural Diversity? But also, what about the American strategy?

Gilbert Gagné revisits these debates in detail, and the way in which digital technology has profoundly changed their terms. More importantly, he shows how American positions, far from being static, have, to the contrary, never ceased to evolve under the influence of interest groups and their associations (often clustered together), but also under the impetus of economic and technological change. This is perhaps the most striking element: In the course of agreements it has concluded over the years, American trade policy has shown an extraordinary capacity to adapt. Thus, instead of remaining entangled in the intricacies of the WTO, the United States effectively took the debate on services out of the multilateral framework and engaged a large coalition of countries (fifty) in a large-scale negotiation on services, the *Trade in Services Agreement*. Similarly, bilateralism, which today has become somewhat dated, has given way to a new model of negotiation that is both plurilateral and interregional, resolutely turned towards interconnection and regulations. This model has ultimately given rise to two mega-negotiations: one, completed, that is directed towards the Pacific, the *Trans-Pacific Partnership* (TPP), and the other, still in progress, directed towards Europe, the *Transatlantic Trade and Investment Partnership* (TTIP).

Three elements have made it possible for the United States to advance its trade agenda in the area of services in general and cultural services in particular. First, it has systematically resorted to the negative list approach. Unlike the positive list approach, which confines the scope of negotiations to previously chosen topics, the negative list approach has the double advantage of covering a wide territory ("everything but") and of setting aside contentious topics, treating them as exceptions. Introduced during the negotiations for the NAFTA, this method eventually imposed itself, notably during transatlantic and transpacific negotiations. Second, the United States has applied a standard model in all trade negotiations. The model can evolve or change, but having one to begin with presents a double advantage. On the one hand, all agreements must conform to a common framework, and only the exceptions that are listed in annexes (I and II) differentiate them. On the other, precedents created through dealings with a more lenient partner make it possible to enhance the level of engagements from one negotiation to the next, or can at least serve as a starting point for future negotiations. The third element is the negotiation of exceptions and annexes. As we have stated, the negative list allows for exceptions. Nevertheless, these must be negotiated and, in this regard, the United States has always sought to reduce their scope. Thus, it is noteworthy that the United States has ended up conceding to demands for local content, subsidies, and other traditional support measures promoting cultural services, in particular within the audiovisual field, while remaining inflexible with regard to everything that pertains to digital technology and new media. To quote Gilbert Gagné: "Digital networks should be free of cultural protectionism." This amounts to saying that it is one thing to accept what already exists, but with digital technology, the game has changed and, henceforward, only the principle of competition should prevail!

Gilbert Gagné takes up these three elements to analyze in detail the content of the different US trade agreements, beginning with the ones concluded within the framework of the *Trade Promotion Authority Act* of 2002 and ending with those that are currently being negotiated. We are at the heart of the book.

It has often been said that the United States does not negotiate with developing countries in the same way it does with developed ones, but without always giving a clear demonstration of this or providing robust arguments, except perhaps in the case of investment. One of the most original features of this book is that it shows us precisely how the agreements differ from one another. Indeed, bargaining power is certainly not the same in both cases, nor do services in general and cultural services in particular hold the same importance for each of these two categories of countries. Thus, it is scarcely surprising to note that bilateralism has largely allowed the United States to assert its views with regard to trade, depriving developing countries of many of their means and leaving them little room to pursue their cultural policies. However, an analysis of their content also reveals significant differences between agreements in terms of the exceptions deemed reasonable by US authorities, suggesting that some countries, for example Costa Rica, are able to get a better deal than others out of bilateral negotiations with the United States.

The situation of developed countries is different. There are fewer trade agreements, while cultural services and the audiovisual sector are more sensitive issues, both in public opinion and for the parties concerned. Furthermore, the issue of new media and of e-commerce also holds more importance, particularly for a country like Korea, which has made information and communication technologies, as well as culture, two of its great economic priorities. This is apparent in the agreements: exceptions and special provisions are more numerous and their scope is broader. These countries have thus managed to retain more leeway and a certain amount of flexibility in pursuing their cultural policies, even where new media are concerned. Proof positive that compromise is always possible.

What has changed with the current negotiations? That is the question raised in the last chapter of the book. First, they have shifted from a bilateral frame to a plurilateral one. Second, new media, the neutrality of Internet, digital freedom, and e-commerce now occupy a central position in negotiations. And, finally, the method of negotiation has changed yet again. We are faced with a new model, of which the TPP is emblematic. In a hurry to conclude negotiations, the United States agreed to the preservation of a large number of exceptions and other traditional support measures, to the great satisfaction of the countries involved. But these concessions were only obtained at the cost of a quasi-absence of regulations in the new media and digital sectors. We have yet to see what will come of the two important ongoing negotiations, on services and with the European Union. However, the question remains: What scope can an instrument such as the UNESCO Convention on Cultural Diversity still hope to achieve, and what means will governments dispose of to pursue their cultural policies if, as is the aim of the United States, the principle of digital freedom prevails?

The problem is directly stated in the *Comprehensive Economic and Trade Agreement* (CETA) concluded between Canada and the European Union in 2013. In the preamble to the agreement, both parties clearly affirm "their commitments as Parties to the UNESCO Convention on the Protection and Promotion of the Diversity of Cultural Expressions," and recognize "that states have the right to preserve, develop and implement their cultural policies, and to support their cultural industries for the purpose of strengthening the diversity of cultural expressions, and preserving their cultural identity, including through the use of regulatory measures and financial support." While this in itself is a great novelty, one may note in parallel that within the main text of the agreement, cultural exemption is not treated as a general exemption, but as a specific one, in other words as an exemption that relieves cultural industries of certain obligations contained in the treaty. Canadian negotiators justified their point of view by claiming that the result is the same. Maybe so, but in a context where Europeans are also negotiating a trade treaty with the United States (the TTIP), the formula takes on a different meaning, in that it is no longer a matter of agreeing on the extent of protections to be granted to cultural industries, but a matter of bargaining, on a case by case basis, for exceptions to the general principle of the free circulation of cultural products. As was the case for the TPP negotiations! If these negotiations are "writing the rules for 21st century trade," one can readily understand the concerns of cultural milieus and coalitions on cultural diversity!

Gilbert Gagné has accomplished a painstaking task, examining in detail all provisions pertaining to culture and cultural products, treaty by treaty, chapter by chapter, with remarkable precision. In so doing, he has produced a book that is destined to be a landmark in its field. However, it is not so much on that point I wish to insist in concluding this foreword, as on the exemplary nature of such a work. Whether they deal with the US-Canada softwood lumber dispute, international investment, or, as is the case here, with culture and cultural products, the works of Gilbert Gagné are embedded in the field of international political economy, with a special interest for American trade policy. This field has considerably evolved, increasingly forsaking the old debates between liberal internationalists, realists, and constructivists to privilege pluralistic analyses instead, these being no doubt more conducive to quantitative methods. That is not the case here. In his own way, Gilbert Gagné stands in the tradition of institutionalism—more precisely he remains faithful to the spirit and method of one of its great founders in the field of political economy, John Commons.

As an inventor of modern industrial relations who was strongly inspired by labor legislation and by his experience of collective negotiation, Commons not only put institutions back at the center of economic analysis, he also developed an original work method that rests on a continuous back-and-forth between facts and theory. While institutions evolve and are transformed under the influence of ideas and interests (the bargaining power), they are also influenced by facts, which is something Peter Hall has tended to neglect in his three "I" model. While science is always in flux, it also has its own demands. Social sciences in particular require that facts be dissected and reconstructed, in order to make sense of them. In this book, Gilbert Gagné has done just that, taking apart the content of each US trade agreement and "reading" it line by line rather than between the lines, as jurists like to remind us. Thus, he shows us how the rules and institutions guiding collective action are constructed. Or at least, how the United States tries to export its own rules and build a world in its image. We are here in the best tradition of John Commons's institutionalism, not in the current institutionalism of the rules of the game!

Christian Deblock
Professor
Department of Political Science
University of Quebec in Montreal

Introduction

Trade is not usually associated with culture and one may wonder how there could be a debate involving these two notions. According to the Cambridge Dictionary, in American English, trade is generally understood as "the activity of buying and selling goods and services, especially between countries." As for culture, it mainly refers to "the arts of describing, showing, or performing that represent the traditions or the way of life of a particular people or group" (*Cambridge Dictionaries Online*). If the two concepts of trade and culture belong to different spheres, they are considered to intersect when they involve cultural goods and services. Alongside visual, performing, and literary arts, the latter also encompass printed, audiovisual, and, now, multimedia products. To the extent that these reflect the way of life of specific communities, issues have arisen as to whether or the extent to which cultural products (encompassing goods and services) should be exempted from trade disciplines. Some states, such as the United States and Japan, important exporters of cultural products, have held that they should not be treated differently from other products. On the other hand, states, such as France and Canada, concerned about the impact of foreign cultural products on their cultural identity and/or insistent on the pursuit of cultural policies and measures to foster their national cultures, have sought to wholly or partially exempt cultural products from economic liberalization.

The so-called trade and culture debate, thus, refers to the conflicting views between states as to the treatment of cultural products in international economic law. Essentially, the debate stems from the difficulties in conciliating, on the one hand, the need to maintain sufficient policy space and flexibility for states' cultural policies and measures, and, on the other, non-discrimination (national treatment and most-favored-nation [MFN]) obligations[1] in trade agreements (Richieri Hanania and Ruiz Fabri 2014, 1). The terms of this long-standing debate have evolved with the advent of the twenty-first century. Now acknowledging the concerns for cultural identity in international trade negotiations, the position of the United States in particular has somehow softened, from outright liberalization to an acceptance of circumscribed and clearly defined exceptions. This new US strategy has been materialized in the conclusion of a series of negotiations for preferential trade agreements (PTAs) under the Trade Promotion Authority (TPA) or Trade Act of 2002. Yet, for other key protagonists of the debate, such as Canada and France, exclusion in whole or in part of the cultural sector is essential to ensure the diversity of cultural expressions in the context of economic globalization and the digital revolution. Their stances have been pursued not only in the PTAs Canada and the European Union have respectively concluded, but also in the adoption in 2005 of the Convention on the Preservation and Promotion of the Diversity of Cultural Expressions (hereafter the CDCE or the Convention), recognizing the special character of cultural goods and services, as well as the right of states to implement cultural policies.

Although prominent and problematic, the trade and culture debate is but one of the "trade and" or trade-linkage issues. These also involve public services, intellectual property, the environment, labor standards, development, and human rights, among the main ones. The trade-linkage debate prompts questions about the relationship between economic and non-economic values in global governance. The increase in "trade and" problems is attributable to more issues being regarded as trade-related as their associated regulations affect trade and a growing number of areas becoming subject to international agreements.[2] For liberal trade economists, such as Bhagwati (1995, 122–30; 2000), non-economic objectives constitute an important element of free trade theory. While insisting on the value of free trade, they insist that values other than economic, such as culture, must be duly taken into account. For Patricia Goff (2007, 14–15, 35), states' insistence on sheltering cultural industries from liberalization, while simultaneously promoting a liberal economic order, rather than protectionism in a new guise, represent efforts in favor of an evolving and reconfigured embedded liberalism compromise; this time to prevent cultural, instead of socioeconomic, dislocation.[3]

The new US strategy with regard to the treatment of cultural products in international trade agreements has four main elements or characteristics: 1) the most liberal approach possible should be used to make trade commitments, i.e., the negative-list approach; 2) existing financial support schemes for cultural content production need not be dismantled; 3) local content requirements and other trade barriers in audiovisuals need not be totally eliminated, at least where traditional technologies are involved; and 4) digital networks should be free of cultural protectionism (Wunsch-Vincent 2003, 11; see also Bernier 2004, 3). The multilateral negotiations on services resumed in 2000 under the auspices of the World Trade Organization (WTO), as mandated under the General Agreement on Trade in Services (GATS). These were soon subsumed within the Doha Round, launched in 2001, but which has been in stalemate for quite some years (see, e.g., Evenett 2014). Alongside these multilateral efforts, many countries, including the United States, have pursued their own trade liberalization agenda, through the conclusion of PTAs, almost all of which have taken the form of bilateral free trade agreements (FTAs). Under the top-down or negative-list approach, used for the US PTA negotiations, sectors and measures not specifically excluded are covered by liberalization commitments. On the other hand, under the bottom-up or positive-list approach, as is the case in the GATS negotiations, only sectors and measures specifically designated are subject to liberalization commitments. The latter approach, clearly, better provides for the exclusion or particular treatment of key sectors, such as audiovisual services.

Many studies have focused on the negotiations and provisions of the multilateral agreements under the aegis of the WTO and the increasingly broader and deeper ones under the series of PTAs concluded by countries throughout the world (Bartels and Ortino 2006; Bhagwati 2008; Buckley, Io Loo, and Boulle 2008; Lester and Mercurio 2009; Heydon and Woolcock 2009; Horn, Mavroidis, and Sapir 2010; WTO 2011; Krist 2013; Dür and Elsig 2015; Lester, Mercurio, and Bartels 2015). Others have considered more specifically states' negotiations and commitments on services, including cultural services, both within the WTO and PTAs (Roy, Marchetti, and Lim 2007; Marchetti and Roy 2008a; Roy 2011; Sauvé and Shingal 2011; Hoekman 2012; Hoekman and Mattoo 2012; Sauvé 2013; Marchetti and Roy 2013; Lim and De Meester 2014; Sauvé and Shingal 2014). Most of these studies have been conducted within international organizations or institutes, such as the WTO. Yet, if they sometimes go beyond a mere inventory of commitments in the cultural sector, their analysis remains limited, mainly because no particular attention is paid to so-called cultural services.

Some books and articles dealing with the trade and culture debate consist of overviews of the evolution of tensions surrounding the treatment of cultural goods and services in international trade law (Goff 2007; Voon 2007; Richieri Hanania 2009; Singh 2011b; Neuwirth 2013, Shi 2013). Others, published either as books, policy reports, book chapters, or articles, concentrate on the negotiations and provisions regarding cultural products in the WTO and PTAs (Pauwels and Loisen 2003; Bernier 2004; Graber, Girsberger, and Burri-Nenova 2004; Gagné, Côté, and Deblock 2004; Guerrieri, Iapadre, and Koopman 2005; Formentini and Iapadre 2007; Roy 2008; Singh 2008a; Gagné 2011a; Richieri Hanania 2012; Chase 2015). Some others look at the debate in light of the digital revolution, which profoundly alters the way cultural contents are created, distributed, and accessed, with serious implications for the conduct of cultural policies (Wunsch-Vincent 2006; Burri-Nenova 2009; Breen 2010; Burri 2011; Burri and Cottier 2012; Gagné 2014).

Concurrently, the CDCE has been thoroughly studied, with an emphasis on its negotiations, provisions, and operational guidelines, and the way these may impact the evolution of the trade and culture debate (Bernier 2005; Gagné 2005a; Kolliopoulos 2005; Lemieux 2006; Hahn 2006; Graber 2006; Obuljen and Smiers 2006; Voon 2006; Carmody 2007; Craufurd Smith 2007; Lachapelle 2008; Germann 2008; Wouters and De Meester 2008; Bernier 2009; Neuwirth 2010; Vlassis 2011; Kono and Van Uystel 2012a; Vlassis 2013; Richieri Hanania 2014; Vlassis 2015). Such studies are often accompanied by considerations of the latter debate, now addressed within both the WTO and the United Nations Educational, Scientific and Cultural Organization (UNESCO), as a case of fragmentation of international law.[4]

With the delays and problems in multilateral negotiations, PTAs undoubtedly have proved the main determinants and indicators of the evolution of the trade and culture debate. Yet, the relevant studies that have considered and compared the details of the provisions concerning cultural products in PTAs, notably those concluded by the United States, the European Union, and Canada, have essentially been published as policy reports, books chapters, and journal articles. When books have pertained to US PTAs, none of these has focused specifically on cultural products. This book, thus, analyzes the specifics of the provisions relating to cultural products in the various US FTAs, with an emphasis on those concluded under the 2002 TPA. Considering the full roster of US FTAs allows drawing broader conclusions on the implementation of the US trade strategy on cultural products. In particular, analyzing various US FTAs makes it possible to compare and contrast the terms of each one in the wider context of US negotiating objectives pertaining to the cultural/audiovisual sector. Furthermore, it provides an opportunity to highlight and account for variations in the deals states parties struck with the United States. Of all major players in the trade and culture debate, by far, the United States is the main exporter of cultural products and the country that has pushed for the highest level of liberalization of the cultural sector. As a result, the US PTAs are those most consequential as for states' remaining latitude to conduct public policies benefiting the cultural sector, known as cultural policies. Hence, the book purports to be most informative of the evolution and actual situation of the trade and culture debate.

The United States had already concluded four PTAs before the 2002 TPA. These are with Canada and Mexico, its two North American neighbors, as well as Israel and Jordan, two relatively small Middle Eastern countries. The one with Canada was later superseded by the North American Free Trade Agreement (NAFTA), which also includes Mexico. Yet, it is really under the 2002 TPA, in effect until June 30, 2007, that the United States has entered the PTA path. Besides the PTA comprised of Costa Rica, the Dominican Republic, El Salvador, Guatemala, Honduras, Nicaragua, and the United States (CAFTA-DR), the US trade agreements negotiated between late 2000 and 2007 are bilateral. These involve Singapore, Chile, Australia, Morocco, Bahrain, Oman, Peru, Colombia, Panama, and South Korea. Thus, eleven US PTAs, with sixteen countries, most from the developing world, were concluded under the 2002 TPA and are all in force.[5] Although some of the negotiations overlapped, these FTAs have been negotiated sequentially. The usual bilateral character of such PTA negotiations, coupled with the asymmetry of the negotiating parties and the resort to the negative-list approach, make them interesting, and indeed better, venues for securing US views and interests on the treatment of cultural products in international trade law.

Among the states parties to the above US PTAs, seven (the Dominican Republic, El Salvador, Nicaragua, Oman, Panama, Singapore, and South Korea) had already made liberalization commitments relating to the audiovisual sector within the WTO. These US PTAs were also essentially negotiated alongside the mobilization that led to the adoption and entry into force of the CDCE. In particular, the US-Korea FTA was seen as a first test for the CDCE, as the US-Korea negotiations began shortly after the adoption of the Convention, while their conclusions coincided with the CDCE's coming into force. Interestingly, Australia has been among the countries most resistant to liberalization requests for the audiovisual sector within the multilateral setting. Australia, Honduras, and Nicaragua were among the only four countries to abstain during the vote on the CDCE, clearly as a result of US pressure in the case of the latter two. Among the states parties to these US PTAs, Guatemala and Peru ratified the Convention in 2006; Chile, Oman, and Panama in 2007; Australia, the Dominican Republic, and Nicaragua in 2009; Honduras and South Korea in 2010; Costa Rica in 2011; as well as Colombia, El Salvador, and Morocco in 2013; leaving only Bahrain and Singapore as non-parties to the CDCE. Yet, for countries that had already concluded an FTA with the United States, the ensuing constraints on their ability to pursue cultural policies remain, as the Convention does not have any retroactive effect.

A significant evolution in the trade and culture debate may also be about to unfold as the United States has taken part in three major sets of trade talks: the Trans-Pacific Partnership (hereafter TPP) negotiations, which took place between 2010 and 2015, and, alongside the United States, included eleven other countries of the Pacific Rim; the Trade in Services Agreement (TiSA) negotiations, assembling twenty-three WTO members (with the European Union [EU] counted as one), belonging to the informal group "Really Good Friends of Services"; and, finally, the US-EU Transatlantic Trade and Investment Partnership (TTIP) negotiations. In each case, the treatment of cultural products, as well as the growing impact of the digital revolution in the diffusion of cultural contents and on the effectiveness of cultural policies, is bound to be considered. In the TTIP in particular and, to a lesser degree, the TiSA negotiations, serious confrontation is to be expected in view of the historical US and European perspectives on the treatment of audiovisual services. The renewal of the TPA by the US Congress in June 2015 significantly adds to the salience and prospects of these negotiations.

This book consists of a study of the treatment of cultural products in US FTAs, particularly those negotiated under the 2002 TPA, and the main issues surrounding the recent and ongoing plurilateral negotiations in which the United States has been involved. It does so by identifying and analyzing the provisions and exceptions in US FTAs relating to cultural products, including digital trade. The objectives of the book are to: 1) highlight the results of the US efforts for liberalizing the cultural sector; 2) assess the implications of US FTAs on the capacity of states parties to pursue cultural policies; and 3) draw conclusions on the evolution of the trade and culture debate. The book concentrates on the provisions secured by states parties to US FTAs regarding cultural products, which is undoubtedly the primary element to focus on for anyone seeking to understand the evolution of the trade and culture debate. The negotiating history of these US FTAs is beyond its scope, due to a lack of available evidence on the specifics of many negotiations, notably those pertaining to cultural products. Nevertheless, the book considers some existing studies on US PTA negotiations, as well as some possible explanations as to why some countries insisted on and secured greater flexibility for cultural policies.

The central argument of the book is that the new US trade strategy on cultural products is the primary determinant of the scope of the provisions and/or exceptions enabling states parties to US FTAs to conduct cultural policies. If US leverage is evident in its ability to get its trade negotiating partners to subscribe to its favored negative-list approach, states' leverage only plays a significant role with respect to some restrictive cultural exceptions pertaining to new or digital technologies secured by few states parties to US FTAs. This, in turn, explains why the book outlines and analyzes the essentials of the US trade strategy and its four key elements and focuses on the actual provisions impacting the cultural sector in US PTAs.

Another main goal of this book, of a pedagogic nature, is to reach out to a wider public beyond those few trained in, and/or knowledgeable about, the intricacies of international trade law and regulations. In so doing, the book seeks to allow not only students of international economic law or international political economy, but in fact any interested citizens, to better grasp the implications of US trade agreements upon the evolution of the trade and culture debate. The book, as a result, aims at the advancement and dissemination of theoretical and policy knowledge on one of the big issues surrounding globalization and the digital revolution.

The book is structured around five chapters. Following this introduction, the first chapter addresses the various elements and the history of the trade and culture debate, as well as the different forums within which it is being played out. The second chapter concentrates on the key issues and elements surrounding the treatment of cultural products in US FTAs. The third chapter focuses on the nine US FTAs concluded under the 2002 TPA with fourteen developing countries and on the exceptions secured by states parties relating to cultural products. The fourth chapter is dedicated to the US FTAs with Australia and South Korea, two industrialized countries, and their more extensive exceptions allowing for the pursuit of cultural policies, including in the digital field. The fifth and last chapter considers the plurilateral trade negotiations in which the United States has recently been involved. A general conclusion ensues, which highlights the main findings of the book.

NOTES

1. The principle of non-discrimination has both external and internal dimensions. The external one consists of the MFN treatment, whereby any trade advantage a country gives to another must be extended, immediately and unconditionally, to all other countries. As for the internal dimension of non-discrimination, it revolves around national treatment, which requires countries to treat imported products no less favorably than domestic products with respect to internal taxes and regulations.

2. On the trade-linkage issues in general, see Leebron (2002) and, with respect to US PTAs more specifically, see Aggarwal (2013).

3. The concept of "embedded liberalism" refers to the compromise struck in the immediate post-war period so as to reconcile free trade at the international level with economic stability and full employment at the domestic level. See Ruggie (1982; 2008).

4. There is a wide literature on the fragmentation of international law, which refers to the multiplication and specialization of regimes and judicial bodies, each with its own rationality and scope. See, notably, UN (2006). Whereas the GATT/WTO was long the principal forum to deal with cultural products, at present, a perplexing and increasing number of international regimes, mainly in the form of PTAs, preside over the trade and culture debate. To the extent that such PTAs allow various countries, and notably the main protagonists in the debate, namely the United States, the European Union, and Canada, to secure their policy preferences, they greatly contribute to the fragmentation of international trade law. Beyond, with the cultural dimension of cultural products being addressed within UNESCO and their economic dimension within the WTO and numerous PTAs, this further complicates the question of the relationship and compatibility of norms and provisions emanating from different regimes (Gagné 2015, 79–80, 89).

5. From the website of the Office of the United States Trade Representative (USTR), http://www.ustr.gov, in which the text and provisions of all US PTAs can be accessed.

ONE

The Trade and Culture Debate

Before delving into the key elements of the new US strategy on cultural products, as well as the specific exceptions that states parties to US FTAs have secured for the pursuit of cultural policies, it is essential to grasp the fundamentals of the trade and culture debate. Indeed, the debate encompasses various components and dimensions that ought to be examined in order to understand it. Central are the concept of cultural identity and the cultural policies pursued by many state governments to foster national identity through the promotion and protection of cultural industries, as well as the main cultural policy instruments, all of which have an impact (although varying and incidental) on international trade. A recent element in the debate relates to digital technological developments, which revolutionize the means by which cultural goods and services are produced and consumed, and, hence, raise questions as to whether they represent either a threat or an opportunity for the diversity of cultural expressions, and whether they imply the end of effective cultural policy regulations. The importance of cultural products in international exchanges also needs to be emphasized, particularly for the United States.

This leads to the more properly political evolution of the trade and culture debate, distinguishing between its three main phases, i.e., before, during, and after the Uruguay Round of multilateral trade negotiations from 1986 to 1993. Since, despite fierce US opposition, the main proponents of cultural exception/diversity secured the adoption in 2005 within UNESCO of the CDCE, which insists on the distinctive character of cultural products, as well as on states' rights to pursue cultural policies. Besides, with the deadlock in the Doha Round, the main protagonists of the trade and culture debate, including the United States, have each concluded their own PTAs, furthering their policy preferences on the treatment of the cultural sector in trade agreements. In turn, the resulting divergences in the provisions on cultural products in such different forums raise questions, notably with respect to their impact on the possibility of progress within the WTO. In particular, the chapter highlights that the lack of any significant advances in the multilateral negotiations on cultural services under the GATS, based on a positive-list approach, not to forget the more general stalemate in the Doha Round and the CDCE, mainly explain that the United States has turned to PTA negotiations to secure far-reaching liberalization.

CULTURAL IDENTITY AND CULTURAL POLICIES

Culture, it has been emphasized, "is one of the two or three most complicated words in the English language" (and in most other languages for that matter) (Williams 1983, 87). From a general anthropological view, culture refers to "a given people's particular set of preferences, predispositions, attitudes, goals, its particular way of perceiving, feeling, thinking, and reacting to objective reality" (Gagné 1972, 526). Throsby (1995, 201–2) suggests a constituent and functional construct of the word *culture*. The former, from an anthropological or sociological perspective, corresponds to "a set of attitudes, practices and beliefs that are fundamental to the functioning of different societies." The latter views culture as "a set of activities, including all those [associated with the] 'cultural industries' . . . [and] represented by the 'cultural sector' of the economy." Following on this latter view, according to UNESCO, culture includes cultural heritage, printed matter and literature, music, the performing and visual arts, cinema and photography, radio, and television, and socio-cultural activities (quoted in Cultural Industries Sectoral Advisory Group on International Trade [SAGIT] 1999, 2). In both its functional and constituent senses, an essential element of culture is its role as an expression of group or collective aspects of people's behavior, as manifested in their activities and belief systems. Thus, in general terms, something may be considered of cultural value if it contributes to these shared elements of human experience (Throsby 1999, 6).

These explanations bring us to a notion related to the one of culture. The idea of identity refers to the tendency of individuals and groups to develop a sense of who they are in relation to their shared psychological, sociological, and political attachments to each other (Brodie 1999, 409). As these two concepts of culture and identity are closely associated, one often reads about cultural identity. The latter is understood as the sum of all cultural references through which an individual, alone or in community with others, defines or constitutes him/herself and his/her community, and by which he/she wishes to be recognized. Even if individuals often have multiple cultural identities, they have a primary identity, usually with their nation (Shi 2013, 21–22; see also Kuper 1999, 2; Acheson and Maule 1999, 7–8).

In some countries, such as the United States, culture tends to be thought of in terms of fine arts, literature, opera, ballet, and classical music—i.e., is primarily associated with "high" culture. On the other hand, in many countries, such as Canada, it also includes books, magazines, newspapers, movies, video and music recordings, radio and television. In fact, what corresponds to mass or popular "culture" in Canada is seen in the United States as the "entertainment industry." Yet, it could be observed that culture in the United States means more than high culture to the extent that reference is made to notions such as pop culture or native cultures. What is certain is that in countries such as Canada more aspects of cultural production at all levels are associated with national identity and, thus, are accorded greater political significance than in the United States, especially in terms of the need to protect them (Gagné 2003/2004, 30).

Cultural goods and services, thus, include not only visual, performing, and literary arts, but also newspapers, magazines, books, movies, video and music recordings, radio, and television, and now multimedia (computers and telecommunications). Yet, cultural products are primarily associated with motion pictures, video discs, television programs, and sound recordings, the grouping of which is known as audiovisual services, the latter historically having proved the focal point of the trade and culture debate.

The goods and services produced by the cultural industries have been at the center of government initiatives in many countries to further a national culture and a feeling of identity among citizens. Indeed, cultural products are the means through which people from different communities can most clearly express and project who and what they are. They also constitute the aspects of national cultures most directly impacted by economic globalization and technological evolution. Although such public initiatives are nearly universal, they have tended to be more significant in political communities that have felt threatened by their exposure to foreign cultural influences. Hence, the political will to support national cultural production in Canada mainly results from pervasive US influence. Most cultural products in Canada have long originated from abroad, and, for both geographical and linguistic reasons, overwhelmingly from the United States. The latter, and particularly Hollywood, has proved for the past century the nucleus of global entertainment.

In an effort to theorize the trade and culture debate, Chase (2014a, 2, 33) contends that it rests primarily on interests and advances a framework to understand how states judge their sovereignty costs[1] and set their trade preferences. The pressure on governments to resist liberalization commitments in audiovisuals tends to be related to concentrated interests in domestic entertainment industries highly exposed to US competition, the latter a function of cultural proximity. On the other hand, smaller countries, whose domestic industries are less politically powerful or less exposed to commercial pressure, show less concern for the cultural sector. Hence, countries with both large markets and cultural proximity to the United States are most insistent on an exception for culture from trade disciplines, while the stakes are lower for smaller and culturally more distant countries, the latter most likely to liberalize audiovisual trade (see also Chase 2015, 238–42).

Public policies to foster national cultural identity, known as cultural policies, inevitably entail restrictions on the exchange of cultural products. This contravenes the principle of free trade, which has been a cornerstone of the post-war international economic order. Thus, there is, on the one hand, the local culture model, or culture-as-identity, which understands culture as a way of life, a public good deserving of state support; and, on the other hand, the global market model, or culture-as-commerce, which sees culture as a commodity to be treated like other commodities (Armstrong 2000, 370; see also Shi 2013, 20–31). These two competing models of cultural policy have led to philosophically and economically grounded tensions between states.

In the United States, any action that interferes with the free flow of ideas is seen as intrinsically wrong. Such a stance owes to US political culture and constitutional regime, its adherence to free trade principles (i.e., trade unfettered by government-imposed barriers), as well as to free speech, holding as valuable diversity of viewpoints and programming. Governments should refrain from intervening in the cultural lives of their citizens, who have the right to decide for themselves what they see, read, listen to, and do (Balassa 2012, 88–90). John Meisel (1986, 165), a key architect of Canada's domestic content regulations, ironized that if Americans really believe in the free flow of information, "this ideological position often miraculously coincides with crass self-serving economic interests."

In fact, the stance of people and governments in favor either of free trade or of an exception for cultural products usually rests on varying combinations of both principles and interests, most often difficult to disentangle. This has had for effect to render the trade and culture debate even more intractable.[2] Yet, apart from major exporters of cultural products, cultural/audiovisual industries are rarely national champions in the commercial sense, nor are they disproportionately large providers of jobs or particularly crucial to a country's Gross Domestic Product (GDP). For Goff (2007, 3), this shows that public policies benefiting the cultural sector are primarily based on genuine cultural identity, rather than protectionist, concerns.

The economic significance of cultural industries for the United States must be pointed out. The United States is the world's largest producer and exporter of cultural products, the latter also constituting one of its most profitable export sectors (Acheson and Maule 1999, 47–50; Bruner 2008, 355–56). As Mulcahy (2000, 181–82) stresses, with a dominant popular culture able to indemnify its costs over a populous and prosperous society largely immune to cultural expressions not projecting an American sensibility, the United States can afford a "cultural open-door policy" as it has little to fear from foreign competition. Moreover, the communication industries have long proved a key element in ensuring US world hegemony and, then, a pillar of American foreign policy (see Schiller 2000; McCarthy 2015; see also Nye and Owens 1996; Nye 2004). The United States strongly objects to what it perceives as restrictions under the guise of cultural concerns in a context of economic globalization. American authorities, therefore, have aggressively voiced and defended the concerns and interests of US cultural industries.

STATES' CULTURAL POLICIES AND MEASURES

Cultural policies in general refer to public measures taken to encourage or to protect activities in fields considered as cultural. At one level, culture is associated primarily with artistic expression and, in this sense, cultural policy is largely concerned with government funding and promotion of the arts. All societies have recognized the importance of art and most have supported artists. In the twentieth century, governments came to fill the role played in previous times by the Church, royalty, or wealthy patrons. At another level, culture is associated with communications and mass culture, through broadcasting, film, book and magazine publishing, sound recording, and new media. In this respect, cultural expression is more and more bound up with the development of cultural industries, which play a key role not only in disseminating works but also in forming the way in which the culture itself is perceived. Culture is often seen as a public good and cultural policies respond to the need to preserve or stimulate cultural identity, or to create an environment in which distinctive cultures can be sustained. Such policies may sometimes be developed in response to dominant foreign influence, as in the case of Canada vis-à-vis the United States (Marsh and Harvey 2006, 1–2).

The goal of cultural policies is to ensure an environment in which a country's cultural products are created, produced, marketed, preserved, and shared with audiences at home and abroad, thereby contributing to a country's economic, social, and cultural growth. Through cultural products, such as sound recordings, books and films, not only are ideas and experiences expressed, but stories and images that are unique to a particular community or nation are shared within that community and with the rest of the world. Cultural products entertain as well as they inform; they help shape people's sense of identity. They also help individuals develop more cohesive societies and a sense of pride in who they are as a people and a nation (SAGIT 1999, 1, 3).

Public authorities in many countries have thus adopted a whole series of policies and measures to protect and promote national cultural goods and services produced by cultural industries. Among the types of cultural policy instruments or measures, one may mention the financial and program incentives. Subsidies, taking the form of grants, preferential loans, or tax credits, usually through specific programs and funds, are most often used to support audiovisual (film and television) production, distribution, and professional training, and, less often, book and magazine publishing. Such financial instruments exist in all countries pursuing public cultural objectives.

The most common regulatory measures reserve the property and/or control of cultural industries to nationals. These usually take the form of foreign investment and licensing restrictions, to control access to radio and television broadcasting (including news media) and, less often, to cinema, as well as book, magazine, and newspaper publishing. Such measures are to be found in most countries, including the United States. Other types of measures set content quotas, typically requiring radio and television broadcast stations (sometimes including pay and specialty television, pay-per-view, and video-on-demand channels or networks) and, less often, publications, to feature a certain percentage of domestically produced television programs, music recordings, or national "stories" or news events. These measures are found notably in Australia, Canada, France, as well as the European Union. Others prescribe television and radio stations and/or networks to contribute financially to national productions, as in Australia and Canada. Some others provide for screen quotas in cinemas, as in France, Mexico, South Korea, and Spain. There are as well tax measures, either levied on box-office revenues (e.g., France and Sweden), receipts of broadcasters (e.g., Australia and Canada), or audio and video recordings, to support domestic audiovisual production.

A cultural policy instrument resorted to in many countries is a coproduction agreement, primarily in film and television. Although in decline, there are also border measures, such as tariffs, as those often applied on foreign magazines; quantitative restrictions, as in the case of China and Egypt regarding the number of foreign films permitted annually; or import bans, as the one resorted to by Canada from 1965 to 1998 on split-run periodicals (SAGIT 1999, 5–20; see also Footer and Graber 2000, 122–26).[3]

On the other hand, in the United States, there is long-standing suspicion of government involvement in the arts and in the production of content viewed by its citizens. There is no Department of Culture and the US government does not normally subsidize and/or regulate (in the latter case, with the exception of obscenity as well as radio and television licenses) cultural industries. Arts policy is rather financed largely through indirect subsidies, such as tax deductions, mainly at the state and/or local level, as well as through contributions and bequests from private donors, the latter activity in turn eligible for tax relief (see Cowen 2006). Yet, if no other country embraces the "pure" market model more fiercely than the United States, under the regulatory oversight of the Federal Communications Commission (FCC), US broadcasters have had "public-interest obligations" and been subject to local and children's programming requirements, closely resembling quotas in their design and impact (Grant and Wood 2004, 212–15).

THE DIGITAL REVOLUTION

People have long bought books, magazines, newspapers, and records, and received radio and television signals. Around the late 1970s, with cable television, they have been able to pick up further channels, and, in the 1980s, directly from satellites. Nowadays, with the development of wireless technology and the Internet, people have even more choices. They can use the Internet not only to listen to music and watch audiovisual materials, but also to read magazine or newspaper articles. Internet can be accessed virtually everywhere from personal computers, laptops, ipads, ipods, and mobile phones. Digital transmission technology, therefore, dramatically expands the capacities to deliver cultural contents by different networks, including terrestrial, cable, and satellite. At the same time, the Internet constitutes a new platform for multimedia services, where the traditional systems for the delivery of text, voice, sound, and images are merged.[4] Multimedia products draw on content produced by the film, television, sound recording, book, magazine, as well as fine and performing arts industries, thus blurring the distinctions between them. They are also truly interactive, as much of the content online, especially on social networks, such as Facebook and Twitter, is made by the consumers themselves, here again blurring the traditional distinctions between creators (including producers and distributors) and consumers.

Hence, new technologies are revolutionizing the way cultural products are created, produced, delivered, distributed, accessed, and consumed, and, as a result, have a tremendous impact on cultural industries. The digital revolution, as it is known, is associated with both opportunities and risks for cultural policies and the diversity of cultural expressions. There are no indicators for the measurement of the impacts of digital technologies and networks on the diversity of cultural expressions (Rioux et al. 2015, 10). As is often the case with complex social phenomena, there is conflicting evidence as to whether the new media further or jeopardize cultural diversity. On the one hand, there could be possibilities for a technological leap, allowing a rapid development of cultural industries, particularly in developing countries. Movies and television programs, among other things, may be less expensive to produce and easier to disseminate. The very nature of the Internet as a medium apparently allows cultural diversity to flourish. Nearly anyone anywhere can access and even produce online cultural contents. Countless instances provide compelling evidence of the Internet as an accessible, democratic platform providing unlimited "shelf-space" for cultural contents from all over the world. At the same time, such global diversity would not be at the expense of distinctive national cultures. For example, an online interactive map which repertories the most popular titles in a thousand cities in 60 countries, downloadable from Spotify, a Swedish music streaming, podcast, and video service, reveals similar preferences among inhabitants of a same city for local and national music (*Culture, commerce et numérique* 2015, 11–12).

On the other hand, there is increasing evidence that the promise of a diversification of cultural expressions in a global digital environment has proved illusory. Abundance does not necessarily mean diversity, especially cultural diversity. Economic and political forces of the globalized market have inevitably seized this seemingly libertarian virtual space the Internet represents. Internet "majors," i.e., Google, Apple, Facebook, and Amazon (GAFA), and other US companies, such as Netflix, are the global driving force of the digital economy and the main beneficiaries of the explosion of content available on the Internet, as they provide the access to services and much of the content (Thiec 2014, 99). The management and governance of the Internet are also outside the regulatory bodies of the United Nations system. The Internet Corporation for Assigned Names and Numbers (ICANN), responsible for domain names and the network's stable and secure operation, is a non-profit organization based in California and dominated by American interests. In 2009, the US Department of Commerce relinquished its oversight of ICANN, which has moved toward a global multi-stakeholder governance model, with input from state governments.

The increasingly large and integrated, mainly American, conglomerates exercise effective oligopoly, if not quasi monopoly, control on the cultural contents offered over the Internet. They can, thus, decide which of these contents to emphasize, likely those whose owners paid for such promotion. The fierce competition between these corporations creates a semblance of diversity, yet they all subscribe to the same cultural and commercial criteria for their products. Like Hollywood majors, dominating world cinema, with the advent of digital technology, they extend their reach to the whole of cultural industries. Early on, the Internet was perceived in Europe as the Trojan horse of US imperialism, which was to impose its Anglo-Saxon values and productions (Thiec 2014, 98; Beaudoin 2014, 3, 5, 10, 15). Already in the mid-1990s, UNESCO pointed that one of the main risks in the trade and culture debate is the standardization of content resulting from the processes of technological convergence and economic globalization (UNESCO 1995, 232). For Grant and Wood (2004, 1), with the growing concentration of media, the distribution of cultural products is in the hands of gatekeepers who reduce choice rather than expand it.

Thus, among the main threats associated with the growing concentration of media, one is the visibility of, and access to, local content in a transnational digital environment (Guèvremont et al. 2013, 50–51). Despite the huge quantity of cultural contents on the Internet, there would not be much effective variety. The film or song titles most downloaded tend to be those of the major entertainment corporations. If this could be interpreted as the result of free individual choice, it may also be attributable to search engines "programmed" to give first exposure to mainstream contents belonging to the "majors." In the first years of the twenty-first century, surveys had confirmed that most web traffic flowed to heavily promoted extensions of existing brands (Grant and Wood 2004, 420).

The challenges associated with the transformations induced by new technologies can be summed up as the five Ds: dematerialization, disintermediation (direct relationship between creators/producers and consumers), decompartmentalization (technological convergence and blurring of frontiers between traditional sectors), delinearization (end of programming top-down by the media), and deterritorialization. In particular, the dematerialization of cultural products challenges the principle of territoriality upon which current states' cultural policies rest (Rioux et al. 2015, 45, 88). There has been growing concern that digital developments in the production and distribution of cultural contents might well be beyond the reach of effective regulation (Shi 2013, 8). Indeed, for some, technological developments mark the end of protectionism and the victory of globalization as they break most remaining barriers, including those resulting from policy measures to protect domestic cultural industries, rendering an increasing number of them obsolescent (e.g., Ibbitson 2014). For others, such developments represent an opportunity to reformulate public cultural policies and adapt regulations to respond to dramatic changes (Grant and Wood 2004, 329–51; Guèvremont et al. 2013; Beaudoin 2014; Rioux et al. 2015).

In the digital environment, enterprises can supply services to citizens in countries without being present within their territories. Courts in Canada and elsewhere have ruled multiple times that assets need not be physically located in a country for an enterprise to be considered to "carry on business" within its territory. Also, to the extent that cultural contents transmitted through satellites or the Internet are subject to copyrights, their enforcement essentially depends on states' institutions as well as collective management societies. Therefore, copyright owners have brought pressure on states to act on the borderless cyberspace (Grant and Wood 2004, 334–37).

A fundamental challenge consists in creating the synergy and interconnections between policies, actors, and institutions at several (mainly national and multilateral) levels, so as to make the digital revolution a genuine catalyst for the diversity of cultural expressions. Governments must rethink their regulatory measures to ensure that the major digital distribution platforms make plenty of room for national and local works in the countries where they operate and, thereby, really foster the diversity of cultural expressions (Rioux et al. 2015, 73). For satellite services, technology allows to transmit to only a portion of a satellite's coverage area, making it possible to enact requirements within specific borders. Also, video-on-demand services (except those on the Internet) are already subject to content regulations in countries such as Canada. For services delivered through the Internet, governments can require that works included on a file server include a proportion of local titles, that the menu provided to consumers promotes local expressions, or that the enterprise supports local creators in other ways (Grant and Wood 2004, 337, 350). In response to a question from a representative of Quebec's music recording industry, the executive of a US supplier recognized that it is easy to program an algorithm for different territories to ensure that for a specific number of titles, one be of local origin.

Yet, how can states' cultural policy regulations be applied to the new media without causing fragmentation of the Internet (Rioux et al. 2015, 95)? To the extent that such regulations confront the US objective of absence of cultural protectionism for digital products, could they be implemented without leading to a most epic and dramatic phase in the trade and culture debate? As pointed out by Grant and Wood (2004, 215–16), although content quotas pertain to *categories* and not the *content* of programming, and are designed to *enhance* and not to *restrict* audience choice, no other measure in the cultural policy "tool kit" raises as much criticism. For the proponents of the culture-as-commerce model, such requirements are antithetical to freedom of expression and the functional equivalents of censorship, and even a form of "command and control" social engineering. Clearly, the main challenges concerning domestic content regulations in digital networks are not to be technical or legal, but political.

CULTURAL PRODUCTS IN INTERNATIONAL AND US ECONOMIC EXCHANGES

As most cultural, notably audiovisual, products take the form of services, data on economic exchanges of such products are mainly to be found under trade in services. Services are now central in global economic activity, particularly in industrial countries, where they account for about 72% of GDP and total employment (Marchetti and Roy 2008b, 1). In 2013, services accounted for $10.6 trillion or 78% of US GDP and for 87 million jobs or 82% of employment (United States International Trade Commission [USITC] 2015, 15–16). A report published periodically in the United States since 1990 for the International Intellectual Property Alliance (IIPA) focuses on the core copyright industries, which include films, music, radio and television, books, periodicals and newspapers, as well as software, in traditional and digital formats (Siwek 2014, 4). Apart from computer software, leisure and business applications, and video games (although the latter may arguably be seen as cultural products), these essentially correspond to the usual understanding of the cultural goods and services produced by the cultural industries. In 2013, the contribution of the core copyright or creative industries to US GDP reached $1,126.59 billion (up from $954.4 billion in 2009), accounting for 6.71% of the US economy (compared with 6.62% in 2009). During the 2009–2013 period, these industries grew at an aggregate annual rate of 3.9%, i.e., 70% higher than for the entire US economy (Siwek 2014, 1–2, 6). The core copyright industries employed nearly 5.5 million people in 2013 (up from 5.1 million in 2009), representing 4.03% of the whole US workforce (3.92% in 2009). The average annual compensation of $87,860 paid to core copyright workers in 2013 was also 34% above the average US annual wage (Siwek 2014, 2, 10–11). According to data from the Motion Picture Association of America (MPAA), as an industry, the production and distribution of motion pictures and television programs supported 1.9 million US jobs and $113 billion in total wages in 2013. The industry also contributed $130 billion in sales to the overall US economy that same year, up 5% from 2012 (MPAA 2015).

World services exports, based on balance-of-payments transactions, reached almost $2.8 trillion in 2006, accounting for about 20% of world trade. Yet, those figures represent a significant underestimation. International trade statistics do not cover all trade in services as defined by the GATS, since they notably ignore the sales of services by foreign affiliates or through commercial presence, linked to foreign direct investment (FDI). These are approximately one and a half times larger than conventional cross-border trade flows measured through the balance of payments (Marchetti and Roy 2008b, 1–2). Between 80% and 90% of all world services are traded under two modes of supply: cross-border (mode 1) and commercial presence (mode 3), which are also the dominant modes of delivering audiovisual services (Chase 2015, 228). Since the 1980s, world services trade has been growing more rapidly than world production and merchandise trade. In 2005, nearly two-thirds of global FDI stock was in services, as compared to about 50% in 1990 (Marchetti and Roy 2008b, 2).

US commercial services exports totaled $662.1 billion in 2013, accounting for 14% of global cross-border exports and about 30% of American exports. While the United States has a huge and increasing trade deficit, in 2013, it had a trade surplus of $230.5 billion in services, the largest according to the WTO, with the foreign sales and exports of core copyright industries being the largest single contributor to that surplus. Services sales by US foreign affiliates reached $1.3 trillion in 2013 (USITC 2015, 15–16). In 2014, the United States had an $88.2 billion surplus in services trade with respect to intellectual property–related licensing (United States, Office of the United States Trade Representative [USTR] 2016a, 8). Apart from estimates, reliable data on services trade present enormous challenges. Despite these caveats, figures on exchanges in cultural services are presented so as to give an overall idea of their economic magnitude and main trends, especially as regards the United States. They provide as well evidence as to the economic and political bases of the trade and culture debate.

The WTO valued world exports in audiovisual and related services at $35 billion in 2007, and the US audiovisual exports at $15 billion, although these figures ignore the dominant forms of exchange, i.e., sales through foreign affiliates, royalties, and license fees (WTO 2010, paras 10–11, 15).[5] As a consequence of digitization, notably with multimedia, which creates a whole new range of products, an explosion in demand for audiovisual content is expected. In turn, this adds to the importance of the cultural sector in overall economic production, employment, and trade. With respect to the United States, the IIPA report notices that the US government's statistics on "exports" of copyright products, from which its estimates are drawn, here again, generally fail to measure adequately the true value of such American works sold abroad. Nevertheless, estimates of the foreign sales and exports of the core copyright industries increased substantially, from $129.5 billion in 2009 to $156.3 billion in 2013, surpassing those for other key US industrial sectors (Siwek 2014, 15–16). For three selected core copyright areas, the estimated figures are as follows: motion pictures, television, and video: $23.25 billion in 2009 and $25.35 billion in 2013; recorded music: $6 billion in 2009 and $7 billion in 2013; non-software publications, including newspapers, books, and periodicals: $4.9 billion in 2009 and $4.7 billion in 2013 (Siwek 2014, 20).

Film and television production and distribution represent one of the most highly competitive US industries, one of the few consistently generating a positive balance of trade in virtually every country in which it does business. In 2013, its exports amounted to $15.8 billion. Exporting six times more than it imported, the industry had a services trade surplus of $13.4 billion, or 6% of the total US private-sector trade surplus in services (MPAA 2015). With regard to the film industry, annual statistics from the MPAA reveal that international box-office revenues for all films released outside the United States and Canada reached $26 billion in 2014, up 4% from 2013 and 24% from 2010, with the growth driven primarily by the Asia-Pacific region. With $4.8 billion, the Chinese box office increased by 34% in 2014, to become the first foreign market to exceed $4 billion (MPAA 2014, 2–4). Since the 1980s, only a part of the total revenues generated by films comes from movie theaters. Yet, films benefiting from an important advertising campaign and that are commercially successful retain a significant advantage on secondary markets, such as television, DVD, or video-on-demand.

THE EVOLUTION OF THE TRADE AND CULTURE DEBATE

Until the Uruguay Round

The differences of perspectives among countries regarding the treatment of cultural products in international trade and investment regulations are not new. At the beginning of the twentieth century, fearing for their culture, Canada and European countries adopted measures to protect their cultural industries from US entertainment exports. In the mid-1920s, as four American magazines had larger circulations than its leading periodical, Canada in 1930 applied a tariff on US magazines (Thompson 1996, 396). As for European countries, they resorted notably to screen quotas in the early 1920s in order to protect their film industry from an influx of American movies. The US motion picture industry then pressed the State Department during the inter-war years to respond to European screen quotas (Bernier 1998, 109; see also Acheson and Maule 1999, 56–59). In the second half of the 1920s, screen quotas were to prove a sore point in the first trade talks under the League of Nations, a forgotten episode in the trade and culture debate (Chase 2014b, 125–33).

In international trade negotiations shortly after the Second World War, the United States requested free or at least enhanced access to the European audiovisual market. Yet, devastated by the war and fearing an invasion of US movies, European countries, especially Britain and France, secured screen quotas for cinematographic films in what became Article IV of the General Agreement on Tariffs and Trade (GATT) (Bernier 1998, 109). Entitled "Special Provisions relating to Cinematographic Films," Article IV of the GATT is the only one named for a product and also entails the sole exception to the principle of national treatment (GATT Article III.10). Yet, by only mentioning screen quotas, the article implicitly banned other measures and by treating screen quotas like tariffs, it made them negotiable (Chase 2014b, 150).

There have been tensions over cultural products throughout the history of the GATT, albeit of varying scope and intensity depending on the period. One such moment was when restrictions came to be applied to television broadcasts. In 1961, the United States requested the establishment of a working party and argued that Article IV only covered "cinematographic films." No agreement was reached, however, as the disagreements centered on whether GATT rules applied to television. During the Tokyo Round of multilateral trade negotiations, the United States also complained, among other things, about the subsidization of cinema and television in no less than twenty-one countries (Bernier 1998, 109). Later in 1991, in the course of the Uruguay Round, the United States challenged the restrictions of the European Union on the televised showing of non-European films and programs under its Television without Frontiers Directive. In the ensuing dispute settlement proceedings, the two parties repeated long held arguments. While the United States invoked GATT Article IV, the European Union responded that television broadcasting was a service and, then, out of GATT purview.

The Uruguay Round

The controversy surrounding the treatment of cultural products peaked during the Uruguay Round between 1986 and 1993 as services for the first time figured on the agenda. As had long been the case, the debate on cultural goods and services involved some key actors and revolved around two contrasting perspectives. For one, primarily advocated by the United States, culture represents an economic sector like any other and should be liberalized, with cultural products subject to standard trade disciplines. Government measures aimed at protecting and promoting cultural products constitute a form of unwarranted protectionism. For the other perspective, although cultural goods and services have commercial value, they are not mere commodities as they carry symbols and values and, thus, touch on the very fabric and identity of states. Mainly defended by Canada and France, this perspective gave rise to the notion of cultural exception, according to which culture should either be exempt from economic liberalization or subject to specific provisions. This perspective was expanded and is now known as cultural diversity, as a result of growing apprehension that economic globalization may have an adverse impact on the world's cultures. The debate has proved ever more salient in the context of the digital revolution. Between these extreme positions, most countries have been favorable to a more or less pronounced form of cultural exception in trade agreements.

While heavily influenced by the GATT, regulating trade in goods, the GATS entails a different normative framework and more modest obligations. Unlike the GATT, market access and national treatment[6] are not general obligations. Following the bottom-up or positive-list negotiating approach, such obligations only apply if and to the extent that specific commitments are listed in a country's schedule. Thus, states that do not want to commit themselves in the cultural sector, and especially audiovisual, only have to abstain from commitments in that area. The pressure, if there is one, comes from states that request commitments in cultural services. In case of refusal to accede to their demand, they may in turn refuse to accede to requests in other sectors coming from countries refusing to liberalize their cultural and audiovisual sectors. The latter countries, ultimately, have the last word. The result is that very few states made commitments in cultural and audiovisual services. Under the GATS, countries could also list exemptions to the MFN treatment pertaining to cultural services.

With regard to proposals concerning the treatment of cultural services in the international trading regime, an all-out exclusion or exemption for audiovisual services was rejected early in the talks. Then, two alternatives were debated. The first consisted of a general exception in the framework agreement for "cultural values or relating to cultural services" (GATT 1990a, 11). Canada sought a "general exception based on cultural values which would apply to all existing and future cultural industries." The second alternative was in the form of a sector annex to adapt the framework rules to the "cultural specificity" of audiovisual services. Sponsored by the European Union, a sector annex for audiovisual services would have allowed "special treatment" for "portions of the audiovisual sector which fell under national cultural policies" (GATT 1990b, 2–3, 8). By the end of the Round, the EU position had hardened and become closer to a request for cultural exception (Chase 2014b, 161–63; see also Kono and Van Uystel 2012b, 11–16). The United States, for its part, refused to recognize the special "cultural" character of cultural services. It notably requested to other state delegations a standstill on existing regulations in audiovisuals (Chase 2014a, 8). The European Union was asked to either cap or remove its Television without Frontiers Directive, and to either cap its generous system of film subsidies or administer them on the basis of national treatment (Balassa 2012, 76–77). A last-minute US request for commitments only for video-on-demand and "new media" proved too little, too late (Grant and Wood 2004, 359).

At the conclusion of the Uruguay Round, Canada did not make any commitments on cultural services, while the European Union did not make any specific commitments with respect to the audiovisual sector. On the other hand, the United States, only followed by the Central African Republic, committed itself almost completely, i.e., in all six subcategories of audiovisual services covered by the GATS. In all, eighteen states undertook commitments concerning audiovisual services. Few of these commitments covered every sub-sector and mode of supply, and several of these states inscribed limitations on market access and national treatment in sub-sectors with bound commitments.[7] Apart from the United States, Japan, and New Zealand, these countries are from the developing world, and, among them, seven (i.e., the Dominican Republic, El Salvador, Israel, Mexico, Nicaragua, Singapore, and South Korea,) are parties to US FTAs. Yet, if relatively few countries committed themselves vis-à-vis this sector, with the United States, Hong Kong, India, Japan, and Mexico, they include the main producers and exporters of audiovisual products. At the same time, thirty-five countries (counting the then twelve-member EU as one) secured close to 100 exemptions from MFN treatment in favor of the audiovisual sector, particularly co-production agreements. With this outcome, hailed as "the agreement to disagree," the debate was set aside and remained completely open (Bernier 1998, 110; Roy 2005, 925–28; Voon 2007, 24–26; Shi 2013, 136–37).

Since the Uruguay Round

GATS Article XIX provides for successive trade negotiations with a view to progressively increase the level of liberalization of services, no sector *per se* being excluded.[8] In preparation for the multilateral negotiations of the Doha Round, in its proposals on audiovisual services, the United States stressed that the cultural sector was not the only one with unique characteristics for the fulfillment of important social policy objectives and that the GATS framework was flexible enough to respond to the concerns related to the preservation and promotion of cultural values and identity (WTO 2000, para 7). Overall, the United States reiterated its request made in the Uruguay Round relating to audiovisual services that governments commit themselves to their current levels of market access, i.e., a standstill on existing audiovisual regulations. Unlike the previous multilateral negotiations, the United States has not put forward rollback requests and has expressed its willingness to accept most existing subsidies in the audiovisual sector (Wunsch-Vincent 2003, 15–16; Balassa 2012, 82). Clearly, the United States has softened its position on audiovisuals. Yet, in view of the competitive advantage of its cultural industries and their importance in terms of export revenue, this country remains the chief proponent of the liberalization of the cultural sector, at most accepting some specified and circumscribed exceptions. The United States is also not as isolated as it was in the Uruguay Round. In the early years of the twenty-first century, a group known as the Friends of Audiovisual Services was formed by the United States and ten other WTO members, i.e., Argentina, Brazil, Egypt, Hong Kong, India, Japan, Mexico, New Zealand, the United Kingdom, and Taiwan. As net exporters of audiovisual services, these states also seek liberalization commitments in this sector.

Launched in 2001 the Doha Round has witnessed serious difficulties to the point of impasse. By 2008, only nine countries had made offers regarding audiovisual services so as to expand the scope of the GATS, six of which with existing commitments in the sector (Roy 2008, 361). In June 2005, five of the Friends of Audiovisuals issued a joint statement to the WTO Council for Trade in Services in which they emphasized the benefits of greater commitments in audiovisual services and expressed concerns over the efforts by some key participants in the negotiations to create an *a priori* exclusion of the sector (WTO 2005). These Friends (Hong

Kong, Japan, Mexico, Taiwan, and the United States), as well as Singapore, asked in 2006 for commitments in motion picture and video tape production and distribution, motion picture projection, and sound recording (Chase 2015, 231). Concurrently, the European Union had made it clear to prospective member states that their membership would be compromised if they made any WTO commitments for audiovisual services. Other states have justified their refusal to discuss audiovisual or cultural services by referring to the CDCE (Roy 2005, 928–30; Balassa 2012, 83–84).

In December 2005, in order to bring a new momentum, WTO members agreed on holding plurilateral negotiations on services. A group of developed and developing countries, most Friends of Audiovisuals, presented a plurilateral request for audiovisual services. Up to twenty-four WTO members, including the European Union counted as one, were involved in the ensuing negotiations (*International Trade Daily* 2006; Marchetti and Roy 2008a, 717; Roy 2008, 361–65). In 2013, outside of the WTO, a group of now twenty-three members (involving most industrial states, with the EU counted as one member) undertook the plurilateral TiSA negotiations (*Inside US Trade* 2013a; Marchetti and Roy 2013; Sauvé 2013). Yet, as far as audiovisual and cultural services are concerned, Canada, the European Union, and the United States, the main protagonists of the trade and culture debate, are not expected to change their respective positions.

If, unlike the Uruguay Round, audiovisual and cultural services have not been a hot topic in the Doha talks, it is partly because the trade and culture debate has unfolded in other settings, i.e., accession negotiations to the WTO and the proliferation of PTAs principally concluded by the United States. Hence, between 1996 and 2013, sixteen among twenty-five new members of the WTO made liberalization commitments in audiovisual services, mainly as a result of US pressure (Rioux et al. 2015, 31; Vlassis and Richieri Hanania 2014, 27, 37). These include Oman and Panama, which later both concluded a bilateral FTA with the United States. Although, as of June 2016, the total number of countries with audiovisual commitments was thirty-six, given that the WTO counted 162 members, this service sector remains one in which the fewest WTO members have obligations.[9] Besides, the United States has concluded a whole series of PTAs with various countries throughout the world, with key implications for the evolution of the trade and culture debate.

There are stark differences in the treatment of cultural products between the GATT and the GATS. Not surprisingly, the United States has favored an interpretation of cultural products as goods, whereas the European Union and Canada have made a case for defining them as services. The American government introduced the term "virtual good" to capture audiovisual products, as well as software and electronic commerce, in the hopes that such recategorization may bring these sectors under GATT auspices (Goff 2007, 133–34).

Because they often have both goods and services features, cultural products may also be subject to diverging rules (see Shi 2013, 185–93). This was revealed notably by Canada's measures for the protection of periodicals, which led in 1996 to a complaint to the WTO from the United States. The periodicals dispute, the first involving the cultural sector to be subject to a ruling under the WTO Dispute Settlement Understanding, proved a landmark on states' tensions over the treatment of cultural products in international trade law. WTO authorities found the policy measures complained against to contravene Canada's international trade obligations. This episode raised serious fears as to the incompatibility of many cultural policy measures with the world trading regime. The case was followed by many countries also wary of their cultural identity and their ability to intervene in the cultural field. Finally, this was to lead the proponents of cultural exception/diversity to reflect on the manner to legitimize cultural policies in the context of economic globalization and to ensure a better balance between cultural and economic concerns.[10]

Alongside state governments, national associations of cultural industries, themselves grouped, as within the International Network for Cultural Diversity and the International Federation of Coalitions for Cultural Diversity, have proved instrumental in the mobilization efforts in favor of cultural diversity. Such efforts have aimed both at securing an international convention with provisions on cultural products and influencing international trade negotiations, so that states preserve latitude to pursue cultural policies.

THE CONVENTION ON THE PROTECTION AND PROMOTION OF THE DIVERSITY OF CULTURAL EXPRESSIONS

The efforts of the protagonists of cultural exception/diversity were to culminate with the adoption on October 20, 2005, within UNESCO of the CDCE (UNESCO 2005a). The move toward the Convention was a major factor that brought the United States to rejoin UNESCO in 2003. The adoption of the CDCE is by far the most politicized initiative to emerge from the first decade of the twenty-first century at UNESCO (Singh 2011a, 98; see also Ruiz Fabri 2014, xvi). The Convention was adopted almost unanimously, with the approval of 148 states, the opposition of the United States and Israel, and four abstentions. It became effective on March 18, 2007, and, in June 2016, had been ratified by 142 countries. Both the adoption and the ratification processes of the CDCE have proved the fastest ever in the history of the organization.

The CDCE was adopted under the auspices of the specialized agency of the United Nations in charge of culture and outside the WTO. Aside from the fact that it was deemed impossible to agree on the treatment of cultural products within the latter forum, a properly cultural instrument was sought and, thus, one that would constitute more than mere exceptions to trade laws and the principle of economic liberalization. In the same manner as multilateral environmental agreements exist on their own authority and set their own norms, the choice of UNESCO is attributable to a concern to enshrine the principle of cultural diversity in international law.[11]

The provisions of the CDCE notably recognize the specific or dual (economic and cultural) nature of cultural goods and services, which because they convey identities, values, and meanings, must not be treated as solely having commercial value. The Convention reaffirms the sovereign rights of states to resort as they see fit to a wide array of policy measures in the conduct of cultural policies. This must be done with a view to furthering the diversity of cultural expressions both within their territory and at the international level, while seeking to promote openness to other cultures. The CDCE also includes a non-exhaustive list of cultural policy measures.

The issue that most divided states and was only agreed in the last stage of negotiations pertains to the relationship of the Convention to other instruments, particularly trade agreements. This concerned not only the United States, but also other countries, such as Australia and Japan, some of which belong to the WTO Friends of Audiovisual Services. In the end, without modifying their rights and obligations under any other treaties to which they are parties, states agreed on non-subordination and mutual supportiveness between the Convention and these treaties and to take into account the provisions of the Convention when interpreting and applying other treaties or entering into international obligations (CDCE, article 20). States parties also agreed to consult each other to promote the objectives and principles of the Convention in other international forums (CDCE, article 21).[12]

The United States fiercely resisted and formally objected to the dual nature of cultural products during the CDCE negotiations, although by then it had implicitly recognized their cultural and economic characteristics in a series of communications within the WTO (Neuwirth 2012, 56). Just before the adoption of the Convention, the United States mentioned that it had "very serious concerns about the potential of the [CDCE] to be misinterpreted in ways that might impede the free flows of ideas by word and image as well as affect other areas, including trade" (UNESCO 2005b, 221). It also stressed that the proposed text was deeply flawed because it dealt with trade rather than culture, thus, that it was outside UNESCO's mandate, and that its adoption would weaken UNESCO's reputation as a responsible international organization (Martin 2005). Some of the Friends of Audiovisuals, such as Argentina, Brazil, India, Japan, Mexico, and New Zealand, also had reservations toward the

CDCE, alongside other states, such as Australia, Colombia, Israel, South Korea, and Turkey. In general, the United States and these countries apprehended the trade-restricting effects of the international efforts in favor of cultural diversity (see Balassa 2012, 85–87; Vlassis and Richieri Hanania 2014, 26).

In the words of Craufurd Smith (2007, 53), the CDCE was primarily designed by its promoters, notably Canada and France, to maintain the status quo in the field of trade and culture. It serves to justify not only their culturally motivated trade restrictions, but also their refusal to make commitments in existing and developing communications sectors. Indeed, for many states parties to the Convention, its proper implementation requires that the cultural sector not be subject to trade negotiations and that governments preserve all latitude to pursue cultural policies. Otherwise, why would states have secured the right to adopt or maintain cultural policy measures if it were to sacrifice this right through binding trade commitments? It remains a party's political choice under the Convention whether or not to liberalize its cultural sector. Brazil and Mexico, exporters of cultural products, seek liberalization commitments, although assorted with more or less important exceptions or conditions allowing for the pursuit of cultural policies. If they are of the view that this is compatible with the tenets of the CDCE, others argue that such commitments do not respect the specific character of cultural products, compromise the efficiency of cultural policies and, thus, the proper implementation of the Convention. At the other extreme, with a view to preventing the application of the CDCE, the United States insists on wide-ranging liberalization of the cultural sector with, at most, clearly defined exceptions.

THE TRADE AND CULTURE DEBATE IN PREFERENTIAL TRADE AGREEMENTS

The stalemate in the Doha Round has led states to increasingly turn to PTAs to serve their economic and trade objectives and secure their policy preferences. The number of PTAs has been steadily increasing. At the end of 2014, the WTO had received notification of 445 PTAs, with 258 of them currently in force. Most are bilateral, cross-regional, and take the form of FTAs. All WTO member states, with the exception of Mongolia, are now parties to one or more PTAs, with some countries belonging to as many as thirty, creating what has been described as a tangled "spaghetti bowl" of overlapping trade regulations (WTO 2015, 75). The states most active on the PTA front include the United States, Canada, Chile, China, India, Japan, Peru, Singapore, and Turkey; as well as groupings, such as the European Union, the European Free Trade Association, and the Association of Southeast Asian Nations.[13]

Although some PTAs only apply to trade in goods, they are increasingly broader and deeper in their coverage, notably with provisions on services and electronic commerce. As a result, PTAs often go beyond the rules contained in the multilateral agreements under the aegis of the WTO, encompassing both more advanced rules in areas covered by the WTO (WTO+ provisions), such as industrial and agricultural tariffs, technical barriers to trade, services, trade-related investment measures, intellectual property rights, and policy areas not covered in WTO agreements (WTO-X provisions), such as competition policy, electronic commerce, investment, environmental laws, and labor-market regulations. Most PTAs also include their own provisions for dispute settlement.

If cultural products, and especially audiovisual services under the GATS, have not been subject to a significant number of commitments following the Uruguay Round and of offers in the Doha Round, some PTAs have provided for major advances. In fact, the audiovisual industry is one of the sectors in which the contrast between multilateral and preferential or bilateral commitments is the greatest, especially in PTAs involving the United States (Roy 2008, 340). Among all PTAs, there are, however, varying degrees in the liberalization of cultural products. Indeed, the treatment of cultural products in the hundreds of bilateral, regional, and multilateral trade agreements negotiated over recent decades varies as greatly as the historical circumstances, national interests, and relative negotiating leverage of the parties (Bruner 2008, 366). In particular, the United States and other Friends of Audiovisual Services, including Japan, have been eager to reduce if not eliminate foreign market restrictions on their cultural exports.

Yet, as is the case in the multilateral setting, most states are not keen on liberalizing the cultural sector. In fact, with the high-profile exception of cultural products, not many sectors are singled out for special status in PTAs with any regularity (Chase 2015, 218, 230). Hence, some PTAs do not provide for any liberalization of the cultural sector. This is the case of Canada's PTAs, which include an outright exemption for cultural industries, including in its bilateral FTA concluded with the United States in 1987, which was later incorporated into the NAFTA. At the same time, most PTAs only provide for modest liberalization. Thus, PTAs that only apply to trade in goods do not entail much liberalization of the cultural sector. This is because the main instruments of states' cultural policies, such as domestic content regulations in the media, are associated with "services." As for the impact of PTAs covering goods and services on states' ability to pursue cultural policies, this, of course, depends on their specific provisions. The PTAs concluded by the European Union have systematically excluded audiovisual services.[14]

Another factor is whether PTA negotiations are conducted following a positive-list or negative-list approach. PTAs are roughly split between positive and negative listing, while a majority of services PTAs are based on a negative-list negotiation approach (Sauvé 2010; Chase 2015, 230). For some authors (Low and Mattoo 2000; Sauvé 2010; Mattoo and Sauvé 2011), the positive and negative-list approaches would not be so different from a technical or legal perspective. In principle, the same level of commitment to liberalization can be formulated in either "positive" or "negative" terms or, otherwise stated, the two negotiating modalities can result in identical liberalization levels. In some conditions, positive-listing coverage may even be more liberalizing than negative listing with significant reservations (Mattoo and Sauvé 2011, 252–53). Instead of zero liberalization, positive listing may have as a baseline the current level of regulatory liberalization (standstill) and/or include "ratchet" mechanisms, pegging commitments to future levels of liberalization.[15]

If such considerations contend that both negotiation modalities *may* lead to far-reaching liberalization, they overlook that their points of departure are radically different. Under positive listing, a sector or measure has to be explicitly inscribed in a schedule of commitments, and to the extent of the inscription. On the other hand, under negative listing, all sectors and disciplines are fully committed, unless expressly excluded, to the extent of the exclusion. Following the logic of the latter approach, the pressure is clearly upon countries that wish to exclude certain sectors and measures from their initial PTA proposal. These countries have to justify why this should be the case in order to secure the consent of the other negotiating party or parties. Not surprisingly, the number of reservations generally remains relatively small. Another implication is that states not well prepared to express their preoccupations and concerns in the cultural sector run the risk of ending fully committed by default. The most at risk from that perspective are the developing countries (see Bernier 2004, 3–4).

The positive-list approach is intended to facilitate a *gradual* process of liberalization, echoing the GATT in achieving tariff reductions through sequential rounds of negotiations. Conversely, the negative-list approach is more akin to a *once-for-all* negotiating exercise aimed at maximizing liberalization. Thus, evidence reveals for countries actively engaged in PTAs, such as Chile, that when a positive-list approach has been used, the resulting commitments, both in terms of sectoral coverage and depth of liberalization, have turned out to be less far-reaching than in PTAs based on a negative-list approach (Sáez 2008, 701). Having built an index of commitments in audiovisual services from 113 PTAs involving seventy-three countries, Chase (2015, 226–27, 230, 242) found that positive-list PTAs include no such commitments 53% of the time, compared to 15% of the time for negative-list PTAs. This constitutes powerful evidence that negotiating modalities matter, as negative listing makes commitments harder to avoid. Indeed, if negotiation modalities were not really consequential, why is the United States so insistent on the negative-list approach?[16]

While some countries, such as the United States, Canada, and Japan, have negotiated all or most of their PTAs under the negative-list approach, others, such as China and the European Union, have primarily resorted to the positive-list approach. In the case of Australia, Chile, Singapore, and South Korea, depending on their trading partners, some of their PTAs, negotiated under a positive-list approach, entail *specific commitments* on cultural products, while others, owing to the negative-list approach, entail *specific exceptions* pertaining to the cultural sector. The bottom-up or positive-list approach, arguably, leaves greater flexibility for the exclusion or particular treatment of key sectors, such as audiovisual services. The top-down or negative-list approach is, then, most likely to involve the greatest degree of liberalization of cultural products. Aside from specific exceptions or reservations, themselves of varying scope, the cultural sector is entirely liberalized. Yet, for Canada, this does not affect the cultural sector, as the latter is wholly exempted. Interestingly, the negotiations of the Comprehensive Economic and Trade Agreement (CETA), which concluded in 2014 between Canada and the European Union, followed the negative-list approach, a first for the EU. Also, among the recent and current PTA negotiations, while those of the TPP were based on the negative-list approach, the TiSA and the TTIP negotiations subscribe to a hybrid approach, i.e., positive listing for market access commitments and negative listing for national treatment.

Some countries, such as Chile, Mexico, and South Korea, are parties to PTAs concluded with the United States, the European Union, and Canada, the key protagonists in the trade and culture debate. Thus, shortly after concluding its FTA negotiations with the United States, the South Korean government further negotiated and concluded an FTA with the European Union, which aims at implementing the CDCE, notably through a Protocol on Cultural Cooperation.[17] Later, South Korea also concluded an FTA with Canada. These different PTAs entail sharply differing, if not conflicting, outcomes as to the liberalization of the cultural sector and, by consequence, on states' ability to pursue cultural policies. If the latter is significantly curtailed, as is the case under a PTA with the United States, it is hardly of any use to preserve latitude for cultural policies under PTAs concluded with Canada and the European Union. US PTAs are therefore extremely significant with regard to the evolution of the trade and culture debate. Such differing outcomes exemplify the increasing fragmentation of international economic and trade law. When considered in light of the provisions of the CDCE under UNESCO, they contribute more generally to the fragmentation of international law. In view of the multiplication of international regimes, with key multilateral organizations, such as the WTO and UNESCO, alongside an expanding web of PTAs, the institutional trajectories pursued by states for handling the trade and culture debate reveal an ever-increasing and perplexing fragmentation (Gagné 2015, 89).

MULTILATERAL VERSUS REGIONAL/BILATERAL TREATMENT OF CULTURAL PRODUCTS

The existing, sometimes pronounced, divergences in the principles and rules relating to cultural products within the WTO, on the one hand, and PTAs, on the other, raise a lot of questions. A key one is whether such divergences associated with the proliferation of PTAs may further jeopardize the likelihood of an agreement, or even of some progress, on the treatment of cultural goods and services within the WTO. In this regard, there are two different views on the relationships between economic regionalism/bilateralism and multilateralism.

On the one hand, as some states further liberalize their trade, the overall outcome of PTAs is freer trade, as long as these do entail new barriers to trade with third countries and trade creation (when consumption shifts from high-cost producers to low-cost producers within the union, leading to an increase in efficiency) outweighs trade diversion (when consumption shifts from low-cost producers outside the trading bloc to high-cost ones within it, leading to a decrease in efficiency). Also, inasmuch as the trade principles and provisions at the basis of such PTAs are essentially similar and consistent with WTO rules, and PTAs now involve nearly all countries, this would result in *de facto* multilateral liberalization. Moreover, many liberalization commitments between PTA partners often involve changes in their domestic laws that apply indiscriminately to third parties. PTAs would then act as vanguards of trade liberalization, which could later be more easily emulated and formally multilateralized (see Baldwin 2006). On the other hand, to the extent that PTAs necessarily involve discrimination vis-à-vis third countries and result in trade diversion, they hinder world trade. Furthermore, as various PTAs have their own particular scope and content, usually reflecting the objectives and interests of their most important states parties, thus allowing these states' preferences to be more easily pursued, this would complicate, if not prevent, the possibility of such differences later being harmonized at the multilateral level (see Bhagwati 2008).

It is this latter view that is of particular concern with respect to the evolution of the trade and culture debate. PTAs have proved for the United States, Canada, and the European Union more suitable venues than the WTO to secure their policy preferences on the treatment of cultural goods and services in international trade law. Thus, it appears increasingly unlikely that the main protagonists of the trade and culture debate would accept to see their respective positions being compromised by multilateral negotiations, when they have successfully pursued their preferences in the bilateral/regional setting with an ever greater number of partner countries.[18]

SUMMARY AND CONCLUSIONS

The trade and culture debate mainly results from different conceptions of culture as well as divergent economic interests among states. The series of measures pursued by governments as part of cultural policies can essentially be distinguished between financial and regulatory ones. Even though these are meant to foster states' cultural identity, they are not without involving restrictions upon international trade. The technological developments mark a revolution in the way cultural products are created and consumed, as well as a challenge for the diversity of cultural expressions and the effectiveness of states' cultural policies. With the digital revolution, cultural products, and especially audiovisual services, are to occupy an even more central place, particularly for US economic and trade interests.

The evolution of the trade and culture debate has been chiefly influenced by the outcome of the Uruguay Round of multilateral trade negotiations in the early 1990s, summed up as "the agreement to disagree." If audiovisual services were not formally subject to any exceptions, very few countries entered into commitments regarding the cultural sector. Although cultural products have not figured so prominently in the long blocked Doha Round, still few states seem willing to liberalize their cultural sector, despite requests to that effect from the WTO Friends of Audiovisual Services. This situation may be partly attributable to the use of the bottom-up or positive-list negotiating approach, as well as the mobilization within UNESCO that led to the CDCE, the latter insisting on the specific character of cultural products. The primary instruction among the states parties to the Convention is to abstain from trade commitments and maintain the ability to conduct cultural policies. This has had for consequence to encourage the main protagonists of the trade and culture debate, and notably the United States, to pursue their preferences on the treatment of cultural products through a series of PTA negotiations. In turn, the proliferation of PTAs raises questions as to the prospects for multilateral negotiations.

With respect to the United States, the next chapter discusses the evolving American position on the trade and culture debate, in particular its negotiation strategies and priorities, as revealed in key features and provisions of its PTAs.

NOTES

1. Sovereignty costs are calculated as loss of support among particular constituencies that may value policy autonomy highly (Kahler 2000, 668).

2. On the economics of cultural products and economic rationale for cultural policies, see Caves (2000); Baker (2000); Sauvé and Steinfatt (2000, 323–39); Grant and Wood (2004, 42–136); Voon (2007, 37–60); Shi (2013, 51–64).

3. For more on cultural policy instruments, see Shi (2013, 64–86). For a comparative analysis of cultural policies in different countries, see Guerrieri, Iapadre, and Koopmann (2005); Poirrier (2011). On the trade effects of various cultural policy measures, see Roy (2005, 941–47).

4. As an illustration of convergence, an online magazine is not only less expensive to produce, but can integrate sound and film, making "reading" a magazine a very different experience from what it used to be.

5. Chase (2015, 220) also mentions that no data are available on audiovisual services trade for more than 100 countries that make up a quarter of the world economy.

6. Market access refers to the conditions set by countries for the entry of specific goods and services into their territory. According to the national treatment principle, imported and domestic goods and services, as well as foreigners and locals, should be treated equally.

7. Under the United Nations Provisional Central Product Classification (UN CPC) code, used as an optional guiding tool by states for the GATS negotiations, "audiovisual services" are classified as a sub-sector of "communication services" and divided into six sub-categories: motion picture and video tape production and distribution (CPC 9611); motion picture projection (CPC 9612); radio and television (CPC 9613); radio and television transmission (CPC 7524); sound recording; and "other" unclassified audiovisual services, such as multimedia. The first four sub-categories, with their corresponding codes, are also further divided. Most cultural services other than audiovisual are included within "recreational, cultural and sporting services." These comprise: entertainment (including theater, live bands, and circus) (CPC 9619); news agency (CPC 962); libraries, archives, museums, and other cultural services (CPC 963); sporting and other recreational services (CPC 964); and an "other" sub-category. Among the remaining cultural services, advertising (CPC 871) as well as printing and publishing (CPC 88442) belong to "other business services."

Given the specifics of services, compared with goods, the WTO has defined trade in services to span four modes of supply: Mode 1—cross-border, where a service is supplied from the territory of a country into the territory of another; Mode 2—consumption abroad, where a service is supplied in the territory of a country to the consumers of another; Mode 3—commercial presence, where a service is supplied through the establishment of a legal entity of a country in the territory of another (i.e., foreign direct investment); Mode 4—movement of natural persons, where a service is supplied by a national of a country in the territory of another.

Under the GATS, a sector or sub-sector included in a country's list of specific commitments does not automatically entail full compliance with the market access (Article XVI) and national treatment (Article XVII) obligations. States rather decide, for each mode of supply, whether to undertake full commitments (i.e., without any limitations), partial commitments (i.e., inscribing in their schedules measures or types of measures inconsistent with Articles XVI or XVII to be maintained or adopted in the future), or no commitment at all (i.e., keeping flexibility to maintain or adopt any measure inconsistent with Articles XVI and/or XVII with regard to a given mode of supply).

8. Cultural services are sometimes included in different, overlapping sectors: audiovisual services; telecommunications services; and recreational, cultural, and sporting services. The United States and other countries have stressed that the classification of audiovisual services under the GATS no longer corresponds to current realities and technologies in the audiovisual sector, where, for instance, films and music are provided directly to consumers online or via cable. The WTO Secretariat has noticed that it can be difficult to distinguish "radio and television transmission services" classified under "telecommunications" from those under "audiovisual services," although it is generally accepted that the latter involve content programming while the former only involve the transmission of information, despite US disagreement with this interpretation (WTO 1998a, para 5; Voon 2007, 70–73).

9. For more on states' negotiations and commitments in the audiovisual sector within the WTO, see Roy (2005).

10. On the periodicals dispute, see Gagné (1999); Armstrong (2000); Bruner (2008, 388–89).

11. For an account of the initiatives in different forums that led to the adoption of the CDCE, see Gagné (2005c). On the CDCE negotiations and provisions, see Bernier (2005); Craufurd Smith (2007); Shi (2013, 105–17). On the US objections to the CDCE, see also Bruner (2008, 397–404).

12. The differences and links between the CDCE and other, especially economic, treaties constitute a vast and fascinating topic, of course, beyond the scope of this book. For more on the history, negotiations, provisions, and implementation of the CDCE and on its relationship with, or impact on, the WTO and PTAs, see Gagné (2005b); Hahn (2006); Graber (2006); Voon (2006); Wouters and De Meester (2008); Gagné (2008); Bernier (2009); Vlassis (2011); Kono and Van Uystel (2012a); Richieri Hanania (2014).

13. For a discussion on the interrelationship between PTAs and the international trading system and a comparison of US, European, and Asian approaches to PTAs, see Bartels and Ortino (2006); Buckley, Io Loo, and Boulle (2008); Heydon and Woolcock (2009); WTO (2011); Dür and Elsig (2015). For an overview and comparison of states' liberalization commitments in the services sector more specifically, see Marchetti and Roy (2008a); Roy (2011); Hoekman and Mattoo (2012).

14. For a discussion of US, Canadian, and European stances on the trade and culture debate as translated in PTA negotiations, see Richieri Hanania (2012).

15. A standstill provision ensures that a measure will not become more restrictive in the future, while a ratchet mechanism automatically binds all future unilateral liberalization measures. In the latter case, this means that if a measure is later amended to become less restrictive, the new, more favorable treatment will apply. The standstill and ratchet mechanisms are associated with both positive-list and negative-list negotiation modalities.

16. For more on the bottom-up and top-down negotiation modalities and their implications, see Broude and Moses (2015).

17. Similar to audiovisual co-production agreements, the protocols on cultural cooperation concluded by the European Union with some third countries, even though they may involve some liberalization, correspond to cultural rather than commercial arrangements. On the EU-Korea cultural cooperation protocol, see Loisen and De Ville (2011).

18. On the relationship between multilateral and preferential agreements, with a focus on intellectual property and services, see Cottier, Sieber-Gasser, and Wermelinger (2015).

TWO

The Treatment of Cultural Products in US Free Trade Agreements

In the trade and culture debate, the United States has traditionally held that cultural products are no different and ought to be subject to the same trade obligations as any other products. Yet, given the ensuing confrontation at the international level, the position of the United States has evolved. If chapter 1 showed that US efforts in favor of the liberalization of cultural services have encountered strong resistance from most WTO members, this chapter focuses on the revised US strategy so as to increase the liberalizing prospects of the cultural/audiovisual sector. Chapter 2 also examines how, in comparison with the multilateral negotiations, the PTA path has better enabled the United States to meet its objectives regarding the treatment of cultural products in trade agreements. This is mainly attributable to the essentially bilateral setting of such PTA talks and the US ability to secure its preferred negative-list negotiating approach.

The first section of this chapter relates the evolution of the US position on the trade and culture debate. This is followed by the negotiating strategies and priorities of the United States, as revealed from the 2002 TPA, the US trade institutions and advisory committees, the main characteristics of the revised US policy concerning cultural products, as well as its FTA program. Then, the key features and provisions of US FTAs regarding cultural products are analyzed, with an emphasis on the main relevant chapters of these agreements, i.e., those on trade in services, investment, and electronic commerce, as well as those dealing with telecommunications, intellectual property rights, regulatory transparency, and movement of key personnel. The chapter ends with the exceptions pertaining to the cultural sector taken by the United States in its FTAs, as well as those of its FTA partners before the 2002 TPA. This serves as a preliminary to the examination, in the two subsequent chapters, of the cultural reservations secured by states parties to the US FTAs concluded under the 2002 TPA.

THE EVOLUTION OF THE US POSITION ON THE TRADE AND CULTURE DEBATE

In the early 1980s, in preparation for the negotiations that were to lead to the GATS, motion pictures, together with telecommunications and advertising, were among different services sectors for which the Office of the United States Trade Representative (USTR) drafted a series of internal reports (Balassa 2012, 72–73). Since motion picture was the only sector with services features covered by the GATT, the United States saw it as a model for the application of international trade rules to services. Besides, because of the convergence between developing technologies in the motion picture industry and other services sectors, particularly telecommunications and advertising, the United States foresaw that extending trade disciplines to motion pictures "may help to assure an orderly expansion of economic relations in other dynamic services—and related merchandise areas too." Outlining a position largely abandoned in the heat of the Uruguay Round negotiations, the motion picture report recognized that screen time quotas and subsidies "permit governments to pursue legitimate social objectives without unnecessarily distorting international trade." Quoting industry sources, the report added that "reasonable screen time quotas are a relatively straightforward and acceptable means of protecting a domestic film industry; subsidies, when paid from general revenue (and not from box-office receipts) have little impact on trade patterns" (Balassa 1981, 6, 35).

The motion picture report also started from the dual nature of motion pictures—i.e., both a commercial product and the embodiment of a nation's cultural identity—therefore leading to special treatment under the GATT (Balassa 1981, 29). Then, in a communication to the WTO in 1998:

> The United States wishes to join the [WTO] Secretariat in underscoring that audiovisual services reflect the social and cultural characteristics of a nation and its peoples—as a source of entertainment and education, as a means for helping to integrate a nation domestically, and in presenting to the rest of the world a nation's unique identity. (WTO 1998b, 2)

Yet, up until 1998, the official US position was that cultural products were no different from other goods and services and, as a result, must be treated exactly like any other products in trade agreements (Bernier 2004, 1). A first indication that this position was subject to a significant change in both tone and substance came at the end of 2000 in the US communication on audiovisual and related services submitted at the invitation of the

WTO Group on Negotiating Services (WTO 2000). This revision translates serious concern from both government and industry that the US position in the Uruguay Round on content quotas and subsidies had hardened opposition to future liberalization commitments in the audiovisual sector. In particular, demands for non-discriminatory access to European film subsidies are reported to have helped Europe's film associations to mobilize by arousing widespread fears that trade rules could be used to restrict the aids upon which most national film industries depended. The United States was also mindful of ongoing discussions led by Canada and France to create a new international instrument to tackle cultural issues within UNESCO. The perspective of having the audiovisual sector entirely removed from multilateral trade disciplines was not taken lightly, and the United States set about to improve its image on the trade and culture debate (Balassa 2012, 79–80).

In order to cast the Doha Round in a new light, the US government emphasized that the audiovisual sector in 2000 was "significantly different from the audiovisual sector of the Uruguay Round period when negotiations focused primarily on film production, film distribution, and terrestrial broadcasting of audiovisual goods and services" and went on to stress that "[e]specially in light of the quantum increase in exhibition possibilities available in today's digital environment, it is quite possible to enhance one's cultural identity and to make trade in audiovisual service more transparent, predictable, and open" (WTO 2000, paras 2 and 9). Directly referring to the trade and culture debate that marked much of the Uruguay Round discussion, the US communication refutes the notion that the controversy over the audiovisual sector in the WTO is an "'all-or-nothing' game" in which "the only available options were to exclude culture from the WTO or to liberalize completely all aspects of audiovisual and related services" (WTO 2000, para 5).

In an attempt to lay the groundwork for a constructive negotiation, the communication, acknowledging the "public concern for the preservation and promotion of cultural values and identity," outlines a proposal where the promotion and preservation of a nation's cultural identity and liberalization of trade in audiovisual services may in fact "reinforce each other" (WTO 2000, paras 1 and 9). It is recognized, in particular, that public funding of audiovisual services is "a sensitive issue for many [WTO] Members where local theatrical film production . . . is dependent on government support" (WTO 2000, para 8). The earlier 1998 communication mentioned that "[t]he U.S. delegation is of the view that development of trade disciplines for the audiovisual sector need not necessarily restrict government subsidies for domestic film production and distribution, as long as these are not derived from discriminatory practices" (WTO 1998b, 3). Many governments provide substantial financial support to their cultural, especially audiovisual, industries. Although the elaboration of subsidy disciplines under GATS Article XV has proved difficult, subsidies are not completely beyond the reach of the GATS. A key illustration is that the latter applies to (discriminatory) subsidies when states list a sector in their schedules of commitments without any limitation regarding national treatment. This explains why the United States, in one of few limitations on its commitments in audiovisual services, specifies that grants from the National Endowment for the Arts are reserved to individuals with US citizenship or permanent resident alien status, and non-profit companies (Bernier 2004, 5–6).[1]

In three concluding sub-paragraphs, the 2000 US communication itemizes specific negotiation proposals. One calls for a "clear, accurate and comprehensive" classification of audiovisual services, respecting the principle of technological neutrality. This is accompanied by two annexes, the first describing the set of activities that may be considered to belong to the audiovisual sector, including sub-sectors not covered or likely covered by more than one classification under the GATS (many of which "new" services); while the second follows with an indicative listing of the international scope of the activities and services providers in the sector. The second proposal reiterates that "GATS disciplines are relevant to the audiovisual sector, as they are to virtually any services sector" and the US objective of "negotiated commitments . . . that establish clear, dependable, and predictable trade rules with due account taken of the sector's specific sensitivities." The third suggests "developing an understanding on subsidies that will respect each nation's need to foster its cultural identity by creating an environment to nurture local culture . . . while ensuring that the potential for trade distortive effects is effectively contained or significantly neutralized," although this was made contingent on "negotiated commitments for audiovisual services" (WTO 2000, para 10; Grant and Wood 2004, 372–73; Balassa 2012, 82–83).

By contrast to its Uruguay Round audiovisual request to the European Union, which sought removal of content quotas and access to subsidies on a national treatment basis, in the Doha Round the United States has made no rollback request, and has only demanded that the European Union commit itself to its current level of market access. With a few notable exceptions, similar requests have been formulated to most other WTO members as regards audiovisual services. Yet, some countries were quick to point out that the US standstill request was less benign than it appeared. It would notably involve a legally binding commitment on the part of states not to impose any further restrictions in the new and more lucrative technologies, such as video-on-demand and pay-per-view television (Balassa 2012, 81–82; Bernier 2004, 1; see also Wunsch-Vincent 2003, 16; Grant and Wood 2004, 373–74).

A similar US stance combining increased flexibility and concern for digital trade was reflected in a presentation by the MPAA before the US Congress in May 2001:

> Many countries around the world have a reasonable desire to ensure that their citizens can see films and [television] programs that reflect their history, their cultures, and their languages. In the past, when their towns might have had only one local cinema and received only one or two [television] broadcast signals, the motivation for foreign governments to set aside some time for local entertainment products was understandable. In today's world, with multiplex cinemas and multichannel television, the justification for local content quotas is much diminished. And, in the e-commerce world, the scarcity problem has completely disappeared. There is room on the Internet for films and videos from every country on the globe in every genre imaginable. There is no "shelf-space" problem on the net. (MPAA 2001)

The MPAA went on to explain to Congress its understanding of such development for trade negotiations:

> Fortunately, to date, we haven't seen any country adopt this form of market-closing measure for digitally delivered content. We hope this market will remain unfettered—and hope we can count on your support as we work with our international trade partners to keep digital networks free of cultural protectionism. Congressional authorization of Trade Promotion Authority will also be very helpful in empowering the Administration to negotiate these commitments in the WTO and other trade agreements. (MPAA 2001)

Then, in July 2002, in the US proposals for liberalizing trade in audiovisual services in the context of the GATS negotiations, while countries were requested to schedule "commitments that reflect current levels of market access in areas such as motion picture and home video entertainment production and distribution services, radio and television production services, and sound recording services," the US government at the same time strongly insisted on the need to keep free of trade barriers in electronically delivered audiovisual products (US Mission—Geneva 2002). A month later, the US Congress enacted the TPA or Trade Act of 2002, with the specific instruction to anticipate and prevent new trade barriers in the digital environment. Trade agreements having proved impossible in the multilateral setting, it is only in its PTAs that this new US approach has been translated for the first time into legal rights and obligations (Bernier 2004, 2).

US TRADE NEGOTIATION STRATEGIES AND PRIORITIES

The US Trade Promotion Authority of 2002

The US Congress has express Constitutional authority over the regulation of foreign trade. Although the US Constitution assigns no specific responsibility for trade to the President, the latter has exclusive authority to negotiate international agreements. Thus, both legislative and executive branches of the US government need to cooperate in the negotiation and implementation of trade agreements. Until the 1960s, Congress sometimes authorized the President to bargain tariffs. In particular, during the 1930s, the consequences of the Smoot-Hawley Tariff Act of 1930[2] soon led to the Reciprocal Trade Agreements Act of 1934, which enabled the President, for a limited-time period, to enter into agreements to reduce tariffs, on an MFN basis and within pre-approved levels, by proclamation without additional legislation.

After Congress renewed such authority eleven times until 1962, notably for the GATT multilateral negotiations, the issue of non-tariff barriers[3] appeared on the international trade agenda. Because adherence to agreements on such matters was to require changes to US law beyond tariff reductions, this brought Congress to adopt the Trade Act of 1974, which created the "fast-track trade negotiating authority." Through such legislation, Congress defines American negotiating objectives and priorities for trade agreements, accompanied by consultation and notification requirements for the President to follow throughout the negotiation process. Once concluded, such agreements are to be approved or rejected by Congress without possibility of amendments. Although to expire in 1980, the fast-track authority was in effect from 1975 to 1994. It was extended for eight years in 1979, then prolonged in 1988 until 1993 to accommodate the NAFTA and Uruguay Round negotiations, and further extended to April 16, 1994, a day after the conclusion of the Marrakesh Agreement establishing the WTO. Following an eight-year hiatus, in June 2002, fast track was renewed, from then known as TPA, to be effective until June 30, 2007.[4]

After emphasizing the importance of international trade to US security and prosperity, the TPA or Bipartisan Trade Promotion Authority Act of 2002 mentions, notably, information technology, telecommunications and other leading technologies, services, and intellectual property among the critical sectors and building blocks of the US economy, whose opportunities can be maximized through trade agreements (2002 TPA, section 2101(b)(2)). Unlike previous fast-track legislations, the 2002 TPA incorporates more specific negotiation objectives on issues like the protection of US trade remedy laws, the inclusion of labor and environmental standards, and digital trade,[5] as well as a Congressional Oversight Group (made up of key members of the House of Representatives and Senate) to ensure Congress's involvement in trade negotiations. Throughout the difficult Congressional negotiations that led to the TPA, the strong mandate for digital trade was one of the few topics marked by unconditional bipartisan support (Wunsch-Vincent 2003, 8–10).

Among the "principal trade negotiating objectives," the 2002 TPA highlights many areas, particularly trade in services, foreign investment, intellectual property, and electronic commerce (section 2102(b)). On services, the main US objective "is to reduce or eliminate barriers to international trade in services, including regulatory and other barriers that deny national treatment and market access or unreasonably restrict the establishment or operations of service suppliers" (section 2102(b)(2)). With respect to electronic commerce, the objectives are to ensure that: a) current WTO provisions apply; b1) electronically delivered goods and services receive no less favorable treatment under trade rules and commitments than like products delivered in physical form, and b2) the classification of such goods and services guarantees the most liberal treatment possible; c) governments refrain from implementing trade-related measures impeding electronic commerce; d) where legitimate policy objectives require domestic regulations affecting e-commerce, to obtain commitments that any such regulations are the least trade restrictive, non-discriminatory, transparent, and promote an open market environment; and e) to extend the WTO duty moratorium on electronic transmissions (section 2102(b)(9)).

The ambitious US digital trade agenda owes to a powerful alliance of American business associations representing high-tech firms (e.g., the Information Technology Industry Council) and content-producing firms (e.g., the MPAA), the contribution of these sectors to US growth and employment, as well as the strong competitive advantage of the United States in services trade in general and, notably, information technology (especially software), entertainment products, and activities related to royalties and license fees. The US comparative advantage in the services sector is reflected both in its rising share in total exports and in its positive and increasing net export balance (Wunsch-Vincent 2003, 9).

The 2002 TPA was intended to facilitate a parallel series of multilateral and preferential trade negotiations, principally to ensure that the United States was not losing out in the race for PTAs. Yet, one knows the serious difficulties confronting the multilateral trade negotiations of the Doha Round. In particular, the continuing stalemate over services liberalization within the WTO has been a key factor in bringing the United States to pursue its revised trade strategies and priorities through PTAs. The US service industries, especially the so-called copyright ones, were also instrumental in this shift in strategy. Yet, the PTA path represented a new approach for the United States. Before 2002, the American government had only concluded four PTAs, involving four countries (Israel, Canada, Mexico, and Jordan), the two with its North American neighbors by far being the most significant.

Thus, between 2002 and 2007, a series of US PTAs, all in the form of FTAs, have been concluded with countries from different continents. In fact, FTAs have proved a central element in securing liberalizing norms and provisions that the United States is determined to see adopted at the international level. Such FTAs, most of these bilateral, fit into the great liberalization principles figuring in the multilateral agreements under the ambit of the WTO. However, they often go beyond rules agreed upon in the WTO agreements. The essential US strategy has been to obtain concessions in sectors considered crucial, such as cultural and audiovisual services, from which to set precedents for its next trade liberalization endeavors. In this regard, a broader goal of the US FTA program has been to stimulate competitive liberalization to extend to the multilateral arena.[6]

US Trade Institutions and Advisory Committees

In consultation with the relevant government departments and agencies, US international trade negotiations are conducted by the USTR, which comes under the Executive Office of the President of the United States. A trade negotiation advisory committee system was put in place under the Trade Act of 1974. The purpose of advisory committees is to ensure that the Administration receives advice and assistance from a broad range of stakeholders in setting US trade policy and developing US positions in trade negotiations. The advisory system is run jointly by five federal agencies: the USTR, acting as the lead agency, the Departments of Commerce, Agriculture, and Labor, as well as the Environmental Protection Agency. There are around thirty advisory committees, comprising over 700 practitioners representing diverse interests and views, from business, labor, environmental and consumer groups, state governments, as well as academic experts and retired US government officials. These committees meet and keep regular contact with US trade officials to provide advice on proposed and ongoing trade initiatives.

The committees are required to prepare reports on proposed trade agreements (mostly FTAs) subject to TPA for the Administration and Congress. The reports must include an advisory opinion as to whether and to what extent an FTA promotes the economic interests of the United States and achieves the applicable overall and principal negotiating objectives set forth in the TPA. Each committee report must also include an advisory opinion as to whether an FTA provides for equity and reciprocity within its particular area(s). Hence, the comments from the advisory committees are indicative of the extent to which US objectives, as stipulated in the TPA, have been met in US FTAs. Their reports are also more likely to point to elements where US objectives have only partly, or not at all, been satisfied than the USTR, as the US agency responsible for negotiating the FTAs, would be willing to acknowledge.

The advisory committee reports most relevant for this book centered on cultural products are primarily those from the Industry Sector Advisory Committee on Services for Trade Policy Matters (ISAC–13) and, to a lesser degree, from the Industry Functional Advisory Committee on Electronic Commerce (IFAC–4) and the Industry Functional Advisory Committee on Intellectual Property Rights for Trade Policy Matters (IFAC–3).

In 2004, the advisory committee system was restructured. The sectoral composition of ISAC–13, which represented virtually all services sectors, was changed, to become the Industry Trade Advisory Committee on Services and Finance Industries (ITAC–10). In relation to US FTAs, the objective of ISAC–13 and later ITAC–10 is to achieve substantial additional market access for US service industries. This means commitments to greater access to foreign markets for US cross-border trade, to investment abroad, as well as to the temporary movement of persons who provide services. As for IFAC–4, it gave place to the Industry Trade Advisory Committee for Information and Communications Technologies, Services and Electronic Commerce (ITAC–8), while IFAC–3 became the Industry Trade Advisory Committee on Intellectual Property Rights (ITAC–15).

The New US Trade Strategy on Cultural Products

There are four main characteristics to the new or revised US negotiating stance or strategy pertaining to the treatment of cultural products in trade agreements (see Bernier 2004, 3–19; Wunsch-Vincent 2003, 11). The first is the adoption of the most liberal approach possible for making trade commitments. The United States seeks wide-ranging liberalization assorted with a predictable trade framework based on clearly defined provisions. To serve this objective, the US FTA negotiations are conducted following the top-down or negative-list approach. The latter implies that, in the fields of services and investment, all sectors and measures are liberalized, save for those subject to reservations or exceptions in a list or schedule. This was the approach proposed by the United States for the multilateral negotiations on services, notably for the Doha Round. The WTO members, however, decided to keep the positive-list approach, whereby only sectors and policy measures that are specifically included are subject to liberalization commitments. Then, the United States resolved to use its favored approach in its FTA program, which had already been resorted to for the NAFTA negotiations. The implications of this approach for international negotiations on services and investment can hardly be overstated.

The negative-list negotiating method or approach has been praised by the US Advisory Committee on Services. The parties to US FTAs agree to texts, or chapters, spelling out rules for liberalization. The parties then list in separate annexes those elements that they want to exclude from the rules set forth in the chapters. Thus, when texts have been agreed, the negotiations focus on the exclusions or non-conforming measures. Negotiators of each party seek to reduce the scope of such exclusions so as to obtain greater commercial opening. A crucial aspect of this method is that, unless a party succeeds in excluding a future service, all new services are to be automatically covered and, consequently, freely traded. This is particularly important in rapidly evolving sectors such as computer and related services. Such a negotiating method clearly leads to much greater liberalization than would be possible under the positive-list method of negotiation. If there is a disadvantage, it is that the negotiation of separate FTAs results in different lists of exclusions for each party, reflecting the particular economic and political forces at work within that country. Hence, while the texts of FTAs may be similar or nearly similar, the non-conforming measures are often quite different. This often means different rules in each country for US businesses operating in a same sector (DRFTA, ISAC–13 Report, 2–3).

The second characteristic of the new US strategy refers to the broad acceptance that financial support schemes for culture and content production need not be dismantled. Except for very trade-distorting financial support schemes, the United States has come to a more detached view of subsidies. Yet, the United States already excluded subsidies from the services chapters of its PTAs prior to the 2002 TPA. When considered in context, the US concession on subsidies is more apparent than real. Production of audiovisual and cinematographic content in most countries is practically impossible without financial support. The United States is aware that any attempt to seriously curtail the resort to subsidies for audiovisual products is to be fiercely resisted. Besides, the United States itself has offered considerable subsidies to its audiovisual sector, although often at the state level, as the US federal government has no history of direct subsidies to its profit-making arts sector (Bernier 2004, 6–7; see also Balassa 2012, 82).

Unlike the first two characteristics of the revised US strategy, which are common to all its FTAs in the twenty-first century, the scope of the last two depends on the specific exceptions or reservations secured by states parties. The third characteristic, perhaps the most surprising, as Bernier (2004, 3) points out, consists in the abandonment of traditional demands that local content requirements and other barriers to trade in the audiovisual sector be entirely suppressed, so far as traditional technologies are concerned. As will be seen from recent US FTAs, the exact significance of this third element is that the domestic cultural quotas subject to reservations are mostly the existing ones; they may only be maintained, and it is often on condition that they are reduced. Far less common are reservations leaving latitude to states to adopt future content requirements and, even more so, in the digital field. The fourth and last characteristic, at the core of the new US strategy, is that states commit themselves to keep digital networks free of cultural protectionism. With respect to this fourth element, it will be seen that if three states parties to the US FTAs negotiated under the 2002 TPA obtained reservations pertaining to digital trade, these are consorted with such strict conditions as to raise questions regarding their applicability.

Actual and Envisaged States Parties to US Free Trade Agreements

Before 2002, the United States had concluded an FTA with Israel in 1985, with Canada in 1987, with Mexico (and Canada) in 1992, and with Jordan in 2000. Under the 2002 TPA, besides the FTA which, with the United States, comprises Costa Rica, the Dominican Republic, El Salvador, Guatemala, Honduras, and Nicaragua (CAFTA-DR), the other US FTAs, all bilateral and effective, are with Singapore, Chile, Australia, Morocco, Bahrain, Oman, Peru, Colombia, Panama, and South Korea.

Yet, in the first decade of the twenty-first century, the United States had an ambitious FTA program, which came to involve close to fifty countries, many with which the United States had concluded bilateral investment treaties (BITs) and Trade and Investment Framework Agreements (TIFAs). Thus, the eleven FTAs, covering sixteen countries, concluded under the 2002 TPA represent about one-third of the trading partners with which the US government at that time was involved in FTA negotiations. Formally launched in 1998, the negotiations for a Free Trade Area of the Americas (FTAA), which would have included all thirty-four countries of the Americas except Cuba, ceased after the missed 2005 deadline. In the first half of 2004, the United States had begun FTA negotiations with Colombia, Ecuador, and Peru, members of the Andean Community and beneficiaries of the US Andean Trade Promotion and Drug Eradication Act, as well as Panama. More or less at the same time as the start of its FTA negotiations with Morocco, the United States had launched its Middle East Free Trade Area (MEFTA) initiative. Other regional negotiations involved the South African Customs Union, grouping Botswana, Lesotho, Namibia, South Africa, and Swaziland, these being "on hold" since 2006. Bilateral US FTA negotiations were as well conducted, notably with Malaysia, Qatar, Thailand, and the United Arab Emirates.

The United States has also been party to three major preferential trade negotiations. The first are those of the TPP, with twelve countries of the Pacific Rim, notably Australia, Canada, and Japan. Six of the parties (Australia, Canada, Chile, Mexico, Peru, and Singapore) already have an FTA with the United States; while, in the 2000s, Malaysia was involved in bilateral US FTA negotiations and New Zealand considered for such possibility. The second major negotiations are those of the TiSA, so far assembling twenty-three WTO Really Good Friends of Services, among which are Australia, Canada, the European Union, Japan, and South Korea. Ten of these countries (Australia, Canada, Chile, Colombia, Costa Rica, Israel, Mexico, Panama, Peru, and South Korea) count among US FTA partners, while three (Mauritius, New Zealand, and Taiwan) were already envisaged for an FTA by US authorities. Finally, the third correspond to the TTIP being negotiated with the European Union. The United States had concluded BITs with eight Central and Eastern European countries in the 1990s, but such agreements had to be amended when these countries joined the European Union.

KEY FEATURES AND PROVISIONS OF US FREE TRADE AGREEMENTS

The preambles of the American FTAs negotiated between 2000 and 2007 are to a great extent similar as to their stated objectives and revealing of the priorities of the US government with respect to international trade. There is no specific reference to trade in cultural goods and services or to the importance of preserving cultural diversity. The closest to a reference to cultural products pertains to intellectual property rights. In the CAFTA-DR, as well as in the US-Chile, US-Morocco, and US-Panama FTAs, it is stressed that governments are resolved to "foster creativity and innovation, and promote trade in goods and services that are the subject of intellectual property rights." In the US-Bahrain and US-Oman FTAs, one rather reads "desiring to foster creativity and innovation, improve technology, and enhance the protection and enforcement of intellectual property rights." The US-Australia FTA mentions "foster creativity and innovation and promote stronger links between dynamic sectors of their economies," while, in the US-Peru and US-Colombia FTAs, one finds "foster creativity and innovation and promote trade in the innovative sectors of our economies."

The texts of the US FTAs conform to a standard model or template and, thus, are quite similar. Although the numbering of the chapters as well as their scope and content may vary slightly, they address basically the same issues more or less in the same order. What really differ from one FTA to another are the lists of exceptions and, at times, some precedents. With the use of the top-down or negative-list approach, what is most relevant in US FTAs are the lists of exceptions, in annexes, which indicate the specific sectors and measures that states parties have secured for the conduct of cultural policies.

Two types of lists are provided. Exceptions in Annexes I allow the maintenance and renewal of measures in a given domain. Yet, when including an exception in its Annex I, a state limits its ability to intervene in a sector. Following the standstill clause, any renewed or revised measure could not be more trade restrictive than the existing one. In addition, under the ratchet mechanism, any subsequent liberalization of measures is to be automatically bound. On the other hand, exceptions in Annexes II, also known as reservations for future measures, are much broader. Under these, states keep full discretion to not only maintain existing, but adopt new or more restrictive, measures in a sector or sub-sector.[7]

The chapters in US FTAs most relevant as regards the treatment of cultural products and, hence, states' ability to pursue cultural policies, are those on cross-border trade in services, investment, and electronic commerce. To a lesser degree, the chapters on telecommunications, intellectual property rights, regulatory transparency, and, when applicable, temporary entry for business persons, are also to be considered. By concentrating on these chapters, this book deals primarily with cultural "services." The latter are most significant as they relate to measures such as domestic content regulations in the media. As far as cultural "goods" are involved, tariffs and quotas on items such as books have not figured among the main instruments of states' cultural policies. The concerns over cultural products in trade agreements are essentially associated with services. Cultural goods are rarely singled out for special treatment in PTAs and usually treated like any other merchandise. Thus, the exclusion of the audiovisual sector in the European Union's PTAs only applies to services (Chase 2015, 222–23). More revealingly, at the same time as Canada insisted on and finally secured an exemption for cultural industries in its FTA with the United States in 1987, it agreed to abolish its tariffs on US cultural goods (books, records, magazines, films, and tapes) (Grant and Wood 2004, 361). Furthermore, unlike services, regulated by the GATS and in which few countries have made commitments relating to the cultural sector, cultural goods come under the general disciplines of the GATT.

Chapters on Cross-Border Trade in Services

As is the case of the chapters on investment, the chapters on services are accompanied by two lists of exceptions or reservations contained in Annexes I and II. "[S]ubsidies or grants provided by a Party, including government-supported loans, guarantees, and insurance," i.e., most financial instruments of cultural policy, are exempted from these chapters, as they are from the investment chapters (e.g., CAFTA-DR, article 11.1.4(d)). In this respect, recent US FTAs follow on those concluded before the 2002 TPA and, as Bernier (2004, 6) points out, are even less constraining than the GATS. As formulated, the exemption seems to encompass preferential or low-interest loans from public authorities, but not indirect and less transparent forms of subsidization, such as tax credits or incentives. Yet, the cultural sector in the United States is mainly subsidized through such means, albeit at the "regional" or state level. This is not to have much effect on the United States, anyhow, since "[a]ll existing non-conforming measures of all states in the United States, the District of Columbia, and Puerto Rico" have been systematically excluded from the disciplines of the investment and services chapters of its FTAs (e.g., US-Morocco FTA, annex I-US, 16; US-Korea FTA, annex I-US, 12).

The key obligations in the services chapters pertain to national treatment, MFN treatment, market access, and local presence. Under the first, national treatment, service suppliers of another party should be treated, in like circumstances, no less favorably than national ones. The second key obligation, MFN treatment, entails that service suppliers of another party and of any non-party shall receive, in like circumstances, equal treatment. The third, market access, refers to the conditions set by states parties allowing for service suppliers to access their markets. The latter obligation forbids measures limiting: a) the number of service suppliers; b) the total value of transactions or assets; c) the total number of service operations or the total quantity of services output; d) the total number of natural persons who may be employed in a particular service sector or that a service supplier may employ; and e) measures restricting or requiring specific types of legal entity or joint ventures through which a service supplier may supply a service. As for the fourth obligation, local presence, it relates to FDI, as well as the physical presence of another party's service suppliers, in a party. It provides that "[n]either Party may require a service supplier of the other Party to establish or maintain a representative office or any form of enterprise, or to be resident, in its territory as a condition for the cross-border supply of a service."

Investment Chapters

The investment chapters also involve four key obligations. National treatment ensures that another party's investors or investments are treated no less favorably than national ones. MFN treatment supposes that investors or investments of another party and of any non-party receive equal treatment. Under the third, performance requirements are prohibited, such as those in the form of reviews by governments of foreign investments to determine whether these are to be to a country's net benefit and which require the achievement of a given level or percentage of domestic content. Finally, a fourth obligation prevents restrictions based on nationality for the directors and senior managers of enterprises. The provisions on national treatment, MFN treatment, and the nationality of directors or managers do not apply to subsidies in general, including for the promotion of a state's cultural industries.

The chapters on investment recognize the close link between investment and trade. FDI is particularly important for trade in services because many services can only be "traded" by establishing a commercial presence (investing) in a foreign market. US FTAs provide strong protections for American investors and investments that are critical to promote greater participation of US service providers in states parties' markets. Such protections notably encompass the investor-state dispute settlement mechanism. The latter refers to the right of US investors to direct, binding, and enforceable international arbitration, enabling them to be compensated in case a state party's measure(s) is/are found to contravene treaty obligations and adversely affect their returns.[8]

As in the case of its FTA with Jordan, the US-Bahrain FTA does not contain a chapter on investment. Instead, investment continues to be governed by the BITs reached beforehand with these two countries. The US-Jordan BIT was signed on July 2, 1997, and has been effective since June 13, 2003; while the one with Bahrain was signed on September 29, 1999, and has been in force since May 30, 2001. The United States also has BITs with three other of its partners with which it concluded an FTA under the 2002 TPA. One with Panama was signed on October 27, 1982, and came into effect on May 30, 1991; another with Morocco was signed on July 22, 1985, and was in force on May 29, 1991; while a third with Honduras was signed on July 1, 1995, and became effective on July 11, 2001. In these cases, the BITs were suspended after the applicable FTAs came into force. The US government concluded BITs with El Salvador and Nicaragua, but these two had not entered into force. In the late 1990s, the United States also conducted negotiations for a BIT with South Korea, but these never concluded.

Temporary Entry of Business Persons

Like investment, the temporary entry of key business persons is one of the most important ways by which services are traded. The speedy and agile movement of skilled personnel is essential to international trade and investment, since this is a key means by which enterprises can provide services to their customers. Only the US-Singapore and US-Chile FTAs, the first two trade agreements negotiated under the 2002 TPA, include chapters on trans-border movement of natural persons. To the extent that US immigration policy was affected, such provisions were not in the mandate given to the Executive for negotiating FTAs and have not figured in subsequent FTAs due to Congressional opposition. Without temporary entry provisions in most US FTAs, parties' nationals who have to travel to provide services can only do so under the relevant provisions of the services chapters, as well as through the existing states' work permit and visa systems. The US Advisory Committee on Services has deplored the hurdles faced by service providers as a result of this situation.

Chapters on Electronic Commerce

A core objective of the new US trade strategy concerning the cultural/audiovisual sector is to adapt it to the new communication technologies or digital environment. Hence, US FTAs include chapters on electronic commerce, which are closely related to the chapters on services and pertain to trade in digital products. The latter concept reflects increasing technological developments in the last three decades and the need for predictability in how such products are treated in trade agreements. Digital products include computer programs, texts, videos, images, sound recordings, and other products that are digitally encoded and produced for commercial sale or distribution, regardless of whether they are fixed on a carrier medium (CD, DVD, or other) or transmitted electronically. This definition was gradually refined or fine-tuned as successive US FTAs were being negotiated. Whereas cultural goods and services come under different WTO agreements, i.e., the GATT and the GATS, the term "digital products" in US FTAs encompasses both cultural goods and services and makes them subject to similar rules.[9] The provisions of the chapters on electronic commerce must be considered in conjunction with the measures of liberalization in telecommunications, computer and related services, as well as in high technology products. Parties to US FTAs are required to join the WTO Information Technology Agreement, when not already full participants in this plurilateral agreement, as provided under the 2002 TPA (section 2102(b)(7)(B)).

The e-commerce chapters prevent the application of customs duties, fees, or other charges on digital products transmitted electronically. This follows on the 1998 WTO moratorium on customs duties on electronic transmissions, adopted at US initiative. Most US FTAs also provide for the customs valuation of physically delivered digital products on the basis of the value of the carrier medium alone. In this regard, many countries apply customs duties on content-based products using a wide variety of different standards, many of which based on projected revenues from the sale of content-based products. On the other hand, while the US-Chile FTA provides that customs duties may not be applied on digital products of the other party, the US-Australia and US-Korea FTAs stipulate that neither party may impose customs duties, fees, or other charges on the importation or exportation of digital products, regardless of their method of delivery—electronic or physical (US-Chile FTA, article 15.3; US-Australia FTA, article 16.3; US-Korea FTA, article 15.3.1). If this constitutes a broader commitment than in other FTAs, which provide only for zero duties on electronic transmissions, duties may have rather been eliminated on physical products in the goods chapters of these other FTAs. Subsidies or grants provided by a party are also specifically exempted from the e-commerce chapter's national treatment and MFN obligations in the US-Australia FTA (article 16.4.3(c)) and from the national treatment obligation in the US-Korea FTA (article 15.3.5(a)).

In the final text of the US-Chile FTA, Chile dropped its reservation on new services not identified in the UN CPC, which would have allowed it to adopt or maintain any measure with respect to such new services, including Internet-based services. Chile dropped as well its reservation relating to services provided by electronic means (US-Chile FTA, ISAC–13 Report, 10). One could presume that the United States would not have accepted to conclude an FTA had Chile kept such reservations. Broadcasting services are excluded from the national treatment and MFN treatment obligations of the e-commerce chapters in the US FTAs with

Singapore (article 14.3.6) and South Korea (article 15.3.6). In both cases, broadcasting services are understood as "measures affecting the electronic transmission of a series of texts, videos, images, sound recordings, and other products scheduled by a content provider for aural and/or visual reception, and for which the content consumer has no choice over the scheduling of the series." As Bernier (2003b, 12) emphasizes, since this definition excludes subscription-based and pay-per-view radio and television, it appears to confirm the greater US interest and concern for the developing online on-demand audiovisual services than for conventional television and radio. Interestingly, in the US FTAs with Latin American countries, there are special provisions on transparency. Parties shall publish or otherwise make publicly available their laws, regulations, and other measures of general application pertaining to electronic commerce (CAFTA-DR, article 14.4; US-Peru FTA, article 15.4; US-Colombia FTA, article 15.4; US-Panama FTA, article 14.4).

With an economy increasingly based on services and knowledge, the United States has sought to prevent any restrictions in digital trade (see Yang 2012; Hao 2013; USITC 2013; 2014). The digital revolution indeed represents growing economic opportunities and is to profoundly alter the ways in which cultural contents are created, distributed, and accessed.[10] As an illustration, movies have traditionally been produced and distributed on film stocks but, in the coming years, most films are to be distributed as digital products, either fixed on a carrier medium or transmitted electronically. As a condition from US authorities for the launching of FTA negotiations with South Korea, this country reduced by half its screen quota for the benefit of its cinema industry, from 146 to seventy-three days a year, effective from July 1, 2006. Although the United States dropped its demand for a further reduction, it asked that films distributed as digital copies be excluded from such quotas (*The Hankyoreh* 2006). For Marcus Breen (2010, 659–61, 669–71), US FTA chapters on electronic commerce reveal "digital determinism." Owing to the absence or lack of both hyper-specialized expertise and political clout, the technological supremacy of the greater power brings its smaller and weaker partners to believe that free trade in digital media will be mutually beneficial. In fact, the United States nearly becomes the sole beneficiary.

Telecommunications Chapters

The US concern for seizing the economic opportunities offered by the digital revolution is also to be found in the measures of liberalization contained in the chapters on telecommunications. This is a field that, until recently, was often the preserve of public monopolies, as in the case of telephone. Whereas the audiovisual, computer, and telecommunications sectors used to differ in terms of contents, networks, and regulations, they now tend to converge. Digital technologies merge the market segments of telecommunications, centered on transmission and networks, and of audiovisuals, centered on programming and contents, so as to relate the availability of contents to network accessibility. As a result, the actors in the telecommunications sector are to play an increasing role in the dissemination of digital cultural contents, notably through the Internet access services they provide.

The telecommunications chapters cover access to, and use of, the public telecommunications networks and services for the provision of services. They deal with all providers of public telecommunications services, focusing on the major suppliers of those services. The levels of liberalization and privatization of the telecommunications sector vary among the states parties to US FTAs. The FTAs with Singapore, Australia, and Morocco are considered to entail strong commitments. On the other hand, with regard to the CAFTA-DR, the US Advisory Committee on Services underlines that the remaining telecommunications barriers prevent important competition and growth that could foster trade in digital products in the Central American markets (CAFTA, ISAC–13 Report, 11; DRFTA, ISAC–13 Report, 12).

The US FTAs insist on the independence and impartiality of a state's telecommunications regulatory body toward the suppliers of public telecommunications services, particularly foreign ones. Each party must notably ensure that its regulatory decisions and procedures, including those relating to licensing, interconnection with public telecommunications networks and services, tariffs, and assignment or allocation of spectrum for non-government public telecommunications services, are impartial with respect to all market participants. Enterprises may also have regulatory decisions reviewed by an impartial and independent judicial authority. There are also provisions regarding transparency in public rulemaking, notably to ensure that regulations, including the basis for these, are promptly published or made available to all interested persons, coupled with an opportunity to comment on proposed rules by such persons, and that any measure in public telecommunications is made publicly available.

Transparency

An important element in US FTAs is their provisions for transparency in domestic regulatory processes, including licensing decisions. Such provisions are deemed absolutely essential for services industries, because they are generally the most highly regulated. Thus, the US FTAs considered in this book guarantee a high standard of transparency in administrative, licensing, and adjudicatory proceedings. The transparency provisions are laid out in five parts. There is a general chapter, applying to all trade under the FTAs. It provides, notably, for each party to establish or maintain independent tribunals or procedures for prompt review of administrative actions, and to ensure parties to a proceeding the right to a decision based on evidence. In the chapter on cross-border trade in services, there are additional provisions, which, in particular, offer further assurance that administrative decisions related to licensing are prompt and fair. In the investment chapter, there are provisions pertaining to the transparency of arbitral proceedings. Some further provisions are to be found in the financial services chapter, while those in the telecommunications chapter have just been summarized.

Intellectual Property Rights

As for intellectual property rights, since these are meant to sustain creativity and innovation, they have a role in the creation, distribution of, and access to, cultural contents. They are understood as exclusive rights granted to creators and inventors to control the use made of their productions. Such rights may be divided into two main categories: a) copyright and related or neighboring rights, for literary and artistic works, the most relevant for cultural products; and b) industrial property, which includes trademarks, patents, industrial designs, geographical indications, and the layout designs of integrated circuits. The United States is the world's first producer and exporter of products to which intellectual property rights apply, such as sound recordings, books, movies and videos, broadcast signals, as well as software. The intellectual property-intensive industries accounted for about $5 trillion in value added or 35% of US GDP in 2010, while directly supporting 27 million jobs or 19% of all American employment (US 2012, vi–vii). US artists, inventors, and other innovators received $128 billion in royalties, license fees, and payments related to audiovisual services in 2013, i.e., 39% of the world total (USTR 2016a, 8).

The United States also loses more revenue from piracy, counterfeiting, and other infringements of intellectual property rights than any other country. This explains the US emphasis on strengthening the protection and enforcement of such rights, especially copyrights in the digital media (Pham 2010; US 2013; 2015). Each party to the US FTAs should have ratified or acceded to the main existing, mostly multilateral, treaties dealing, notably, with patents, trademarks, and copyrights. On copyrights, while the WTO Agreement on Trade-Related Aspects of Intellectual Property Rights provides for a minimal protection of fifty years following the publication or the death of an author, recent amendments to US domestic law have extended this period to ninety-five years. In its FTAs the United States has obtained an extension to seventy years (e.g., US-Korea FTA, article 18.4.4).

Of all US FTAs, the one with Morocco is considered to entail the strongest commitments to intellectual property protection. The intellectual property provisions in the US-Peru, US-Colombia, and US-Panama FTAs are virtually identical, but fall short of those in the US-Morocco,

US-Bahrain, and US-Oman FTAs (US-Morocco FTA, ISAC–13 Report, 3; US-Panama FTA, ITAC–8 Report, 12). The intellectual property chapters in the US-Australia and US-Korea FTAs, i.e., with developed countries, are considered to be very strong (US-Australia FTA, IFAC–3 Report, 2; US-Korea FTA, ITAC-8 Report, 13).

US CULTURAL RESERVATIONS IN FREE TRADE AGREEMENTS

Before turning to the exceptions in favor of cultural policies secured by states parties to US FTAs, let us begin with the United States as the party to all the trade agreements considered in this book. As it seeks extensive liberalization, the United States has relatively few reservations in the FTAs it has concluded with its partners. The US reservations, including those pertaining to cultural products, are also largely identical in all its FTAs.

Under Annex I, in the field of radiocommunications, consisting of all communications by radio, including broadcasting, the United States reserves the right to restrict ownership of radio licenses in accordance with its statutory and regulatory provisions on foreign participation (e.g., US-Chile FTA, annex I-US, 12). The latter provisions are further described in the US-Korea FTA (annex I-US, 10), while the whole exception, applying to investment, is absent in the FTA with Bahrain. These US provisions have applied to free-to-air broadcasting, and not to cable ownership (Grant and Wood 2004, 360).[11]

Under Annex II, the US government reserves the right to adopt or maintain any measure according differential treatment to persons of other countries due to application of reciprocity measures or through international agreements involving sharing of the radio spectrum, guaranteeing market access, or national treatment with regard to the one-way satellite transmission of direct-to-home (DTH) and direct broadcasting satellite (DBS) television and digital audio services (e.g., US-Chile FTA, annex II-US, 1). The US-Korea FTA (annex II-US, 1) further describes the elements considered by the US FCC in applying reciprocity measures. Another reservation provides that equivalent treatment may be accorded to persons of any country that limits ownership by US persons in an enterprise engaged in the operation of a cable television system in that country (e.g., NAFTA, annex II-US; US-Australia FTA, annex II-US, 2). The latter exception is included in the NAFTA and the CAFTA-DR, as well as in the US FTAs with Singapore, Australia, Oman, and Panama.[12]

US FREE TRADE AGREEMENTS PRIOR TO THE 2002 TRADE PROMOTION AUTHORITY

The first-ever PTA concluded by the US government in the post-war period, the United States—Israel Free Trade Agreement (US-Israel FTA), only covers trade in goods. In force since September 1, 1985, the treaty itself is a short document, with only twenty-two articles, four annexes, and no provisions relating specifically to cultural goods. Israel, however, has been among the few countries to make commitments regarding cultural services during the Uruguay Round.

As for the United States—Jordan Free Trade Agreement (US-Jordan FTA), effective since December 17, 2001, if it covers sectors now included in US PTAs, such as services, intellectual property rights, electronic commerce, as well as labor and the environment, it also consists of a short text of only 19 articles. Interestingly, services commitments have been entered into following the positive-list approach. Yet, the agreement provides for significant liberalization of the whole of cultural services. Similarly to the United States, Jordan has maintained exceptions for subsidies and, generally, has no commitments relating to the movement of persons (mode 4). Some restrictions on foreign investment have been maintained in advertising (CPC 871) as well as printing and publishing (CPC 88442). With respect to audiovisuals, except for radio and television transmission services (CPC 7524), where major restrictions have been kept, the other four sub-sectors are only subject to limited foreign investment restrictions (US-Jordan FTA, Services Schedule, 10, 13, 15–16, 26).

If the US FTAs with Israel and Jordan are relatively modest in terms of provisions and partners, the US FTA with Canada, and later the NAFTA, grouping the two countries with Mexico, have been two important PTAs concluded by the American government before the 2002 TPA. The negotiations for the United States—Canada Free Trade Agreement (US-Canada FTA) began in May 1986 and concluded in October 1987. The FTA was effective from January 1, 1989, to December 31, 1993, when it was superseded by the NAFTA, in force since January 1, 1994. During the negotiations, Canada insisted on exempting the cultural industries and was ready to jeopardize the whole FTA unless this sector was excluded from the treaty. Thus, under the US-Canada FTA (article 2005.1), "[c]ultural industries are exempt from the provisions of this Agreement, except as specifically provided."[13] This exemption is assorted by a party's right to retaliate, with "measures of equivalent commercial effect in response to actions that would have been inconsistent with this Agreement but for paragraph 1" (US-Canada FTA, article 2005.2).

In the course of the NAFTA negotiations, which took place from June 1991 to August 1992, the United States tried to reopen the issue. Yet, the general exemption for the cultural sector secured in the US-Canada FTA was incorporated into the treaty, so as to apply between Canada and the

United States, as well as between Canada and Mexico (NAFTA, article 2106, annex 2106).[14] The definition of cultural industries was slightly modified to refer to *persons*, and not anymore to *enterprises*, working in those industries.[15] Much has been written about the NAFTA's "conditional" cultural exemption clause and it has led to many misunderstandings. In fact, the United States and Canada agreed to disagree on the treatment of cultural industries, essentially leaving them out of NAFTA's purview, while they remained subject to GATT/WTO disciplines.[16]

The NAFTA, unlike its predecessor the US-Canada FTA, is the first US PTA to include specific chapters on telecommunications and intellectual property. In contrast with Canada's stance, Mexico did not seek to exempt its cultural industries under the NAFTA and undertook GATS audiovisual commitments during the Uruguay Round. The NAFTA was negotiated following the negative-list approach, so that Mexico's significant commitments pertaining to cultural products under this PTA may best be understood by pointing to the relevant exceptions taken by the Mexican government.

Reminiscent of the provision of the US-Canada FTA relating to retransmission rights (article 2006), documentation showing the granting of licenses by copyright holders is required for the *Secretariá de Gobernación* to authorize the import in any form of radio or television programming for broadcast or cable distribution within Mexico (NAFTA, annex I-MX, 9–10). Unless otherwise authorized by the same Secretariat, the use of the Spanish language is required for the broadcast or cable distribution of radio or television programming, while radio or television announcers or presenters must be Mexicans to perform in the country. A majority of the time of each day's live broadcast programs must also feature Mexican nationals (NAFTA, annex I-MX, 12). The use of Spanish language or subtitles is as well required for advertising broadcast or otherwise distributed in Mexico. Advertising included in programs transmitted directly from outside Mexico may not be distributed in those programs when retransmitted in Mexican territory (NAFTA, annex I-MX, 13).

In the case of cable television, investors of another party or their investments may only own, directly or indirectly, up to 49% of the ownership interest in an enterprise in this field. The latter exception was subject to discussion by the parties five years after NAFTA's entry into force (NAFTA, annex I-MX, 14). A concession to construct and/or to operate a cable television system may only be granted to Mexican nationals and enterprises (NAFTA, annex I-MX, 15). A quota of up to 30% of the screen time of every theater, assessed on an annual basis, may be reserved for films produced by Mexican persons, either within or outside Mexico's territory (NAFTA, annex I-MX, 16). Foreign governments and state enterprises or their investments are forbidden to invest, directly or indirectly, in Mexican enterprises engaged in communications, transportation, and other general means of communication (NAFTA, annex I-MX, 19). Investors of another party or their investments may own, directly or indirectly, 100% of the ownership interest in an enterprise in Mexico engaged in the simultaneous printing and distribution within Mexico of a daily newspaper published outside Mexican territory, but only up to 49% in the case of the printing or publication of a newspaper written primarily for a Mexican audience and distributed in Mexico (NAFTA, annex I-MX, 41).

Mexico has taken relatively few reservations for future measures, on the other hand. It has reserved the right to adopt or maintain any measure concerning investment in, or provision of, broadcasting, multipoint distribution systems, uninterrupted music, and high-definition television services. This reservation does not apply to measures regarding the production, sale, or licensing of radio or television programming (NAFTA, annex II-MX). There has been a similar reservation in the case of telecommunications transport networks and services (NAFTA, annex II-MX), excluding enhanced or value-added services, the latter otherwise subject to temporary reservations under Annex I (NAFTA, annex I-MX, 17–18). There has been, as well, an exception in favor of the provision of satellite communications services (NAFTA, annex II-MX).

Under Annex III, pertaining to activities reserved to the state, the Mexican government has included satellite communications, telegraph, and radiotelegraph services (NAFTA, annex III-MX). Lastly, under Annex IV, relating to MFN exceptions, all NAFTA parties have included telecommunications transport networks and services. The latter exception does not apply, however, to measures covered by the telecommunications chapter, as well as to the production, sale, or licensing of radio or television programming (NAFTA, annex IV).

Thus, Mexico has maintained restrictions regarding the use of the Spanish language in radio and television, as well as the resort to nationals in the majority of broadcast programs and to act as announcers or presenters. There have also been restrictions concerning: the ownership of, and concessions for, cable television enterprises/services; theatrical screen quotas; and the printing or publication of daily newspapers for a Mexican audience. Reservations for "future measures" have included the right to adopt or maintain any measure relating to investment in, or provision of, broadcasting, multipoint distribution systems, uninterrupted music, and high-definition television services. The United States has also had a similar reservation concerning radiocommunications. Finally, Mexico has reserved satellite communications to the state.

Without conceding to any of the broad cultural exemptions secured by Canada under its FTA with the United States and NAFTA, the 2002 TPA was designed to extend, both in number and scope, the liberalization achieved under the NAFTA and the GATS. At the same time, it strengthened the intellectual property and added the digital components, which had become so important in the preceding years. For its part, the new US trade strategy on cultural products shows continuity with the

NAFTA template, as regards negotiation modalities, subsidy exemptions, as well as liberalizing commitments and reservations.

SUMMARY AND CONCLUSIONS

Until the late 1990s, the official US position was that cultural goods and services were no different from other products and to be subject to similar trade disciplines. In the course of the Uruguay Round, the US requests to remove or at least cap existing cultural regulations and subsidies were strongly resisted by most countries. This, in addition to the efforts of the advocates of cultural exception/diversity to prevent further liberalization of the cultural sector, brought the United States to soften its stance and to acknowledge states' concerns for cultural identity. Following this new or revised strategy, elaborated in concert with the American industry, the United States seems content with states maintaining their present level of market access, as long as no barriers are adopted affecting digital trade. With the stalemate in the Doha Round, it is in its recent PTAs that the modified US strategy on the treatment of cultural products in trade agreements has led to formal treaty obligations. There are eleven of these PTAs currently in force, all in the form of bilateral FTAs, with the exception of the CAFTA-DR concluded with six Central American and Caribbean countries.

The new US strategy encompasses four main elements or characteristics. The first consists of the most liberal approach possible for making trade commitments. This is ensured through the resort to the top-down or negative-list negotiating method, whereby all sectors and policy measures are wholly liberalized unless subject to specific reservations. The second is the broad acceptance on the part of the United States of the financial instruments of cultural policy, while the third does away with the traditional US demand that local content quotas and other barriers to audiovisual trade be completely removed, at least where traditional technologies are concerned. At the center of the new US strategy, the fourth and last element refers to the absence of cultural protectionism in the new and expanding digital networks.

The way the new strategy has been translated in recent US FTAs can be evaluated by examining the chapters most relevant for the treatment of cultural products. These deal primarily with services, investment, and electronic commerce, and, to a lesser extent, telecommunications, intellectual property rights, regulatory transparency, and the movement of business people. Finally, as the chief proponent of the liberalization of cultural goods and services, the United States has secured few exceptions toward the cultural sector in its FTAs negotiated under the 2002 TPA.

After chapter 1 revealed that the intractable nature of the trade and culture debate owes much to the intermingling of economic/trade and cultural/identity concerns, chapter 2 concentrated on the revised US trade strategies and priorities. These are characterized by both a softened stance concerning cultural products and a shift toward PTAs, whose relevant key features and provisions were emphasized. The first two chapters, thus, set the table for us to now turn to the specific cultural exceptions secured by states parties to the US FTAs negotiated under the 2002 TPA, beginning with developing countries.

NOTES

1. For sake of clarification, if sectors and modes of supply are "positively" listed in GATS schedules, the content of schedules is "negative," as derogations from full liberalization of market access and/or national treatment in those listed sectors.

2. This act set very high tariff rates in favor of US producers seeking protection at the outset of the Great Depression. In response, major US trading partners adopted retaliatory tariffs, which severely restricted trade and added to the severity of the crisis, at a time the US government looked to expand exports as a means to address the crisis.

3. Non-tariff barriers or non-tariff measures refer to all kinds of measures, other than tariffs, that have for objective or effect to restrict or distort trade. These notably include quotas, border taxes, and subsidies.

4. On US trade policy, see, among others, USITC (2009) and on US domestic trade politics, see Destler (2005).

5. On the US digital trade agenda or policy, see Wunsch-Vincent (2003).

6. On the US PTA objectives and strategies, see Schott (2004); Evenett and Meier (2008). On the security and economic dimensions of US PTAs, with the US-Singapore FTA as a case study, see Pang (2011).

7. Under the negative-list approach, as used in US PTAs, each specific exception usually refers to the *sector* to which it applies; the *obligations concerned*, i.e., either national treatment, MFN treatment, market access, local presence, performance requirements, as well as senior management and boards of directors; the *measures*, i.e., the laws and regulations of a party for which the exception is made; and a *description* of the exception, which normally indicates the chapter(s) to which it applies, either investment or cross-border trade in services or both, and sets out the scope of the sectors or activities covered by the exception. It is on this latter element that the book concentrates, since it indicates the specific exceptions secured by states parties to US FTAs relating to cultural products.

8. On the evolution of US policy on foreign investment protection, see Gagné (2011b).

9. Although it is specified in a footnote that "(t)he definition of digital products should not be understood to reflect a Party's view on whether trade in digital products through electronic transmission should be categorized as trade in services or trade in goods." Consistent with US objectives, this concept of digital product is without prejudice to the ongoing classification debate within the WTO.

10. Most cultural products, including books and newspapers, and especially audiovisual ones, such as movies, television programs, multimedia productions, and music, are now available in digital format. The digitization of cultural products is almost fully achieved in the case of music and multimedia productions and well under way in the case of television and films. For a more thorough discussion on trade in digital products, see Burri-Nenova (2009).

11. Such exception is broader and figures in Annex II relating to future measures within the NAFTA. Under the latter agreement, the US government has kept latitude with regard to investment in, or the provision of, telecommunications transport net-

works and services, as well as radiocommunications. This reservation does not involve neither enhanced or value-added telecommunications services (subject to an exception under Annex I) nor the production, sale, or licensing of radio or television programming.

12. Such reservation is provided in the NAFTA with another of the same type applying to the publication of daily newspapers primarily written for audiences and distributed in the country.

13. These provisions in the form of commitments relate to: the elimination of tariffs for cultural goods (article 401); the requirement for any US investor having to divest him/herself of assets in Canada because of ownership restrictions in cultural industries to receive fair market value (article 1607.4); amendments to Canadian law so as to ensure authorizations from, and payments to, US copyright holders for retransmission of program signals (article 2006); and the removal of the requirement for a Canadian magazine or newspaper to be printed or typeset in Canada in order for advertisers to deduct expenses for advertising space (US-Canada FTA, article 2007).

14. On the US-Canada FTA negotiations, see Doern and Tomlin (1991); Hart (1994). On the NAFTA negotiations, see Cameron and Tomlin (2000).

15. Cultural industries are understood as persons engaged in any of the following activities: a) the publication, distribution, or sale of books, magazines, periodicals or newspapers in print or machine readable form but not including the sole activity of printing or typesetting any of the foregoing; b) the production, distribution, sale, or exhibition of film or video recordings; c) the production, distribution, sale, or exhibition of audio or video music recordings; d) the publication, distribution, or sale of music in print or machine readable form; or e) radiocommunications in which the transmissions are intended for direct reception by the general public, and all radio, television and cable broadcasting undertakings and all satellite programming and broadcast network services (US-Canada FTA, article 2012; NAFTA, article 2107).

16. For more on the negotiations, provisions, and implementation of the cultural exemption clause under the US-Canada FTA and the NAFTA, see also Ritchie (1997, 215–38); Acheson and Maule (1999, 23–38); Gagné (2003/2004, 36–38); Goff (2007, 126–29).

THREE

US Free Trade Agreements with Developing Countries

Under the 2002 TPA, the US government successfully negotiated nine FTAs with fourteen developing countries. All of these are bilateral, except for the CAFTA-DR, which groups six US FTA partners. In chronological order, these FTAs have been concluded with Singapore, Chile, five Central American states (Costa Rica, El Salvador, Guatemala, Honduras, Nicaragua) and the Dominican Republic, Morocco, Bahrain, Oman, Peru, Colombia, and Panama. Although Singapore is undoubtedly a rich city-state and Chile is sometimes considered a developed country since it joined the Organization for Economic Cooperation and Development in May 2010, their respective FTAs with the United States do not differ significantly from those concluded by (other) developing countries.

This chapter looks at the details of the exceptions regarding cultural products taken by developing states parties to the US FTAs concluded under the 2002 TPA. Depending on countries, the reservations under Annexes I and II are subject to separate sub-sections. This is followed by a summary and analysis, with the exception of CAFTA-DR parties for which such comments apply to their whole regional FTA. Then, a summary and comments in reference to all the US FTAs considered conclude the chapter.

The revised US trade strategies and priorities on cultural products constitute the main determinants of the associated provisions and exceptions found in the FTAs negotiated with the American government. As the United States insists on wide-ranging liberalization, this entails the resort to the negative-list approach, whereby everything is liberalized save for sectors and measures specifically exempted. For countries eager to enhance their development prospects through FTAs with a rich major power, it involves that they must formulate and hold on to requests for exceptions in favor of cultural policies. Yet, not only are financial instruments exempted from US FTAs, but a varying array of regulatory measures may be maintained, as long as they do not significantly distort trade and no restrictions apply in new or digital media.

THE UNITED STATES—SINGAPORE FREE TRADE AGREEMENT

The negotiations for the United States—Singapore Free Trade Agreement (US-Singapore FTA) were announced during the Asia Pacific Economic Cooperation (APEC) summit on November 16, 2000. They started on December 4, 2000, and ended on January 16, 2003. The agreement was signed on May 6, 2003, and entered into force on January 1, 2004.

Cultural Reservations

The government of the Republic of Singapore has reserved the right to adopt or maintain any measure pertaining to broadcasting services[1] receivable by Singapore's domestic audience and to the allocation of spectrum in relation to such services. This exception does not apply to the sole activity of transmitting licensed broadcasting services to a final consumer (US-Singapore FTA, annex 8B, 8). Singapore has also secured a similar reservation with respect to the distribution and publication of printed media[2] (US-Singapore FTA, annex 8B, 17).

Summary and Analysis

If there are few reservations relating to cultural products in the US-Singapore FTA, these two figure in "Annex II" and, thus, leave significant margin of maneuver in the relevant sectors. There is uncertainty, however, about the effectiveness of the reservation for printed media. Reminiscent of the periodicals case, since the two services involved, i.e., distribution and publication, are related to the provision of a good, i.e., the printed medium itself, the measures associated with these services could be challenged under the GATT 1994 (Bernier 2003b, 4–5).

For the US Industry Sector Advisory Committee on Services for Trade Policy Matters (ISAC–13), "[w]hile Singapore took a fairly broad reservation that limits its obligations for television content broadcast to local audiences, its obligations in all other forms of [audiovisual] services, where US commercial interests are strongest, are excellent" (US-Singapore FTA, ISAC–13 Report, 8). In Singapore, a number of the media, i.e., newspapers, free-to-air broadcasting, and cable television stations, are government-owned and remain among the few services sectors either closed or only partially open to foreign investment (Mukherjee 2008, 604, 623). Beyond, Chase (2015, 240) points out that, alongside Singapore,

Hong Kong and Japan have also refused to commit television and radio services, both in the WTO and PTAs, despite having undertaken commitments in films and videos, something which is puzzling and in need of proper explanation. What is certain is that a wholesale exclusion of broadcasting services, including from the e-commerce chapter, is arguably something the American government does not like. Among other US FTAs negotiated under the 2002 TPA, only Korea, another Asian country, has secured such exclusion. Yet, as defined, broadcasting services do not include key "new" services and, thus, do not seem to materially affect US trade interests, as signified in the report of the US Advisory Committee on Services.[3]

THE UNITED STATES—CHILE FREE TRADE AGREEMENT

Chile was originally supposed to join the NAFTA, but, as the Clinton administration failed to secure fast-track authority from the US Congress, this could not come about. Meanwhile, Chile had concluded FTAs with Canada in 1996 and with Mexico in 1998. On November 29, 2000, the United States and the Republic of Chile announced that they were to enter into negotiations for an FTA. These began in early December 2000 to conclude on December 11, 2002. The United States—Chile Free Trade Agreement (US-Chile FTA) was signed on June 6, 2003, and took effect on January 1, 2004.

Cultural Reservations under Annex I

In the communications sector, Chile has maintained the right to require a quota of up to 40% of national production in programs broadcasted through public (open) television channels (US-Chile FTA, annex I, 3). Both parties to the FTA confirmed, by exchange of letters, their understanding of this provision, and, notably, that this percentage does not apply to cable television (US-Chile FTA, Side Letter on Television). Then, the provision arguably covers only conventional television and neither cable nor satellite television. The owner of a social communication medium, such as sound and image transmissions, newspapers, magazines, regular texts whose publishing address is located in Chile, or national news agencies, must, in the case of a natural person, be domiciled in Chile and, in the case of a juridical person, be constituted with domicile in the country or have an agency authorized to operate within the national territory. Only Chilean nationals may be president, administrators, or legal representatives of the juridical person. The legally responsible director or his/her substitute must be Chilean with domicile and residence in the country (US-Chile FTA, annex I, 3, 17).

In the case of public radio broadcasting services, a majority of the members of boards of directors should be Chilean nationals. As to requests for radio broadcasting concessions, submitted by entities in which foreigners hold more than 10% of the capital, these are only to be granted if similar rights and obligations are enjoyed by Chilean nationals in the applicant's country of origin. Only juridical persons duly constituted in Chile and domiciled in the country may be the titleholders, or make use of permits, for limited radio broadcasting telecommunications, as well as limited cable or microwave television services. The president, directors/managers/administrators, or legal representatives of such juridical persons may only be Chilean nationals (US-Chile FTA, annex I, 3–4).

Cultural Reservations under Annex II

Chile reserves the right to adopt or maintain any measure related to cross-border trade and US investors or investments in one-way satellite broadcasting of digital telecommunication services, whether direct home television broadcasting, direct broadcasting of television services, or direct audio broadcasting, and supplementary telecommunication services (US-Chile FTA, annex II, 4–5). With regard to cultural industries, Chile may accord differential treatment to countries under existing or future bilateral or multilateral international agreements, such as audiovisual cooperation agreements. For greater certainty, it is emphasized that government-supported subsidy programs, here seemingly encompassing all forms of aid including tax incentives, for the promotion of cultural activities are not subject to the limitations or obligations of the FTA. The definition of cultural industries[4] included in this reservation is essentially identical to the one in NAFTA's Article 2107 (US-Chile FTA, annex II, 11). Unlike the NAFTA, which includes an exemption for cultural industries;[5] what is exempted in the US-Chile FTA are subsidy measures and co-production arrangements; these constituting only a facet, although important, of cultural policies. Consequently, the latitude preserved by Chile to promote its cultural identity is mostly limited to financial measures, while regulatory measures are significantly constrained.

Chile finally reserves the right to adopt or maintain any measure relating to market access in all sectors, except for certain specified services sectors and sub-sectors, including advertising, printing and publishing, entertainment (encompassing theater, live bands, and circus), news agencies, libraries, archives, museums, and other cultural services. For all of these specified culture-related fields, the condition pertains to the supply of a service by a national of a party in the territory of the other party (mode 4), as indicated in Chile's Labor Code restriction (US-Chile FTA, annex II, 15–19).

Summary and Analysis

As the communications sector, which includes audiovisual services, is not mentioned in the above market access reservation, it would apparently be covered. Yet, the reservation taken under Annex I for television quotas does not refer to the obligation of market access, but, rather, comes under national treatment (Bernier 2003b, 6). Since for the MPAA and its then chair and chief executive officer (CEO), Jack Valenti, the US-Chile FTA "represents a landmark achievement on market access for the filmed entertainment industry," this provision does not seem to have much impact on audiovisual services. For the US Advisory Committee on Services,

> The [US-Chile] FTA ensures that all U.S. audiovisual services will enjoy national treatment and MFN status, with reservations. While Chile did take several reservations with respect to this sector, the reservations are narrow, specific, and unlikely to disrupt existing commercial trade in audiovisual services. For example, Chile limits foreign ownership of media, but the U.S. has similar reservations. Chile preserves the right to impose a quota on local content carried on broadcast [television], however, market forces have historically resulted in higher levels of local content than would be required by the quota, so the impact of imposing such a quota would be negligible. Moreover, the [US-] Chile FTA avoids the "cultural exceptions" approach that has flawed several prior trade agreements, while demonstrating that a trade agreement has sufficient flexibility to take into account countries' cultural promotion interests. (US-Chile FTA, ISAC-13 Report, 8–9)

As Ivan Bernier points out, when one considers the provisions of the US-Chile FTA concerning investment, services, and electronic commerce altogether:

> What is revealed by the agreement is that in exchange of "concessions" regarding the maintenance of existing measures for the protection of cultural industries, the maintenance or the adoption of international agreements on cultural cooperation, and the exclusion from the agreement of existing or future programs of cultural subsidization, the United States obtains the inclusion into the agreement of a chapter concerning the electronic commerce of digital products, which, according to Jack Valenti, should for a long time assure benefits to the entertainment industry considering the developed infrastructure of Chile in the field of telecommunications and the open content of this chapter (my translation). (Bernier 2003a, 6)

In the course of the FTA negotiations with the United States, a Coalition for Cultural Diversity was formed in Chile in October 2001. The group, composed of the film, television, theater, and publishing industries, was very active during the negotiations and received support as well as inputs from similar coalitions in Canada and Australia. The Chilean Coalition proposed a broad exemption for cultural industries, along the one in the Canada-Chile FTA. Even though the sector was not excluded, it is suggested that the cultural reservations under the US-Chile FTA resulted from the mobilization of Chilean cultural industries (Sáez 2008, 695).[6]

THE DOMINICAN REPUBLIC—CENTRAL AMERICA—UNITED STATES FREE TRADE AGREEMENT

On September 24, 2001, during a meeting of the FTAA Negotiations Committee, representatives of five Central American countries met with their US counterparts to discuss possibilities for deepening their trade and investment relations. On January 16, 2002, the US President, George W. Bush, announced his administration's intention to work on an FTA with the five member states of the Central American Common Market, i.e., Costa Rica, El Salvador, Guatemala, Honduras, and Nicaragua. The Central America (CA)FTA negotiations started on January 8, 2003, and ended on January 25, 2004, for Costa Rica and one month earlier, on December 17, 2003, for the other four countries. From January 12, 2004, the Dominican Republic had joined the negotiations which concluded, for the latter, on March 15, 2004.[7] The Dominican Republic—Central America—United States Free Trade Agreement (CAFTA-DR) was signed on August 5, 2004. From March 2006, the United States implemented the CAFTA-DR on a rolling basis as countries completed their ratification procedures. Hence, the agreement entered into force on March 1, 2006, for El Salvador; on April 1, 2006, for Honduras and Nicaragua; on July 1, 2006, for Guatemala; and on March 1, 2007 for the Dominican Republic. On January 1, 2009, the FTA became effective for Costa Rica and, consequently, for all its states parties.[8]

The CAFTA-DR constitutes the first and only FTA between the United States and a group of developing countries. Yet, it has all the key features of other, bilateral US FTAs. Its obligations apply to each party, save for exceptions and undertakings of a particular state included in annexes. The five Central American countries joined together to negotiate as a team with the United States, under the coordination of Costa Rica, although each also had its own negotiating team. In this regard, the CAFTA-DR is essentially an agreement between the United States, on the one hand, and six small states, on the other. The reservations relating to cultural products are described in the following pages, in the English-language alphabetical order of states parties' names.[9]

Costa Rica

To join the Professional Association of Journalists, all foreign journalists must prove that, in their home jurisdiction where they are allowed to practice, Costa Rican nationals can exercise their profession under like circumstances. Subject to the conditions and terms of the applicable legislation, that professional association may provide temporary licenses for the practice of journalism in Costa Rica. Enterprises may otherwise employ foreign journalists in accordance with Costa Rican law in order to carry out contracts (CAFTA-DR, annex I-CR, 4–5). Except as authorized, a journalist who is a foreign national may cover events in the country only if he/she is a resident of Costa Rica. Non-resident foreign nationals may be granted a special permit by the Board of Directors of the *Colegio de Periodistas* to cover events in Costa Rica for up to one year, with a possible extension of that period, taking account of the interests of members of the *Colegio*. If the latter decides that an event of international importance will or has occurred in Costa Rica, it may grant a non-resident foreign national a temporary permit to cover the event for the foreign media the journalist represents (CAFTA-DR, annex I-CR, 39).

The sectors of telecommunications, radio, and television are reserved to Costa Rica's citizens or enterprises with nearly two-thirds national ownership. Only a Costa Rican national or enterprise with at least 65% of capital owned by Costa Rican nationals may: 1) establish or manage an enterprise supplying wireless services (this restriction does not apply to the setting up and operation of ham radio stations, although rights are not to be granted to a foreign national residing in Costa Rica when his/her country of origin does not grant that same right to Costa Rican nationals); 2) obtain a license or be awarded a free over-the-air broadcast television channel for signals originating in Costa Rica; 3) obtain a license to operate radio, ham radio, radio-television, and private broadcasting stations. Only a Costa Rican national or enterprise with nominal capital stock and owned by Costa Rican nationals may be issued a license for ultra-high frequency radio broadcasting. Directors and administrators of enterprises supplying radio and television services must be Costa Ricans by birth or have been naturalized for at least ten years (CAFTA-DR, annex I-CR, 22–23).

Mass media and advertising services are only to be provided by enterprises incorporated in Costa Rica with nominative stock or established as *sociedades personales* under national law. Radio and television programs should conform to a series of rules. If commercials consist of jingles recorded abroad, a lump sum must be paid every time the commercial is aired on domestically transmitted television and only 30% of the commercials aired on each domestic television station or projected in each cinema may originate from abroad. Commercials imported in a physical medium from outside the Central American region and aired on domestically transmitted television are subject to a tax equivalent to 100% of the declared value of the production of the commercial. Radio, movie, or television commercials are deemed national when produced in a Central American state with which there is reciprocity in the matter. Commercials are considered national when: 1) at least 90% of the jingle has been composed or arranged by Costa Rican nationals; 2) at least 90% of the image is attributable to such nationals; and 3) at least 90% of the technical personnel are Costa Ricans. The number of radio programs and radio soap operas recorded abroad may not exceed 50% of the total number aired per domestically transmitted radio station daily, while the number of programs filmed or videotaped abroad may be limited to 60% of the total number of programs aired, per day, on domestically transmitted television (CAFTA-DR, annex I-CR, 37–38).

As regards cultural industries, similarly to Chile, Costa Rica has taken a reservation as to MFN treatment with respect notably to audiovisual cooperation agreements. It is also specified that public subsidy programs for the promotion of cultural activities are exempted from the FTA obligations. The definition of cultural industries is identical to the one in the US-Chile FTA (CAFTA-DR, annex II-CR, 2). In all, as for Chile, Costa Rica reserves, to a large extent, the responsibility of cultural industries to national citizens and enterprises. Yet, unlike Chile, it exempts a relatively wide range of regulatory measures, notably with national content quotas for radio, television, and advertising services.

The Dominican Republic

Only Dominican nationals may serve as announcers for a radio or television broadcast to a national audience in the Dominican territory. However, in special cases and for a six-month period, the *Comisión Nacional de Espectáculos Públicos y Radiofonía* may authorize enterprises making such broadcasts to hire foreign nationals. This authorization may be extended at the Commission's discretion. As well, only Dominican nationals may work as narrators, including commercial announcers and commentators, in transmitting sporting events for a national audience in the Dominican Republic. Yet, foreign nationals may serve as sports narrators, on condition that their country of origin allows Dominican sportscasters to do so. In all radio programs originating in the Dominican Republic, 50% of the music played must be by national authors, composers, and singers. For every three soap operas broadcasted for a national audience in the Dominican territory, one must be by Dominican authors and made in the country (CAFTA-DR, annex I-DR, 11). As for advertisements, if produced in the Dominican Republic, 75% of all artists, announcers, singers, and other participants involved in any jingle, video, tape, script, advertisement for use in cinemas, or commercial transmitted and presented on radio and television, must be Dominicans. In case a commercial for Dominican goods and services to be sold in the country needs to be produced abroad, 25% of the artists and production personnel must be Dominican nationals (CAFTA-DR, annex I-DR, 12).

The senior manager of every newspaper or periodical produced in the country must be Dominican (CAFTA-DR, annex I-DR, 13). Having a legal domicile in the country and being a stock company or a non-profit organization incorporated under Dominican laws is required to obtain an authorization to install and operate broadcast networks and to provide broadcast services in the Dominican Republic. Only Dominican nationals may own and control an enterprise providing public radio broadcasting services that originate in the country. It is specified that this entry does not apply to content providers (CAFTA-DR, annex I-DR, 14). Variety shows in theaters, nightclubs, and other entertainment venues performed by foreign artists must include the performance of one Dominican artist for each foreign one (CAFTA-DR, annex I-DR, 18).

Finally, in the communications sector, like the United States, the Dominican Republic reserves the right to adopt or maintain any measure that accords differential treatment to persons of other states owing to the application of reciprocity measures or through international agreements that involve sharing of the radio spectrum, guarantee market access, or national treatment with respect to the one-way satellite transmission of DTH and DBS television services and digital audio services (CAFTA-DR, annex II-DR, 4).

El Salvador

At least 90% of the production and recording of any commercial for use in El Salvador's public media, i.e., over-the-air television and radio broadcasts as well as printed material originating in El Salvador, must be carried out by enterprises organized under national law. An advertisement produced or recorded by an enterprise organized under the law of another Central American party may be used in the Salvadoran media, as long as similar treatment is extended by that party to Salvadoran advertisements. The broadcast in El Salvador's public media of an advertisement for an international product, brand, or service imported into or produced in El Salvador under license and not satisfying the above requirements is to be permitted and may be subject to a one-time fee (CAFTA-DR, annex I-ES, 7). Concessions and licenses for free reception broadcasting services are only granted to Salvadoran nationals born in El Salvador or enterprises organized under national law whose equity capital is at least 51% owned by Salvadorans (CAFTA-DR, annex I-ES, 8).

No foreign artist may give paid performances of any kind without the prior express authorization of the *Ministerio de Gobernación*, which consults with the legally established craft union of the artistic field in which the artist is involved. Foreign artists must pay, to the relevant union, a performance fee deposit of 10% of the gross income likely to be earned in the country. If it is not possible to make the advance payment, the artist[10] must pay an adequate amount as a "security deposit" to the relevant union. No foreign artist or group of artists may perform in El Salvador for more than 30 days consecutively or intermittently within a year from the date of the first performance (CAFTA-DR, annex I-ES, 9). Foreign circuses or other similar shows must pay to the relevant circus union a performance fee equal to 2.5% of the gross income likely to be earned daily from ticket sales. Such fee must be paid in full through the withholding system. All foreign circuses must be authorized by the appropriate Ministry and, once authorized, notify the *Asociación Salvadoreña de Empresarios Circenses* and pay the Association 3% of the gross income earned from ticket sales for each performance, as well as 10% of total earnings from sales to the audience, inside the circus, of flags, caps, tee shirts, balloons, photographs, and other paraphernalia. The foreign circus should pay an adequate amount as a security deposit to the Association. A foreign circus entering El Salvador may only work in the city of San Salvador for a period of 15 days, which may be extended for a further 15 days. A foreign circus having performed in the country can only return to El Salvador after at least one year from the date it left the country (CAFTA-DR, annex I-ES, 10). Lastly, in the case of public performances involving the live participation of artists of any kind, the participation of Salvadoran nationals should amount to 20% of the number of participating foreigners (CAFTA-DR, annex I-ES, 11).

Guatemala

The only reservation in favor of the cultural sector listed in Guatemala's schedule relates to performing arts. In order to contract with foreign groups, enterprises, or artists, prior authorization from the *Dirección de Espectáculos* is required. To perform in Guatemala, foreign artists or artist groups must have a consent letter from any of the legally recognized nongovernmental national artist unions. In mixed performances, made up of one or more films and variety shows, preference is to be given to Guatemalans if the circumstances of the cast, schedule, and contract so permit (CAFTA-DR, annex I-GU, 9).

Honduras

Only Honduran nationals by birth may exercise senior management of newspapers or free over-the-air broadcast (radio and television) news media, including its intellectual, political, and administrative orientation, this reservation not applying to newspapers or news media established outside Honduras (CAFTA-DR, annex I-HO, 7). To perform individually or as a group in the country, foreign music artists must pay 5% of the contracted fee to the Artist Union of Honduras and the manager or leaser shall, if possible, contract local artists during the same performance. Foreign music artists must also register with the Union for each performance in Honduras (CAFTA-DR, annex I-HO, 15).

Nicaragua

Foreign artists or musical bands may perform in Nicaragua solely by means of a prior contract. Foreign artists or artistic groups performing shows or reviews of a commercial nature should include in their program a Nicaraguan artist or group that performs similar shows, or else should pay 1% of the show's net receipts to the *Instituto Nicaragüense de Cultura,* unless such tax is not levied on Nicaraguan artists in the foreign artists' country of origin (CAFTA-DR, annex I-NI, 1). Enterprises supplying radio and television broadcast services in Nicaragua shall only resort to announcers who are Nicaraguan nationals for narration, commentary, and live broadcast in sports or similar commercial programs. Yet, foreign nationals are to be permitted to serve as announcers if the laws of their countries allow Nicaraguans to supply such services, except when the transmission of such programs is aimed exclusively at other countries (CAFTA-DR, annex I-NI, 7). Licenses for operating free over-the-air television and radio broadcast services may only be granted to Nicaraguans. In the case of enterprises, Nicaraguan nationals must hold 51% of the capital (CAFTA-DR, annex I-NI, 6).

Finally, similarly to the United States and the Dominican Republic, Nicaragua has secured a "type II" exemption from MFN treatment with regard to the one-way satellite transmission of DTH and DBS television services and digital audio services (CAFTA-DR, annex II-NI, 3).

Summary and Analysis

The CAFTA-DR shows great differences among states parties as far as exception measures for cultural products are concerned. On one side, Costa Rica has secured a range of regulatory measures; on the other side, Guatemala has not taken any meaningful exception in favor of culture. Costa Rica is the country that has best maintained its capacity to protect and promote its culture, by ensuring a wider margin of maneuver as regards the instruments of cultural policy. This appears noteworthy because Costa Rica is, with the Dominican Republic, the only party to the CAFTA-DR to have preserved the possibility of more important measures of regulation concerning culture. The other CAFTA-DR countries, in their lists of exceptions, have not included significant regulatory measures for the benefit of cultural diversity, such as national content quotas in the media, while the reservations taken by El Salvador, Honduras, and Nicaragua are essentially similar (Bernier 2004, 11).

If there is a relatively common type of cultural measures that has been maintained among Central American states, these are the restrictions and royalties to the profit of national artist unions. With the exception of Guatemala, cultural industries' ownership, control, and/or management are, to a large extent, reserved to nationals or domestic enterprises. Only Costa Rica has explicitly excluded from the FTA its subsidy measures for the benefit of cultural activities. In advertising, three parties, i.e., Guatemala, Honduras, and Nicaragua, have completely liberalized this sector; whereas Costa Rica, the Dominican Republic, and El Salvador have maintained restrictions. Yet, for the latter two, foreign commercials for goods and services imported from the United States are exempted (CAFTA, ISAC–13 Report, 8; DRFTA, ISAC–13 Report, 10).

In the view of the US Advisory Committee on Services, none of the exceptions in the audiovisual sector constitute major restrictions on American exports of filmed entertainment. National content quotas on broadcast television in the case of Costa Rica, as well as the flexibility to conclude new co-production agreements and to provide subsidies for the promotion of cultural activities, are targeted in scope and do not significantly distort trade. Costa Rica, El Salvador, and Nicaragua keep local equity requirements for broadcast licenses, as is the case in the United States. Honduras requires that nationals be in charge of local news broadcasts, a measure that the US industry, here again, does not consider as being unreasonable (CAFTA, ISAC–13 Report, 10). In the case of the Dominican Republic, the Committee found that the local content requirements for soap operas and music broadcast on radio, as well as the local domicile and incorporation requirements for broadcast television services, are limited in scope and do not significantly distort trade. Furthermore, in a side letter, the Dominican Republic has pledged action against broadcast piracy, the single largest market access problem faced by the US filmed entertainment industry in that country. This side letter, effective upon signature of the agreement, provides an important litmus test as to the willingness and ability of the Dominican government to meet its obligations under the FTA (DRFTA, ISAC–13 Report, 3, 11).

With respect to advertising, the Committee noticed that while Guatemala, Honduras, and Nicaragua have full commitments in this sector, Costa Rica retains fairly restrictive measures. These reserve 70% of advertising played on domestic broadcast television and cinemas and impose 100% import duties and additional fees on any imported commercials. Although El Salvador also maintains local content quotas for commercials, an exception permitting foreign-made commercials for imported US goods and services substantially reduces the negative trade impact of this measure (CAFTA, ISAC–13 Report, 9). Commercials produced in the Dominican Republic for local television broadcast or exhibition in cinemas should meet 75% local employment requirements. Commercials for Dominican goods and services which are broadcasted or exhibited in the country and produced outside the Dominican territory must meet a 25% local employment requirement. As foreign-made commercials for imported US goods and services are not subject to these restrictions, their negative trade effect is relatively small (DRFTA, ISAC–13 Report, 10).

More than any other US FTA considered in this book, the CAFTA-DR begs the question of the reason for such significant variations in the number and scope of states parties' reservations concerning the cultural sector. Since all US partners in this FTA are small developing countries, none seemed to have much more bargaining power or leverage than another in its dealings with the United States. With scant information on the negotiations, one may wonder if states' exceptions for cultural policies were the object of tough bargains and/or entailed further concessions to the US government. Yet, the overall importance of exceptions for different sectors (other than cultural) also varies greatly across states parties, while the FTA obligations otherwise apply to all. In line with the new US strategy, content quotas and other barriers in cultural services may be kept, as long as trade in digital products is not affected, and such measures are not considered to significantly distort trade. On the latter point, this is indeed the conclusion reached by the US Advisory Committee on Services. This also explains why US authorities may not have felt strongly about such reservations. Thus, more than leverage or negotiation dynamics, the ability of a state party to a US FTA to preserve (some) flexibility to pursue cultural policies depends on the importance it attaches to its cultural sector and to the international efforts in favor of cultural diversity.

THE UNITED STATES—MOROCCO FREE TRADE AGREEMENT

The US government had already signed a BIT with the Kingdom of Morocco in 1985, which had been in force since 1991, followed by a TIFA concluded in 1995. Seven years later, the negotiations on the United States—Morocco Free Trade Agreement (US-Morocco FTA) were officially announced on April 23, 2002. They were launched on January 21, 2003, and concluded on March 2, 2004. The signature of the agreement took place on June 15, 2004, and it became effective on January 1, 2006.[11]

Cultural Reservations

In order to be established in Morocco, cinematographic production and distribution enterprises must be organized as corporations or limited-liability companies with fully paid-in capital, and, in the case of an enterprise engaged in executive production,[12] must fulfill certain conditions, notably to have produced at least one feature-length film or three short films that are cinematographic and filmed in the country (US-Morocco FTA, annex I, 29–31). News agencies, other than the Maghreb Arab

Press, may be established in Morocco if they obtain government authorization. For greater certainty, foreign news agencies may supply their services from outside Morocco to any customers in the country without restriction (US-Morocco FTA, annex I, 32).

Alongside Chile and Costa Rica, Morocco has exempted from MFN treatment international agreements pertaining to "cultural activities" and it is specified that subsidization measures in support of such activities are not subject to the FTA. Unlike the corresponding reservation in the case of these two countries, mention is made of "cultural activities" rather than "cultural industries." In the definition of cultural activities, reference is not made anymore to *persons* engaged in such activities. For the rest, the definition remains essentially the same as the one in the NAFTA and the other FTAs so far considered in this book (US-Morocco FTA, annex II, 4). Morocco has also reserved the right to adopt or maintain any measure relating to investment in facilities for the transmission of radio and television broadcasting, as well as cable radio and television (US-Morocco FTA, annex II, 6). In addition, Morocco has taken a type II reservation for any measure requiring cable service operators, or satellite service suppliers, that provide encryption-based subscription services (for fee or non-fee) to consumers in Morocco, to have a local representative, this measure applying to enterprises that distribute programming to viewers and not to those that produce such programming (US-Morocco FTA, annex II, 7).

Summary and Analysis

Unlike Costa Rica and the Dominican Republic and, to a lesser degree, Chile, Morocco has not ensured much latitude to adopt regulatory measures, such as national content quotas in the media. In the view of the US Advisory Committee on Services, the US-Morocco FTA contains significant commitments in a number of sectors, including cultural products, entertainment, advertising, computer and related services, and telecommunications services. Morocco has committed itself to the whole range of advertising services and applies no restriction in this area. While Morocco has taken a few reservations in audiovisual, these are narrow, specific, and unlikely to disrupt existing commercial trade in such services. For instance, Morocco mandates companies producing films or distributing films and videos in the country to set up a corporate entity. This is not onerous for US firms and is consistent with the way the industry typically conducts business in these fields. Morocco also requires government approval for news agency operations, but this does not apply to foreign news agency services outside of Morocco serving Moroccan customers. Similarly, while Morocco has undertaken no commitments for investment in the facilities for transmission of radio and television broadcasting, the Moroccan government clarified that the reservation does not apply to the provision of programming content, where US industry has commercial interests. The latter reservation also does not appear to relate to satellite television (Roy 2008, 368). Finally, Morocco's MFN exemption for cultural activities agreements is not seen as commercially problematic, since Morocco agrees to national treatment in this area and is not expected to very often provide better terms to third parties than it provides its own producers (US-Morocco FTA, ISAC–13 Report, 4, 10–11).

THE UNITED STATES—BAHRAIN FREE TRADE AGREEMENT

On May 9, 2003, the USTR outlined a strategy for the establishment of a US—MEFTA, to be developed within a decade. One step to this end was the negotiation of BITs as well as TIFAs with Middle Eastern countries. The United States and the Kingdom of Bahrain had already signed a BIT in 1999, in force since May 30, 2001, and a TIFA on June 18, 2002. FTA negotiations proceeded swiftly from January 26 to May 27, 2004. On September 14, 2004, the United States—Bahrain Free Trade Agreement (US-Bahrain FTA) was signed. It came into effect on August 1, 2006.

Cultural Reservations

Except where the service is supplied on behalf of a Bahraini enterprise, persons of the other party must maintain a place of business in Bahrain to supply services in a series of sectors, including advertising, publishing and printing, terrestrial over-the-air radio, television, and satellite transmission and subscription. For terrestrial over-the-air radio, television, and satellite transmission and subscription services in the territory of Bahrain, each US service supplier licensed and authorized in the United States to provide such services may apply for up to three temporary licenses to supply such services through the presence of natural persons in Bahrain without having to maintain a place of business in the country. A temporary license shall be for an initial period of one year, and may be renewed for a further period of up to twelve months. Within three years of the date of entry into force of the FTA, the local presence requirement was to be phased out for advertising services (US-Bahrain FTA, annex I, 1–2).

Persons who are not from Bahrain or a member state of the Gulf Cooperation Council may provide advertising and publishing services in Bahrain only through a) a branch office of a foreign company or b) a 100% foreign-owned company established in the country that is either a joint closed stock company or a with limited-liability company using Bahrain as a main place for the distribution of its services. Such entities must also be managed by a Bahraini citizen who resides permanently in the country. In any case, these measures were to be phased out within five years of the FTA's entry into force. This reservation regarding advertising services only involved the creation or public transmission of advertising in the Bahraini territory. Hence, US service suppliers outside of Bahrain and without an office in the country were allowed to sell advertising space on programming transmitted into Bahrain via satellite to a Bahraini person in the country (US-Bahrain FTA, annex I, 4, 6). The publication of local newspapers and periodicals in Bahrain is reserved to national citizens, to whom the ownership of local media enterprises is also reserved (US-Bahrain FTA, annex I, 5).

Finally, Bahrain reserves the right to adopt or maintain any measure giving differential treatment to persons of other countries due to application of reciprocity measures or through international agreements involving sharing of the radio spectrum, guaranteeing market access, or national treatment with regard to the one-way satellite transmission of DTH and DBS television services and digital audio services (US-Bahrain FTA, annex II, 4).

Summary and Analysis

In many media sectors, local presence is required for the supply of services in Bahrain. For advertising and publishing services, temporary five-year reservations pertaining to commercial presence and nationality of managers also applied. Yet, only Bahraini nationals may publish local newspapers and periodicals and own local media enterprises. Following the United States, Bahrain has taken an MFN exemption for the one-way satellite transmission of DTH and DBS television and digital audio services. For the US Industry Trade Advisory Committee on Services and Finance Industries (ITAC–10), formerly ISAC–13, the restrictions with respect to the advertising sector, due to be phased out in three to five years, did not represent, on balance, onerous obstacles for American service suppliers. The Bahraini government has committed to ensure full market access and national treatment for US audiovisual services. The Committee even reported, seemingly overlooking Guatemala, that of all parties to US FTAs until then negotiated under the 2002 TPA, Bahrain was actually the only country without any exceptions in this sector (US-Bahrain FTA, ITAC–10 Report, 6–7).

THE UNITED STATES—OMAN FREE TRADE AGREEMENT

The United States and the Sultanate of Oman signed a TIFA on July 7, 2004. On November 15, 2004, the US Administration notified Congress of its intent to conclude an FTA with Oman. Negotiations for an FTA began on March 12, 2005, to end by October 3 of the same year. The United

States—Oman Free Trade Agreement (US-Oman FTA) was signed on January 19, 2006, and became effective on January 1, 2009.

Cultural Reservations

Only Oman's nationals and enterprises owned by Omani nationals may publish and print books, newspapers, and other written materials in the country for circulation to the public (US-Oman FTA, annex I, 6). The supply of free-to-air radio and television transmission services in the territory of Oman is also reserved to Omani nationals and enterprises owned by such nationals (US-Oman FTA, annex I, 8). Foreign nationals may own up to 70% of the equity in any enterprise established in Oman supplying news agency services (US-Oman FTA, annex I, 11).

Summary and Analysis

The very few exceptions secured by Oman reserve to Omani nationals and enterprises the publication and printing of written materials, as well as the supply of free-to-air radio and television transmission services. The US Advisory Committee on Services and Finance Industries pointed out that US nationals can enjoy majority control of enterprises supplying news agency services in Oman. Besides, the Committee underlined that the only exception pertaining to audiovisual services taken by Oman is in the area of free-to-air television and radio transmission. This limited national treatment restriction does not prevent American audiovisual products from accessing the Omani market (US-Oman FTA, ITAC-10 Report, 7). Indeed, the latter restriction applies to ownership and/or control of the audiovisual sector, rather than to programming.

THE UNITED STATES—PERU TRADE PROMOTION AGREEMENT

On November 18, 2003, the USTR informed the US Congress of the Administration's intent to pursue FTA negotiations with Bolivia, Colombia, Ecuador, and Peru, member states of the Andean Community, all of which are beneficiaries of the US Andean Trade Promotion and Drug Eradication Act. Except for Bolivia, the negotiations for an Andean Free Trade Agreement started on May 18, 2004. Like CAFTA parties, the three Andean countries often negotiated as a bloc, although most market access issues were addressed on a bilateral basis. There was a defining moment in late 2005, when US and Peruvian negotiators agreed on remaining sensitive issues and to conclude their own bilateral FTA, without waiting for Colombia and Ecuador. The Minister of Foreign Trade and Tourism of the Republic of Peru, Alfredo Ferrero, and the USTR, Rob Portman, then signed the United States—Peru Trade Promotion Agreement (US-Peru FTA) in Washington, DC, on April 12, 2006. Yet, a Protocol of Amendment later had to be signed on June 25, 2007, to follow on the bipartisan agreement on trade reached between US Congressional leadership and the Administration in May 2007.[13] The US-Peru FTA entered into force on February 1, 2009.

Cultural Reservations under Annex I

Free-to-air radio communications may only be offered by authorized or licensed Peruvian nationals or juridical persons organized under Peruvian law and domiciled in the country. Foreign nationals may not own more than 40% of the total shares or equity interest in such a juridical person and must own or hold shares or an equity interest in a radio or television broadcast enterprise in their country of origin. An authorization or a license may not be received or held directly or through a sole proprietorship by a foreign national. If a foreign national is, directly or indirectly, a shareholder, partner, or associate in a juridical person, such juridical person may not hold a broadcasting authorization in a zone bordering that foreign national's country of origin, save in a case of public necessity authorized by the Council of Ministers. Such restriction does not apply to juridical persons with foreign equity and with two or more current authorizations, as long as these are of the same frequency band (US-Peru FTA, annex I, 2).

Free-to-air television broadcasters must ensure that, on average, at least 30% of their total weekly programs between 5:00am and midnight are produced in Peru (US-Peru FTA, annex I, 3). At least 10% of the daily programming of free-to-air radio communications enterprises must be dedicated to folklore, national music, and series or programs produced in Peru on the history, literature, culture, or current issues of the country (US-Peru FTA, annex I, 8).

Cultural Reservations under Annex II

Peru has taken an MFN exception with respect to cultural cooperation or co-production commitments by cultural industries, including audiovisual cooperation agreements. It is emphasized that the national treatment and MFN treatment obligations for investment and the whole services chapter do not apply to government support[14] for the promotion of cultural industries. A definition of such industries is provided[15] (US-Peru FTA, annex II, 4–5). As in the case of the US-Morocco FTA, reference is not made any more to *persons* engaged in such industries. The definition also includes three further elements not found in previous definitions of cultural industries, i.e., the production and presentation of theater arts; the production and exhibition of visual arts; and the design, production, distribution and sale of handicrafts.

Subject to consistency with the WTO Agreement on Trade-Related Investment Measures (TRIMs), Peru may adopt or maintain any measure with regard to the design, distribution, retailing, or exhibition of Peruvian handicrafts (US-Peru FTA, annex II, 6). Peru has also reserved the right to ensure that a specified percentage, of up to 20%, of the total cinematographic works shown annually in cinemas or exhibition rooms in the country should be of national origin. In setting such percentage, the Peruvian government shall take into consideration factors, including the national cinematographic production, the existing exhibition infrastructure in the country, and attendance (US-Peru FTA, annex II, 7).

Peru has preserved its latitude to condition the receipt or continued receipt of government support for the development and production of jewelry design, theater arts, visual arts, music, and publishing upon the achievement by the recipient of a given level or percentage of domestic creative content (US-Peru FTA, annex II, 8). Finally, in the audiovisual, publishing, and music sectors, Peru may adopt or maintain any measure that affords a person of the other party the treatment accorded by the other party to Peruvian persons (US-Peru FTA, annex II, 9).

In a side letter, the United States and Peru clarified that nothing in the FTA chapters on investment and cross-border trade in services prevents Peru from maintaining measures concerning: a) the underwriting by the *Instituto Nacional de Cultura* of costs associated with supervising archeological research projects and emergency projects led by Peruvian archeologists; b) the granting of monetary prizes exclusively to Peruvian cinematographic works; and c) the granting of tax credits and refunds that provide benefits for publishing activities in Peru (US-Peru FTA, Side Letter on Peruvian Measures).

Summary and Analysis

Essentially, only Peruvian nationals and nationally owned and/or controlled enterprises may supply free-to-air radio communications. National cultural content quotas are reserved on free-to-air television and radio communications, as well as for cinematographic works. An MFN exemption is secured for cultural cooperation arrangements, while the definition of cultural industries is slightly expanded. Also, an exception is provided for reciprocal treatment of persons in the audiovisual, publishing, and music sectors.

The US Advisory Committee on Services and Finance Industries thought that Peru's Annex I reservations were to have minimal impact on the access of US service suppliers to that country's market. Since the 40% ownership restrictions and the cultural content requirements only involve free-to-air radio and television broadcasting, American interests are not impacted as they are generally in the pay-television segment. In Annex II, the MFN exemption from Peru for the benefit of cultural industries, for the same reasons as Morocco's, is not perceived as commercially problematic. Similarly, the up to 20% cinematographic screen quota has been significantly limited as local factors have to be taken into account, which would prevent such quota from ever being met. Moreover, the quota does not apply to advertising or movie trailers. A provision that the Committee found troubling, and which should be avoided in future FTAs, is the one whereby Peru takes an exception to national treatment and MFN for audiovisual, publishing, and music services, so as to afford a person of the other party the treatment afforded by the other party to Peruvians. Although this reservation does not apply in the case of a commercial presence, Peru essentially reserves the right to discriminate against US suppliers of such services on a cross-border basis, which is the way most services in these sectors are provided (US-Peru FTA, ITAC–10 Report, 8–9).

THE UNITED STATES—COLOMBIA TRADE PROMOTION AGREEMENT

US FTA negotiations with the Republic of Colombia, a member of the Andean Community, were launched on May 18, 2004, and terminated on February 27, 2006. The United States—Colombia Trade Promotion Agreement (US-Colombia FTA) was signed on November 22, 2006. As a result of the US bipartisan trade agreement, similarly to Peru, a Protocol of Amendment had to be concluded, which was signed on June 28, 2007. Later, on April 6, 2011, the United States and Colombia agreed on the "Action Plan Related to Labor Rights," clearing the way for their FTA to come into effect. The US-Colombia FTA could finally be implemented from May 15, 2012.

Cultural Reservations under Annex I

Only a Colombian national may be the director or general manager of a newspaper published in Colombia focusing on national politics (US-Colombia FTA, annex I, 10). Only Colombia's nationals or juridical persons organized under Colombian law may be granted concessions to supply radio broadcasting services (US-Colombia FTA, annex I, 20). The number of concessions to provide radio broadcasting as well as free-to-air national and local for-profit television services is subject to an economic needs test applying criteria set forth by law (US-Colombia FTA, annex I, 20–21). Concessions to provide free-to-air television services are reserved to Colombian nationals or juridical persons organized under national law, and to corporations in the case of a privately operated national television channel. In any enterprise holding a free-to-air television concession, foreign equity is limited to 40% (US-Colombia FTA, annex I, 21).

The Colombian government subjects the exhibition and distribution of foreign films to the Cinematographic Development Fee, set at 8.5% of the monthly net income derived from such exhibition and distribution. In case a Colombian short film accompanies the exhibition of a foreign movie, the fee applied to an exhibitor is reduced to 2.25%. Until 2013, the fee applied to a distributor was reduced to 5.5% if, during the previous year, its distribution of Colombian full-length films equaled or exceeded the target percentage set by the government (US-Colombia FTA, annex I, 19).

Suppliers (i.e., operators and/or persons granted the right to use programming slots) of national free-to-air television services should at least broadcast nationally produced programs on each channel as follows: a) 70% between 7:00pm and 10:30pm; b) 50% between 10:30pm and midnight; c) 50% between 10:00am and 7:00pm; d) 30% for Saturdays, Sundays, and holidays during the hours described in the three subparagraphs above. Concerning regional and local free-to-air television, suppliers must include a minimum of 50% of nationally produced programming on each channel. Only state-owned entities may supply regional television services (US-Colombia FTA, annex I, 21–22).

As for subscription television services, these may only be supplied by juridical persons organized under Colombian law. The latter must make available to subscribers, at no additional cost, those free-to-air Colombian national, regional, and local television channels offered in the authorized area of coverage. The transmission of regional and local channels is subject to the technical capacity of the subscription television operator. Suppliers of satellite subscription television must only include in their basic programming Colombia's public interest channels. When rebroadcasting free-to-air programming subject to a domestic content quota, a subscription television provider may not alter the content of the original signal. In case of a concessionaire of subscription television transmitting commercials different from those of origin, the domestic content quotas required of national free-to-air television suppliers apply. Yet, the quotas are not to be complied with when commercials are inserted into programming outside Colombian territory. Restrictions on the number of subscription television concessions at the zonal, municipal, and district levels were lifted. Suppliers of cable television services must produce and broadcast in Colombia at least one hour of programming each day between 6:00pm and midnight (US-Colombia FTA, annex I, 23–24).

Finally, community television services may only be supplied by communities organized and legally constituted in Colombia as foundations, cooperatives, associations, or corporations governed by civil law. Such services are restricted with regard to area of coverage as well as number and type of channels; they may be offered to a maximum of 6,000 associates or community members and ought to conform to a closed network local access channel (US-Colombia FTA, annex I, 25).

Cultural Reservations under Annex II

Colombia has reserved the right to adopt or maintain any measure with respect to libraries, archives, and museums (US-Colombia FTA, annex II, 1–2). Similarly to Peru, Colombia has preserved all latitude to grant preferential treatment to persons of any other state pursuant to any agreement between Colombia and such other country involving specific commitments regarding cultural cooperation or co-production in cultural industries and activities. It is also underlined that the national treatment and MFN treatment provisions for investment and the whole services chapter do not apply to government support (as defined in the US-Peru FTA) for the promotion of cultural industries and activities. A definition of such industries and activities is included, essentially identical to the one in the US-Peru FTA. Lastly, as for Peru, Colombia maintains its ability to accord a person of the other party treatment equivalent to that provided by the other party to Colombian persons in the audiovisual, publishing, or music sectors (US-Colombia FTA, annex II, 7–8).

Save for compatibility with WTO TRIMs, Colombia could make conditional government support for the development and production of jewelry design, performing arts, music, visual arts, and publishing on the recipient achieving a certain level or percentage of domestic creative content (US-Colombia FTA, annex II, 9). Also subject to consistency with TRIMs, Colombia keeps its margin of maneuver concerning the design, distribution, retailing, or exhibition of Colombian handicrafts (US-Colombia FTA, annex II, 10).

Colombia may require that a specified percentage of the total cinematographic works shown on an annual basis in the country should be Colombian. This percentage is not to exceed 15% in cinemas or exhibition rooms and 10% on free-to-air television channels. In the latter case, account shall be taken of the availability of national cinematographic works for free-to-air television, and such works are to count toward the domestic content requirements under Annex I. Reminiscent of a corresponding provision in the US-Peru FTA, it is specified that, in establishing a percentage for Colombian cinematographic works, Colombia shall consider national cinematographic production conditions, the existing national exhibition infrastructure, and attendance averages (US-Colombia FTA, annex II, 11).

For community television, the Colombian government has preserved the right to adopt or maintain any measure mandating a specified portion of weekly programming, not to exceed 56 hours per week, to consist of national programming produced by the community television operator. In the case of multichannel free-to-air commercial television, Colombia has reserved the right to impose the minimum programming requirements stipulated under Annex I, with the proviso that these may not be imposed on more than two channels or 25% of the total number of channels (whichever is greater) made available by an individual service provider. The Colombian government could require that a specific percentage, not to exceed 20%, of total advertising orders placed annually with media enterprises based in Colombia, other than newspapers and subscription services with headquarters outside of the country, be produced and created in Colombia. This measure does not apply to the advertisement in cinemas and exhibition rooms of upcoming movies and any media where the programming or content originates outside Colombia or to the rebroadcast or retransmission of such programming within the country (US-Colombia FTA, annex II, 11–12).

Subject to the conditions described below, Colombia reserves the right to adopt or maintain measures to ensure that, upon a finding by the Colombian government that Colombia's audiovisual content is not readily available to domestic consumers, access to such content through interactive audio and/or video services is not unreasonably denied to Colombian consumers. Colombia must publish in advance any proposed measure and provide interested persons a reasonable opportunity to comment. At least 90 days before the adoption of a measure, the other parties (the US government and firms or persons directly affected by the measure) shall be notified, with information on the basis for, and description of, the measure; subject to consistency with Colombia's obligations under the GATS. The other party, the United States, may request consultations with Colombia on the proposed measure, to begin within thirty days of such request. The Colombian government, then, may exercise its "right" under this provision only if: 1) the requesting party (the United States) *agrees* that Colombian audiovisual content is not readily available to Colombian consumers and that the proposed measure is based on objective criteria and has the least trade-restrictive impact possible; 2) Colombia agrees that the measure would be applied only to a service supplied in Colombia by a company *established* in the country; and 3) both parties agree on trade-liberalizing compensation in the interactive audio and video services sector (emphasis added) (US-Colombia FTA, annex II, 14).

Summary and Analysis

In services, US negotiators clearly asked for the elimination of restrictions in audiovisuals, telecommunications, and finance, sectors that were difficult to liberalize for Colombia. In the end, the Colombian government undertook commitments across all areas of audiovisual services, albeit with various limitations, including discriminatory taxes and domestic content provisions (Singh 2008b, 520–22).[16] The senior management of newspapers is reserved to Colombian nationals, while only the latter and/or nationally organized and/or controlled enterprises may supply radio broadcasting, free-to-air, and subscription television services. The exhibition and distribution of foreign movies are subject to a fee for the development of Colombian cinema. Detailed Colombian cultural content requirements apply to the suppliers of free-to-air television services and, to a much lesser degree, of subscription and cable television services.

Under Annex II, Colombia also reserves the right to set content requirements for cinematographic works (in cinemas or exhibition rooms and on free-to-air television channels), community television, multichannel free-to-air commercial television, and advertising orders in most media enterprises based in the country. As for Peru, Colombia has taken an MFN exception in favor of cultural co-production agreements. In the audiovisual, publishing, and music sectors, persons of the other party may be subject to equivalent treatment to that provided to Colombians, this same exception which the US Advisory Committee on Services and Finance Industries deemed troubling in Peru's case and wished it be avoided in future US FTAs. Lastly, in the field of "new" media, the government of Colombia, under onerous conditions, may enhance the availability of national audiovisual content through interactive audio and/or video services.

For the above Committee, while the United States did not achieve the fully open environment that it sought for audiovisual services, the US-Colombia FTA, overall, provides the American film industry with substantial commercial access to the Colombian market. Through its reservations in Annexes I and II, Colombia maintains certain screen quotas, local advertising requirements, as well as exhibition and distribution taxes benefiting national cinema. It has preserved its ability to enter into preferential co-production agreements with other states. Colombia has also reserved the right to take measures, under proscribed circumstances, in order to favor domestic programming delivered over "new platforms." Consequently, the US-Colombia FTA fails to meet US negotiating objectives and cannot be regarded as a template for future agreements (US-Colombia FTA, ITAC–10 Report, 10).

There are, however, important limits to the scope of Colombian cultural reservations. Theatrical and free over-the-air television quotas for films have been capped respectively at 15% and 10% annually, whereas the then existing legislation enabled Colombian authorities to set any level of national content. Films and other programs supplied from outside Colombia for subscription (i.e., cable and satellite) television—a key outlet for American films—are completely free of these restrictions, on the proviso that no alterations or additions are made in Colombia. The FTA also exempts from an advertising quota advertisements for films in theaters (trailers) and in print media, as well as advertising inserted in programs prior to delivery to Colombia. With respect to "new platforms" or interactive media, the Colombian government may act only after it finds that national audiovisual content is not readily available and certain specific conditions have been satisfied. The latter conditions give US industry meaningful assurances that new media opportunities are not to be arbitrarily undercut (US-Colombia FTA, ITAC–10 Report, 10).

This reservation providing for the possibility of content regulations in new technologies overtly contradicts the central tenet of the new US trade strategy on cultural products. Yet, its possible use is assorted with such conditions that the US Advisory Committee on Services and Finance Industries considered that American interests are not to be adversely impacted. This exception involving interactive audio and/or video services secured by a developing state party to a US FTA is later to be further analyzed and commented upon, alongside similar ones in the US-Australia and US-Korea FTAs.

Singh (2008b, 523–24) stresses that the issue of the liberalization of the Colombian audiovisual sector was fraught with controversy during the FTA negotiations with the United States, marked by protests from industry producers and civil society groups. In response, Colombia's negotiators pointed to the country's offensive interests in audiovisual and cultural products, especially *telenovelas*. In the end, the FTA notably allows for funds to be kept aside for film-making and preserves domestic content for broadcasting. Yet, the link between e-commerce and audiovisual is overlooked, as Singh makes no mention of Colombia's efforts to ensure the availability of domestic cultural content in digital or new networks.

THE UNITED STATES—PANAMA TRADE PROMOTION AGREEMENT

On November 18, 2003, the same day that the USTR notified Congress of the Administration's wish to initiate FTA negotiations with countries of the Andean Community, it also communicated its intention to launch such negotiations with the Republic of Panama. For a while it was also contemplated that Panama could join the CAFTA negotiations. US FTA negotiations with Panama began on April 26, 2004, to conclude on December 19, 2006. Although the United States—Panama Trade Promotion Agreement (US-Panama FTA) was signed on June 28, 2007, it only became effective on October 31, 2012.

Cultural Reservations

A concession to operate a public radio or television station in Panama may be granted to a natural person, who must be a Panamanian national, or an enterprise, with at least 65% of its shares owned by Panamanian nationals. Senior managers and directors of an enterprise operating a public radio or television station should all be Panamanian nationals. A foreign government or state enterprise may not supply, by itself or through a third party, public radio or television services or hold a controlling interest, directly or indirectly, in an enterprise supplying such services. A license is required of announcers to make advertisements within Panama to be broadcasted in public radio or television. Such licenses are reserved to Panamanian nationals or nationals of other states where reciprocal rights are granted (US-Panama FTA, annex I, 8).

With respect to enterprises producing print publications, such as newspapers or magazines, they must be 100% owned by Panamanian nationals, and their managers—including publishers, editors-in-chief, deputy directors, and assistant managers—must also be nationals (US-Panama FTA, annex I, 24). Journalism may only be practiced by a Panamanian citizen. Foreign journalists hired as correspondents for wire services or other foreign media are to be accredited and allowed to practice on that basis for the length of their contractual service. Upon registration, any foreign journalist is to be issued a temporary permit to practice journalism in Panama (US-Panama FTA, annex I, 29–31).

Summary and Analysis

Concessions to operate public radio and television stations in Panama are reserved to Panamanian nationals or nationally owned and/or controlled enterprises. The senior management of enterprises operating such stations must be in the hands of national citizens. Licenses to make advertisements in such stations are also reserved to Panamanian nationals and nationals of other states having granted reciprocal rights to Panamanians. In the case of publishing enterprises, complete national ownership and management is required. The practice of journalism is normally reserved to Panamanian citizens.

In the words of the US Advisory Committee on Services and Finance Industries,

> Panama has made high-level commitments without exceptions with respect to audiovisual services (which are not expressly referenced in the [US-Panama FTA]). Panama has declared exceptions only with respect to the transmission of radio and television programs, limiting the grant of broadcast licenses to Panamanian nationals (or 65% Panamanian owned companies), with Panamanian nationals in Board and senior management roles, and precluding the involvement of foreign governments in public broadcasting. Broadcasts of advertisements made in Panama containing announcements by unlicensed (non-Panamanian) announcers are also prohibited. These restrictions will not materially detrimentally affect U.S. audiovisual products and services. (US-Panama FTA, ITAC-10 Report, 10)

SUMMARY AND CONCLUSIONS

Nine FTAs concluded by the United States with fourteen developing countries have been examined in order to identify their provisions relating to cultural products and, thus, assess their implications for the ability of states parties to conduct cultural policies. These FTAs, all in force, have been negotiated with Singapore, Chile, Central America and the Dominican Republic, Morocco, Bahrain, Oman, Peru, Colombia, and Panama. Seven chapters of these agreements, i.e., those dealing with services, investment, electronic commerce, telecommunications, intellectual property rights, regulatory transparency, and, when applicable, the movement of business persons, have been analyzed, with the first three being the most relevant for cultural products, together with the exception lists, of two types, accompanying each FTA. Whereas exceptions or reservations in Annexes I provide for the maintenance of non-conforming measures to the obligations of these agreements (specifically those of the investment and services chapters), other exceptions in Annexes II permit to keep, adopt, or reinforce certain regulations.

Exceptions for the benefit of cultural diversity primarily relate to subsidies. In each US FTA considered, chapters on investment and services include a general exception for subsidization measures. Hence, most state aids to cultural industries are not questioned and subject to obligations such as national treatment. Governments maintain a wide margin of maneuver to adopt financial measures as part of national cultural policies. Chile, Costa Rica, Morocco, Peru, and Colombia, in their lists of exceptions, have specified that government support to cultural industries/activities is not subject to the provisions of their respective agreements. By so doing, these five countries have kept leeway in regard to all subsidy instruments, including tax incentives. Such an exception is significant with respect to the possibility for states to pursue cultural policies, as public subsidies represent one of the principal means of support to national cultural development. The exception, however, is limited to financial measures. Even though important, such instruments constitute only a segment of cultural policies. Unlike regulatory measures, they necessarily entail expenditures on the part of states to sustain their culture. In view of other, often more pressing, needs in the case of developing countries, this could be problematic.

Table 3.1. Main Types of Cultural Regulatory Exceptions across Developing States Parties to US FTAs

Cultural Regulatory Exceptions	States Parties													
	BH	CL	CO	CR	DR	ES	GU	HO	MO	NI	OM	PA	PE	SG
Restrictions re. property/control/management and licensing of cultural enterprises	•	•	•	•	•	•		•		•	•	•	•	•
Domestic content requirements														
- Public (free-to-air) radio and/or television		•	•	•	•								•	•
- Subscription television			•											
- Advertising			•	•	•									
- Cinema (screen quotas)			•										•	
Audiovisual cooperation agreements		•	•	•					•				•	
Digital or new technologies/platforms														
- Interactive audio and/or video			•											

As for measures of cultural regulation maintained by developing states parties to the US FTAs negotiated under the 2002 TPA, these are summarized in table 3.1. Since such exceptions vary considerably in number, scope, substance, and/or details, the table only indicates, under general categories, the most important ones for states' ability to pursue cultural policies. These have been secured by countries either in direct form or through broader exceptions. The most common "type I" exceptions pertain to those reserving, to different degrees, to nationals or domestic firms the property, control, and/or management of cultural enterprises, as well as the licenses for radio and television broadcasting. Except for Guatemala and Morocco, such provisions have been secured by all states parties to the US FTAs studied in this book. In Singapore's case, these have taken the form of a broad "type II" broadcasting exception, while, in Bahrain's case, they have been limited to a local presence requirement. The United States does not seem to mind such restrictions on investment, as it has similar ones. The maintenance of such measures in US FTAs appears favorable to the conduct of cultural policies by states parties. Yet, the reservation of the property, control, and/or management of cultural industries to nationals does not necessarily guarantee a more significant level of national content in such media.

Other regulatory exceptions, also mainly under type I, refer to national content quotas for programming, and sometimes for advertising, in public radio and/or television. A little more than one-third of the states parties to the US FTAs considered have reserved such measures, i.e., Chile, Costa Rica, the Dominican Republic, Peru, and Colombia. In the latter case, quotas also apply to subscription television. Peru and Colombia have also provided for such quotas for domestic cinema. Singapore, for its part, has secured a broad (type II) exception for broadcasting and printed media services.

As well, there exist "type II" exceptions. Chile has taken such a general reservation in the area of one-way satellite broadcasting of digital telecommunication services, whereas, in the case of the Dominican Republic, Nicaragua, and Bahrain, similarly to the United States, the exception secured in this sector pertains solely to MFN treatment. Another such exception provided for audiovisual cooperation agreements is found in the lists of Chile, Costa Rica, Morocco, Peru, and Colombia.

If such exceptions, especially those on domestic content regulations, could be seen as a major concession on the part of the United States, they seem to have been obtained in exchange for the absence of any conditions or restrictions with respect to electronic commerce, a domain where American enterprises enjoy a strong competitive advantage and whose role in the dissemination of cultural contents is deemed to increase. When regulatory measures have been subject to specific reservations, as in the FTAs studied here, the United States has considered that, owing to technological developments, their applicability or effectiveness was to decrease. Colombia is the only developing country to have secured from the United States an exception for the cultural sector pertaining to digital trade. Yet, the latter exception did not mark a precedent. It will be seen that Australia had already insisted on such a reservation, whose potential use in its case is arguably accompanied by less onerous conditions. For Colombia, on the other hand, the US government has tightened it in such a way as to guarantee its trade interests and level of access to the Colombian market.

In light of the negative-list approach adopted for the negotiation of US FTAs, governments enter into obligations simply by not including policies and measures in their lists of exceptions. It is practically impossible to pull back on such commitments, even if a state party realized that their implementation proved prejudicial to its cultural identity. Thus, a state that did not request exemptions in favor either of domestic content quotas or audiovisual co-production agreements, as it is the case for a little less than two-thirds of US FTA partners in this chapter, will not be able subsequently to adopt such measures even after realizing their importance for the development of its own cultural expressions. To the extent that the United States insists on the liberalization of the cultural sector and on clearly specified restrictions, the latter have tended to involve *existing* regulations. Thus, the domestic content quotas and international cultural cooperation agreements exempted in US FTAs essentially belong to state governments that already had such measures in place. Otherwise, such exemptions would have necessarily figured in Annexes II and applied to *future* measures, which is less compatible with a predictable trade framework, as championed by US authorities.

Eight countries—Bahrain, El Salvador, Guatemala, Honduras, Morocco, Nicaragua, Oman, and Panama—have not taken any significant exceptions relating to the audiovisual sector. Yet, Chile, Colombia, Costa Rica, the Dominican Republic, Peru, and Singapore have obtained some reservations for the cultural sector, notably national capital requirements for cultural industries, and domestic content requirements within broadcasting channels (see Vlassis and Richieri Hanania 2014, 28). Among the developing states parties to US FTAs considered in this chapter, Singapore, Costa Rica, the Dominican Republic, Peru, and Colombia are the countries that, arguably, have best preserved their capacity to protect and promote their culture, by ensuring a wider margin of maneuver as regards the instruments of cultural policy. Indeed, besides financial or subsidy measures, they have maintained the possibility of a range of regulatory measures in favor of culture. In the case of the other countries studied, the measures allowed under the FTAs concerning the regulation of the cultural sector prove much narrower. It is the case, among others, of Chile that secured, at the very most, a general reservation for satellite broadcasting and the possibility, under a type I exception, of a minimum national content quota on public television channels. Also to be noticed,

Morocco, Bahrain, and Oman, like most CAFTA-DR parties and Panama, seem to have deprived themselves of any significant possibility as regards the regulation of the cultural sector.

On the whole, this chapter on nine FTAs concluded by the United States with developing countries reveals significant constraints on their ability to pursue cultural policies. If financial measures in support of culture have essentially been exempted from US FTAs, so is the case for government subsidization in general. Mostly limited to the possible use of financial instruments, states parties are therefore confined to pay for preserving their culture. As for the possibility of regulatory measures, it has most often been significantly curtailed. Yet, the CDCE enables states to resort to a wide range of instruments, regulatory as well as financial, in order to respond to the challenges posed to their cultural expressions by the globalization process and the digital revolution. The main consequence of US FTAs is, thus, to markedly limit the range of measures, particularly of a regulatory type, that states can adopt so as to preserve their national cultures and, beyond, to foster cultural diversity.

As emphasized by Vlassis and Richieri Hanania (2014, 28), within bilateral negotiations, developing countries do not have enough resources to require provisions for exceptions that could prevent them from opening up their domestic markets to foreign cultural products. The lack of human resources and of expertise, the lack of pressure from professional cultural associations—often loosely organized and representing a nascent industry—as well as the greater influence of other more powerful sectors lead less developed countries to give in to US demands and to not preserve the cultural sector. Furthermore, bilateralism entails a power asymmetry favoring the United States, due to the absence of alliances, mutual support, and organization that would be possible in a regional or multilateral framework.

On the basis of a study of the US FTAs with Chile, Singapore, Australia, and Morocco, as well as the CAFTA-DR, it is clear for Bernier (2004, 15) that the cultural reservations taken by different states reflect quite accurately their negotiating capacity and that, as usual, the least able to protect itself ends up paying the higher price. If developing countries, in particular, have significant concerns to ensure their economic prosperity through PTAs with the United States, their commitments with regard to the liberalization of the cultural sector and their remaining margin of maneuver to implement cultural policies, nevertheless, vary significantly. Some of the more prosperous developing countries, such as Bahrain and Oman, have only taken exceptions reserving to nationals the property and/or control of cultural enterprises. As one of the wealthiest Central American countries, Panama has also done the same. Concurrently, countries with lower *per capita* GDPs, such as Costa Rica, the Dominican Republic, Peru, and Colombia, have secured a wider range of cultural policy measures, including domestic content requirements in public media. Hence, it seems that, rather than leverage, the continuing ability of US FTA partners to conduct policies benefiting the cultural sector primarily depends on the importance they attach to culture and their considerations of the international initiatives toward cultural diversity.

In fact, the exceptions for the benefit of the cultural sector among developing states parties to US FTAs owe above all to the four key elements at the basis of the new strategy of the American government on cultural products. As it has long sought far-reaching liberalization, the United States favors the negative-list approach for negotiating trade commitments, which involves specific and delimitated exceptions. Among cultural policy instruments, the financial ones are essentially excluded, while regulatory exceptions vary greatly in number and scope across states parties, such differences being primarily dependent on states' expressed concerns relating to their cultural policies. In turn, such concessions are acceptable to the United States, inasmuch as they apply to "traditional" instruments and do not significantly affect American interests, the latter mainly related to the absence of barriers in new media. Although only one "digital" exception has been secured, it is assorted with conditions so as to conciliate it with US cultural trade strategy.

If states' leverage or negotiation dynamics are not the principal explanatory factors for the extent of the exceptions in the cultural sector among states parties to US FTAs, it is different with respect to digital trade. As will be seen in the next chapter, in addition to more extensive "traditional" cultural reservations, exceptions pertaining to new or digital technologies, as secured by Australia and South Korea, openly collide with US trade policy and priorities and, thus, make leverage really come into play as regards both the existence and scope of such exceptions.

NOTES

1. Broadcasting services are defined as the scheduling of a series of literary and artistic works by a content provider for aural and/or visual reception, and for which the content consumer has no choice over the scheduling of the series. Services, such as television-on-demand and pay television, are therefore excluded.

2. Printed media are understood as any publication containing news, intelligence, reports of occurrences, or any remarks, observations, or comments relating thereto, or any matter of public interest, printed in any language and published for sale or free distribution at intervals not exceeding one week.

3. For more on Singapore's experience in services liberalization within the WTO and PTAs, including the one with the United States, see Mukherjee (2008). For an account of the US-Singapore FTA negotiations, with some specific attention given to telecommunications and electronic commerce, as well as intellectual property rights, see Koh and Chang (2004).

4. Cultural industries are understood as persons engaged in any of the following activities: a) publication, distribution, or sale of books, magazines, periodical publications, or printed or electronic newspapers, excluding the printing and typesetting of any of the foregoing; b) production, distribution, sale, or display of recordings of movies or videos; c) production, distribution, sale, or display of music recordings in

audio or video format; d) production, distribution, or sale of printed music scores or scores readable by machines; or e) radio broadcasts aimed at the public in general, as well as all radio, television and cable television-related activities, satellite programming services, and broadcasting networks.

5. To be precise, the exemption only applies to Canada's trade with the United States and Mexico.

6. On Chile's services, including cultural, negotiations in the context of its FTA with the United States, see Sáez (2008, 687–97).

7. Because the Dominican Republic had agreed to the basic framework and provisions of the CAFTA, its negotiations with the United States essentially pertained to market access and reservations.

8. As a result of US pressure, Costa Rica opened its telecommunications sector, until then in a situation of monopoly, and partially liberalized certain telecommunications services, namely direct private network, Internet, and mobile wireless services. The ensuing reform in telecommunications sparked a fierce domestic debate that extended to the general merit of the CAFTA-DR. In the first-ever referendum held in Costa Rica, a slim majority of voters approved of the FTA, which made possible its ratification.

9. For more on the CAFTA-DR negotiations, including the resulting controversy in Costa Rica, see Robert and Stephenson (2008); Salas (2009).

10. An artist is understood as any person acting in El Salvador, individually or in a company consisting of one or more persons, to give performances in music, song, dance or readings, or to present shows, whether in person (i.e., live) or before a large or small audience or on radio or television.

11. On the negotiations and key provisions of the US-Morocco FTA, see Kearns (2009).

12. Executive production refers to the supply of the following services pursuant to a contract with an enterprise not organized under Moroccan law: the management of film production, the supply of services related to the constitution of technical/artistic teams, and filming.

13. The bipartisan agreement also came into play with respect to the US-Colombia, US-Panama, and US-Korea FTAs.

14. Interestingly, it is clarified that, for purposes of this entry, "government support" means tax incentives, incentives for the reduction of mandatory contributions, government grants, government-supported loans, and guarantees, trusts, or insurance provided by a government, irrespective of whether a private entity is wholly or partially responsible for its management.

15. The term "cultural industries" means: a) publication, distribution, or sale of books, magazines, periodical publications, or printed or electronic newspapers, excluding the printing and typesetting of any of the foregoing; b) production, distribution, sale, or display of recordings of movies or videos; c) production, distribution, sale, or display of music recordings in audio or video format; d) production and presentation of theater arts; e) production and exhibition of visual arts; f) production, distribution, or sale of printed music scores or scores readable by machines; g) design, production, distribution and sale of handicrafts; or h) radio broadcasts aimed at the public in general, as well as all radio, television, and cable television-related activities, satellite programming services, and broadcasting networks.

16. For a general account of the US-Colombia FTA negotiations and provisions, see Watson (2015) and for an account of Colombia's negotiations of its FTA with the United States, focusing on services and audiovisuals, see Singh (2008b, 520–27).

FOUR

US Free Trade Agreements with Developed Countries

The US-Australia FTA and the US-Korea FTA are both interesting to examine for many reasons. Australia and South Korea have a long tradition of governmental intervention in favor of their cultural industries and both are known for their extensive cultural policies and measures. After Australia, South Korea is arguably the only developed country and certainly the most important with which the United States has concluded an FTA under the 2002 TPA. As already pointed out, at the multilateral level, Australia has been among the countries unwilling to liberalize the cultural sector. As for the US-Korea FTA, it represented a first test for the CDCE, as it was negotiated shortly after the adoption of the Convention and its conclusion coincided with the CDCE's coming into force.

What most contrasts with the preceding chapter is the number and scope of the reservations relating to cultural products in these two US FTAs, which explains why they are subject to a specific chapter. Again, in chronological order, the US FTA with Australia is to be looked at, followed by the one with Korea. In each case, their exceptions contained in Annex I are first to be examined, then the broader ones under Annex II, followed by a summary and analysis. A specific section is dedicated to the reservations taken by Australia and Korea toward the new media and their assorted conditions. A conclusion sums up the main findings of the chapter.

If the exceptions belonging to traditional instruments of cultural policy are still mostly explained through what the US government is willing to either accept or tolerate under its revised trade strategy, those involving digital networks are rather attributable to parties' leverage and/or negotiation dynamics. In this regard, the developed country status of both Australia and South Korea, as well as their concerns and interests in effective cultural policies, appear to be the key factors behind their respective exceptions pertaining to new media and, compared with Colombia, the less onerous conditions accompanying such reservations.

THE UNITED STATES—AUSTRALIA FREE TRADE AGREEMENT

On November 13, 2002, the USTR informed Congress of the intent to negotiate an FTA with the Commonwealth of Australia. Negotiations began in March 2003 and concluded on February 8, 2004. The United States—Australia Free Trade Agreement (US-Australia FTA) was signed on May 18, 2004, and became effective on January 1, 2005.

Cultural Reservations under Annex I

In the media sector, the Australian government continues to screen, and possibly object to, direct (i.e., non-portfolio) investments irrespective of size, and portfolio investments of 5% or more, by foreign persons in existing Australian enterprises and, in telecommunications, foreign investments whose total assets exceed A$ 50 million. Australia maintains further restrictions on foreign investment in the newspapers, broadcasting, and telecommunications sectors (US-Australia FTA, annex I, 3–6). In telecommunications, the maximum aggregate foreign ownership permitted in Telstra (an Australian telecommunications and media company) is 35% of its shares not held by the Australian government, while the maximum individual foreign ownership is 5%. The chair and a majority of directors must be Australian citizens, and Telstra is required to maintain its head office, main base of operations, and place of incorporation in Australia (US-Australia FTA, annex I, 14). In broadcasting, a foreign person must not be in a position to exercise control of a commercial television broadcasting license. Moreover, in the case of a licensee, two or more foreigners must not have company interests exceeding 20% and no more than 20% of the directors may be foreign persons. A foreigner must not have company interests in a subscription television broadcasting license of more than 20% or that, when added to the interests held by other foreign persons, exceed 35% (US-Australia FTA, annex I, 16). Finally, in newspapers, the maximum allowed aggregate foreign interest direct (non-portfolio) investment/involvement in national and metropolitan newspapers is 30%, with any single foreign shareholder limited to a maximum interest of 25%, while it is less than 50% in provincial and suburban newspapers (US-Australia FTA, annex I, 17).

In the case of free-to-air commercial analogue and digital (other than multichannel) television broadcasting, the Australian government reserves quotas for national content of up to 80% on advertising, and to 55% on programming, transmitted annually between 6:00am and midnight. Sub-quotas for specific program formats, such as drama and documentary, may also be applied within the 55% quota (US-Australia FTA, annex I, 15).

Cultural Reservations under Annex II

With respect to multichannel free-to-air commercial television broadcasting, the Australian government may establish national content quotas of up to 55% (80% for advertising) of the programming transmitted annually between 6:00am and midnight on an individual channel of a service provider. Such a measure may not be imposed on more than two channels or 20% of all channels (whichever is greater) and, in any case (as for ads), on more than three channels made available by an individual service provider. Sub-quotas for particular program formats, e.g., drama, documentary or children's, may as well apply within the transmission quotas. Regarding free-to-air commercial television broadcasting, content quotas may be applied to a rebroadcasted or moved channel over another transmission platform (US-Australia FTA, annex II, 5–6).

As for subscription television broadcasting (pay-per-view TV), providers of arts, children's, documentary, drama, and educational programs may be required to assume up to 10% of total program expenditure for Australian production. Yet, no channel is subject to an expenditure requirement for more than a single program format. For drama, if the Australian government finds such requirement insufficient, it may be increased to a maximum level of 20%. Such a finding is to be made through a transparent process that involves consultations with any affected parties, including the United States. Any resulting increase should be non-discriminatory and no more burdensome than necessary (US-Australia FTA, annex II, 6).

In the case of free-to-air radio broadcasting, national content quotas not exceeding 25% of the programming (e.g., of musical items) transmitted annually between 6:00am and midnight may be imposed on individual stations of a service provider. Should the Australian government find that national audiovisual content or genres is not readily available to Australian consumers, it may ensure that access to such programming on interactive audio and/or video services is not unreasonably denied to Australians. Any such measures are to be implemented through a transparent process allowing participation by any affected parties, be based on objective criteria, be the minimum necessary, be no more trade restrictive than necessary, not be unreasonably burdensome, and be applied only to a service provided by an enterprise conducting business activities in Australia in relation to the supply of that service (US-Australia FTA, annex II, 6–7).

Australia has also taken a reservation concerning market access with regard to spectrum management and licensing of broadcasting services, i.e., commercial and community broadcasting, narrowcasting and subscription broadcasting. There is an exception for subsidies or grants for investment in Australian cultural activity where eligibility is subject to national content or production requirements (US-Australia FTA, annex II, 7). Lastly, the Australian government has preserved latitude, under its International Co-Production Program, with respect to any preferential co-production arrangement for film and television productions. National treatment may also be conferred on works covered by such arrangements (US-Australia FTA, annex II, 9).

Summary and Analysis

Under Annex I, Australia maintains foreign investment restrictions in the media sector and tighter ones for telecommunications, newspapers, and broadcasting. In analogue and digital television broadcasting, there are domestic content quotas, including sub-quotas for particular program formats. Under Annex II, in multichannel television, similar quotas and sub-quotas apply, although upon no more than 20% of all channels or three channels of a service provider. Domestic content quotas also apply for radio broadcasting. In subscription-based television, there exists an expenditure requirement of 10% for Australian production in specific program formats, such as documentary and drama, although such requirement may not apply to more than a single format for any channel. In the case of drama, if such requirement is deemed insufficient, under specified conditions, it may be increased to 20%. In new or digital media, here again under strict conditions, the Australian government could ensure that access to domestic content is not unreasonably denied. In this regard, the US Industry Functional Advisory Committee on Electronic Commerce (IFAC–4), restating the relevant principal trade negotiating objectives under the 2002 TPA, stressed that although "[g]overnments should refrain from enacting trade-related measures that impede e-commerce . . . [w]here legitimate policy objectives require domestic regulations that affect e-commerce, such regulations should be least trade restrictive, nondiscriminatory, transparent, and promote an open market environment" (2002 TPA, section 2102(b)(9)(C)(D); US-Australia FTA, IFAC–4 Report, 4).

In its report on the US-Australia FTA, the US Advisory Committee on Services estimated that chapter 10 on cross-border trade in services significantly advances the market access goals of US services industries with a major trading partner. Australia has provided commitments above those made in the GATS for many cultural fields and sub-fields, including advertising, filmed entertainment, printing and publishing, video tape rental and leasing, television and radio broadcast transmission, cable and satellite transmission, live entertainment, news agencies, commercially provided library, archive, museum, or other cultural services.

The FTA also secures access for all "new" services, thereby ensuring the relevance of this agreement into the future (US-Australia FTA, ISAC–13 Report, 2–3).

For the first time in a trade agreement with the United States, Australia has ensured access for a complete range of advertising services, including the production, broadcast, or screening of advertisements for radio, television, or cinema. Although Australia retains significant local content restrictions on commercials for broadcast television, the expansion of Australia's trade commitments in this field are meaningful and important (US-Australia FTA, ISAC–13 Report, 9). As regards audiovisual services, the US-Australia FTA entails continued access to the eighth largest export market for the American film industry. It provides a carefully crafted balance between respect for Australian cultural concerns and predictable access to this important market. The Australian government keeps a number of restrictions, including a national content quota on broadcast television and an investment requirement on subscription television services, which the US industry does not view as unduly burdensome (US-Australia FTA, ISAC–13 Report, 10).

Australia's concessions on broadcasting policy sparked a domestic controversy over the trade deal with the United States (Chase 2015, 218). There were also concerns toward electronic commerce, especially because of its relationship with audiovisual services. As will later be further discussed, since e-commerce encompasses all digital products, it was not missed by representatives of Australian cultural industries that this is a clear back door way to include cultural industries in a trade agreement (Mitchell and Voon 2009, 24).

Finally, in view of uncertainties as to technological change, Australia maintains its ability to take some new measures to ensure continued availability of national audiovisual content, although American trade interests have to be considered in designing any such measures. For the US Advisory Committee on Services, such a special exception for electronic commerce does not constitute a problem in light of Australia's commitments in audiovisual services (US-Australia FTA, ISAC–13 Report, 10–11). At the same time as the new US trade strategy on cultural products seeks to prevent protectionist regulations in digital media, we saw that the 2002 TPA (section 2102(b)(9)) provides for flexibility to respond to "legitimate" policy objectives, in the form of commitments so as to minimize any adverse commercial impact. Interestingly, the Committee did not see as problematic such a "digital" exception in the US-Australia FTA. Yet, the same committee (although restructured) later associated a similar exception subject to stricter commitments secured by Colombia to a failure from the US government to achieve its negotiation objectives on audiovisual/cultural products and something not to repeat in other US FTAs (US-Colombia FTA, ITAC–10 Report, 10).

Overall, as for most US FTA parties already considered, since Australia had no prior commitments under the GATS relating to audiovisual services, the United States was able to secure far-reaching commitments. These involve complete liberalization, except for the cultural sub-sectors or fields for which specific exceptions were taken. In regard to the latter, the United States obtained both standstill commitments, reflecting the then existing level of regulatory liberalization, and stronger ones, as in the case of domestic content regulations, where no specified or higher quotas were in place. In line with US concern for a predictable trade framework, not only are broad exceptions for future measures limited in number, but they are also assorted with conditions regarding their potential use, as in the case of expenditure requirements for Australian drama.[1]

THE UNITED STATES—KOREA FREE TRADE AGREEMENT

The United States and the Republic of Korea announced their intention to negotiate an FTA on February 2, 2006. The negotiations took place from June 2006 to April 1, 2007. The United States—Korea Free Trade Agreement (US-Korea FTA) was originally signed on June 30, 2007. The FTA talks later resumed in June 2010 and a renegotiated version of the FTA was signed in December 2010. None of the amendments pertained to cultural products. The US-Korea FTA finally came into effect on March 15, 2012.[2]

Cultural Reservations under Annex I

Persons who import foreign novels, comics, photo albums, pictorial series, and magazines for domestic distribution must obtain a recommendation from the Minister of Culture and Tourism, while the distributors of domestic publications are subject to *ad hoc* reviews after distribution takes place (US-Korea FTA, annex I, 38). A foreign person who intends to engage in a public performance in South Korea, or a person who intends to invite a foreigner to engage in such a performance, must obtain a recommendation from the Korea Media Rating Board (US-Korea FTA, annex I, 47). A news agency organized under foreign law may supply news communications in South Korea only under a contract with a news agency organized under Korean law and having a radio station license. News agency services may not be supplied in South Korea by: a) a foreign government; b) a foreign person; c) an enterprise organized under Korean law whose CEO is not a Korean national or a person domiciled in the country; or d) an enterprise organized under Korean law in which a foreigner holds 25% or more equity interest. A foreign national or a Korean national not domiciled in the country may not serve as CEO or editor of a news agency, or as member of the boards of directors of

Yonhap News or the News Agency Promotion Committee. A foreign news agency may set up a branch or office for collecting news, but not for distributing news communications, in South Korea. Radio station licenses may not be obtained by a foreign national, a foreign government or its representative, or an enterprise organized under foreign law (US-Korea FTA, annex I, 48–49).

The publisher or editor-in-chief of an enterprise publishing periodicals must be a South Korean national. A foreign government or person, an enterprise organized under Korean law whose CEO is not a Korean national or in which a foreign person holds more than 50% of share or equity interest, may not publish periodicals in South Korea. Subject to authorization from the Minister of Culture and Tourism, a foreign person who publishes periodicals may set up a branch or office in South Korea. Provided that the periodicals are edited in the territory of the other party, such branch or office may print and distribute its periodicals in Korea in the original language (US-Korea FTA, annex I, 51).

A foreign national or a Korean national who is CEO of a foreign enterprise may not serve as CEO or chief programmer of a terrestrial broadcaster, satellite broadcasting operator, cable system operator, program provider, signal transmission network business operator, audio cable operator, or relay-only cable operator. The boards of directors of the Korea Broadcasting System and the Korea Educational Broadcasting System must be made up exclusively of South Korean nationals. Only the government of Korea, a local government, a juridical person organized under Korean law, or a Korean person may be granted or hold a license for communication and broadcasting services. A license is granted through permission in the case of a terrestrial broadcaster, relay-only cable operator, cable system operator, satellite broadcasting operator, or a program provider engaged in multi-genre programming, home shopping, or news reporting. On the other hand, for a program provider not engaged in such activities, a signal transmission network business operator, or audio cable operator, a license is granted through registration (US-Korea FTA, annex I, 54–55).

A foreign government or person, or deemed foreign person may not hold: a) an equity interest in a terrestrial broadcaster, relay-only cable operator, or program provider engaged in multi-genre programming or news reporting; b) more than 33% of the total issued stocks or equity interest of a satellite broadcasting operator; or c) more than 49% of the total issued stocks or equity interest of a cable system operator, signal transmission network business operator, or program provider not engaged in multi-genre programming or news reporting. Yet, no later than three years after the FTA came into effect, South Korea was to allow a deemed foreign person to hold up to 100% of the equity interest in a program provider not engaged in multi-genre programming, news reporting, or home shopping. For transparency purposes, no single person may hold more than 30% of the total issued stocks or equity interest of a terrestrial broadcaster or program provider engaged in multi-genre programming or news reporting, unless such broadcaster primarily provides religious or missionary content. The latter limitations do not apply to the Korean government and a corporation established by a special law, such as Mun-hwa Broadcasting Corporation, created under the *Broadcasting Culture Promotion Act* (US-Korea FTA, annex I, 55–56).

The South Korean authorities require from the providers of communication and broadcasting services, in their quarterly programming hours, the following quotas of national content: a) 80% in the case of a terrestrial broadcaster or program provider using terrestrial broadcasting to provide its programming; b) 50% in the case of a cable system operator or satellite broadcasting operator; and c) 50% per channel in the case of a program provider not using terrestrial broadcasting to provide its programming. In the following genres, in its annual programming, a terrestrial broadcaster must include: a) 45% of Korean content for animation; b) 25% for movies; and c) 60% for music. This latter percentage also applies, per channel, in the case of a cable system operator, satellite broadcasting operator, and program provider, if it provides some music programming. No later than the date the FTA became effective, the latter three types of communication/broadcasting providers shall not be required to ensure, per channel, a percentage of Korean content greater than 30% for animation and 20% for movies, should they provide such programming. Certain separate content quota requirements apply to broadcasters specialized in religious or education programming and to terrestrial digital multimedia broadcasting (DMB) operators, while the satellite DMB operators are subject to the same quotas as the satellite broadcasting operators. When the FTA came into force, South Korea was to allow for terrestrial broadcasters, cable system operators, satellite broadcasting operators, and program providers no less than 80% of their quarterly programming hours of foreign content per genre to be of a single country (US-Korea FTA, annex I, 56–57). Finally, cinema operators should project national motion pictures for at least seventy-three days per year at each screen in South Korea (US-Korea FTA, annex I, 60).

Cultural Reservations under Annex II

The South Korean government, like the US government, has secured the right to adopt or maintain any measure granting differential treatment to foreigners due to reciprocity measures or through international agreements that involve sharing of the radio spectrum, guaranteeing market access, or national treatment with regard to the one-way satellite transmission of DTH and DBS television services and digital audio services (US-Korea FTA, annex II, 12).

South Korea could also: a) limit cross-ownership among media sectors; b) set the minimum percentage of issued stocks or equity interest serving as a threshold to determine whether a juridical person organized under national law is a deemed foreign person (this does not apply to a program provider not engaged in multi-genre programming, news reporting, or home shopping); c) require the members of the board of directors of a supplier of broadcasting services to be Korean nationals or residents; d) require a platform operator (e.g., a cable system or satellite broadcasting operator) to retransmit a terrestrial broadcasting channel or to transmit a public interest channel; e) require a terrestrial broadcaster to include, within its annual programming hours, a certain percentage (historically no greater than 1.5%) of newly produced Korean animation, as long as such measure does not materially impair the level of market access accorded to US animation content as of April 30, 2007; f) require a program provider primarily supplying animation programming or engaged in multi-genre programming to include, in its annual programming hours, a certain percentage of newly produced Korean animation, as long as the measure allows the program provider to ensure a greater quantity of foreign content than specified in Annex I; g) impose an outsourced production content quota, an expenditure requirement for Korean production, or a prime-time quota, provided that, if such a quota or requirement is applied to a cable system or satellite broadcasting operator or program provider, the measure permits such operator or provider to ensure a greater quantity of foreign content than specified in Annex I; h) require a supplier of broadcasting services providing video-on-demand to store a certain percentage of national content, as long as such requirement does not result in the storage of videos for which there is negligible consumer demand; or i) restrict or prohibit foreign retransmitted broadcasting services (including foreign cable channels) in a specific category, on the condition that the foreign equity limitations in Annex I regarding program providers of that category are eliminated, this measure not applying to providers of such services approved on or before the date the FTA was signed (US-Korea FTA, annex II, 24–26).

In view of future regulatory reforms in the broadcasting and telecommunications sectors or of deliberations by the Broadcasting and Telecommunications Convergence Promotion Committee, the South Korean government reserves the right to adopt or maintain any measure with respect to a supplier of subscription-based video services.[3] Yet, any measure limiting foreign equity must be applied according to domestic policy determinations as to the classification of such services and be no less favorable, with respect to a supplier of such services, than a measure applied pursuant to Annex I with regard to a facilities-based supplier of public telecommunications services or cable system operator, as the case may be; and any measure imposing a domestic content quota may not exceed the percentage prescribed pursuant to Annex I with respect to a cable system operator (US-Korea FTA, annex II, 27–28).

As for the Australian government, South Korean authorities also preserve preferential film and television co-productions (US-Korea FTA, annex II, 29). Subject to consistency with the relevant entries under Annexes I and II, South Korea keeps latitude to set criteria for determining whether broadcasting or audiovisual programs are Korean (US-Korea FTA, annex II, 30). The Korean government could also ensure that, in case it finds that domestic digital audio or video content or genres is not readily available to Korean consumers, access to such content is not unreasonably denied and, with regard to such services targeted at a Korean audience, to promote the availability of such content.[4] Any measure adopted under this reservation must be implemented in accordance with the applicable FTA provisions on transparency, be based on objective criteria, and be no more trade restrictive or burdensome than necessary (US-Korea FTA, annex II, 33). With respect to transparency, unlike the US-Australia FTA, the provision specifically refers to the Chapter on Transparency, which not only provides for consultations with the other party, i.e., the United States, but also for appeal of regulatory decisions. Lastly, Korean authorities reserve the right to adopt or maintain any measure concerning the publication, including printing and distribution, of newspapers, as well as motion picture promotion, advertising, or post-production services (US-Korea FTA, annex II, 38, 41).

Summary and Analysis

With regard to cultural regulatory measures in the US-Korea FTA, under "type I" exemptions, governmental recommendations are required for importing foreign novels, comics, and magazines for domestic distribution and for a foreign person to engage in a public performance in South Korea. A foreign news agency is entitled to supply news communications in Korea only under a contract with a radio-licensed domestic news agency, although it may establish a branch for the sole purpose of collecting news. News agency services; the control of, as well as licenses for, communication/broadcasting enterprises; and the publication of periodicals in South Korea are, to a great extent, reserved to national citizens and/or enterprises under Korean management or ownership. The providers of communication and broadcasting services are required, in their programming, to ensure a significant percentage of South Korean content, and cinema operators to project national movies for seventy-three days per year at each screen in Korea. In particular, the relaxation of South Korea's cinematographic quota incited protest rallies by movie industry professionals (Chase 2015, 218).

The South Korean government has secured a "type II" exemption from MFN treatment for the one-way satellite transmission of television and audio services. Korean authorities also preserve a series of measures pertaining, notably, to cross-ownership among media sectors, as well as the management and/or programming of communication/broadcasting enterprises. Finally, Korea maintains either complete or some margin of maneuver with respect to: subscription-based video services; preferential film and television co-productions; criteria for national content; access to (and promotion of) such content in digital audio or video; as well as newspapers and motion picture promotion.

For the US Advisory Committee on Services and Finance Industries, the US-Korea FTA has greater significance than any other trade agreement since the NAFTA, particularly given the importance of the Korean economy (US-Korea FTA, ITAC–10 Report, 1). In the words of the Committee:

> Korea's marketplace offers enormous promise for US audiovisual products and services. However, the Korean government has diminished that promise through the imposition of multiple restrictions at virtually all levels of the industry, including broadcast content, theatrical screen quotas, ownership restrictions on market participants, and a challenging importation and censorship regime. While the [US-Korea FTA] does not sweep away all these restrictions, it does create the framework for improved market access and the potential for economic improvements. (US-Korea FTA, ITAC–10 Report, 8–9)

The Committee also stressed that the US-Korea FTA marks substantial progress toward foreign ownership within the broadcasting sector, as South Korea has committed, for firms setting up a local subsidiary, to phase in 100% foreign ownership of program providers (channel operators) other than those offering multi-genre, news, or home-shopping programming. The halving of the theatrical screen quota was seen by the Committee as the most evident improvement to the treatment of American audiovisual products in South Korea (US-Korea FTA, ITAC–10 Report, 9). Contrary to the reported US government's demand during the FTA negotiations, this latter quota applies regardless of whether movies are distributed on film stocks or as digital products, thereby amounting to a restriction on digital trade. Even though the Korean government keeps the structure of its content quotas on broadcasting, cable and related media, as well as its theatrical screen quota, the Committee pointed that it locked in those quotas at the least restrictive level permitted under existing domestic law. South Korea has also made two further liberalization commitments, decreasing the domestic content quotas applicable to the broadcast of animation programming and films, while increasing the quota applicable to single-country sources of foreign content broadcast (US-Korea FTA, ITAC–10 Report, 9).

As the Committee further mentioned, although Korea could require program providers to reserve time for new domestic animation or impose prime-time or production content quotas, it has conditioned doing so upon parallel increases in the foreign content quotas. New services and delivery platforms are, unsurprisingly, a primary concern and, in the case of video-on-demand and Internet-protocol television, the Committee underlined that the Korean government has reserved, yet again qualified, its right to apply content restrictions (US-Korea FTA, ITAC–10 Report, 9). In fact, many American openings or concessions regarding domestic cultural content have been made while limiting their impact on US access to the Korean market. If "Annex II" reservations usually leave states parties to US FTAs complete latitude to intervene in a certain field, the US-Korea FTA has seen some of these being subject to conditions.

The Committee highlighted the broad cultural reservation secured by the Korean government to promote the availability of national content through digital audio and video services if such content is not found to be readily available. The Committee noticed the rather tight conditions attached to the use of this reservation, but expressed its disappointment that it did not contain more protections against unilateral or arbitrary use. Generally, the Committee was much concerned about the reservations as regards "new platforms" (US-Korea FTA, ITAC-10 Report, 9–10). The Committee's concern echoed the one expressed toward a similar exception in a preceding FTA with Colombia. Yet, the Committee was most wary about Korea's possible abuse of such digital exception, owing to less onerous conditions attached to its use, the latter closer to those figuring in the US-Australia FTA.

Unlike Australia, South Korea had already entered into some specific commitments pertaining to audiovisual services under the GATS. The liberalization commitments made by the Korean government under its FTA with the United States, however, go much further. Nevertheless, as in Australia's case, either such commitments entail full liberalization, in case no exceptions have been taken, lock in existing levels of liberalization, or provide for deeper liberalization, notably with lower quota levels for domestic cultural contents. In particular, broad reservations for the benefit of future measures, henceforth, tend to be designed so as to guarantee a certain level of market access.

THE US-AUSTRALIA AND US-KOREA FREE TRADE AGREEMENTS AND NEW MEDIA

At the end of the negotiations for the US-Australia FTA, the Australian government emphasized that it has preserved sufficient flexibility to not only maintain but to increase the amounts of domestic cultural content, notably as new platforms become more important (Breen 2010, 664). On the other hand, the Culture Research Education and Training Enterprise Australia (hereafter CREATE Australia), an organization representing all the main Australian cultural industries, stressed that most of the reservations in favor of national cultural content pertain to analogue or traditional media. In addition, the concept of "digital products" is wider than the one of "interactive audio and/or video services," under which all the new media are included. As such services are not defined, this could potentially exclude, for instance, e-cinema, as the latter is neither old media nor interactive. Hence, this raises questions as to the scope of this exception with respect to electronic commerce (CREATE Australia 2004, 6, 16, 20). In the US-Korea FTA, there is a definition of "digital audio or video services," although the latter as well does not cover all digital products.

Moreover, Australia's right to introduce national content requirements on new media services is tightly circumscribed. Measures can only be imposed so that access to domestic audiovisual content or genres is not unreasonably denied to Australians, and on companies carrying on business in the country (Breen 2010, 665). The means of delivery of such services, which include satellites and the Internet, do not necessitate any business presence in Australia. Yet, state courts have already ruled that assets need not be physically located in a country for an enterprise to be seen as "carrying on business" within its territory (Grant and Wood 2004, 334). This criterion of business presence is not stipulated in the US-Korea FTA.

Besides, the obligation to invite comment from the United States, also present in the US-Korea FTA, may translate into a *de facto* requirement of approval on the part of the American government. Furthermore, each of the specified conditions, such as "not readily available," "not unreasonably denied," or "no more trade restrictive than necessary" are somehow vague, seemingly onerous, and could be subject to conflicting interpretations from the parties. Then, in case Australia and South Korea proceed with regulations without US agreement, the latter could either demand trade-liberalizing compensation or take retaliatory measures. All these factors led CREATE Australia to conclude that, in practice, such conditions for regulatory action may be difficult to achieve and to have effect in a globalized system of content distribution (CREATE Australia 2004, 6–7, 16–17). Even though the US-Australia FTA has been in place for more than a decade, with no reported use of this exception pertaining to digital trade, disagreements persist over the implications of its associated conditions. The Australian government continues to assert that it has preserved more leeway than what creative industries believe.

A comparison with the three conditions attached to a similar reservation concerning digital media in the US FTA with Colombia may help to better understand those in accordance to which such an exception may be used in the US FTAs with Australia and Korea. Under the US-Colombia FTA, whose negotiations concluded a little more than a year before those of the US-Korea FTA, the Colombian government may act to ensure domestic content in the interactive audio and/or video services sector only if the United States agrees that domestic audiovisual content is not readily available to Colombian people and that the proposed measure is based on objective criteria and has the least trade-restrictive impact possible. Under this first condition, if the latter elements aimed at limiting trade disruption correspond to those found in the US-Australia and US-Korea FTAs, there is no explicit mention in these two FTAs that US agreement is required for this exception to be resorted to. The second condition whereby the measure could only be applied to a service supplied in the country by a company established in Colombia appears to limit its scope to companies physically present in Colombia. Yet, in the digital environment, firms can supply services in countries without being present within their territories. In this respect, we saw that if an enterprise may be considered to be "carrying on business" in a country, as specified in the US-Australia FTA, without being physically located there, the formulation in the US-Colombia FTA seemingly aims at preventing this possibility. Such a question also generally evokes the challenge of ensuring domestic content regulations in a global digital environment. As for the third condition, requiring that both parties agree on trade-liberalizing compensation in the interactive audio and video services sector, in view of the largely unregulated character of the sector, this raises the question as to what could be done to lower another, existing barrier in that sector. The requirement of trade-liberalizing compensation also suggests that the extent of government regulation of the new media in Colombia's case is bound to remain fairly modest (US-Colombia FTA, annex II, 14).

Hence, apparently owing to its developing country status and overall leverage, Colombia was imposed even more restrictive conditions should it seek to foster national cultural content in the new media. Indeed, one could argue that if, under the US-Australia and US-Korea FTAs, the US government's approval were both required and to be followed by trade-liberalizing compensation, as in the US-Colombia FTA, it would have been clearly stipulated. Finally, it is revealing that whereas the US Advisory Committee on Services and Finance Industries expressed concerns about potential unilateral or arbitrary use of such reservation in the US-Korea FTA, it considered, on the other hand, that the conditions in the US-Colombia FTA "give US industry meaningful assurances that new media opportunities will not be arbitrarily undercut" (US-Colombia FTA, ITAC–10 Report, 10).

SUMMARY AND CONCLUSIONS

In the US FTAs with Australia and Korea, the chapters on investment, services, and electronic commerce include a general exception for subsidization measures. As in all US FTAs, states parties maintain wide latitude to use financial instruments of cultural policy. With respect to instruments of regulation, as in most other US FTAs, restrictions on ownership, control, and/or management of cultural industries are found in these two FTAs. The domestic content regulations kept under these agreements, however, are more significant than in most US FTAs. Indeed, among the countries that concluded FTAs with the United States under the 2002 TPA, Australia and South Korea have secured more extensive cultural exceptions or reservations, including with regard to new or digital media, and, hence, have preserved a larger margin of maneuver to pursue cultural policies. Table 4.1 indicates the main types of cultural regulatory exceptions secured by Australia and South Korea in their FTAs with the United States.

Yet, the exceptions enabling Australia and South Korea to ensure the availability of, and access to, domestic cultural content in digital media raise many questions. One relates to the challenge of ensuring domestic content regulations in the digital environment. Another has to do with the conditions underlying the resort to these exceptions that are both unclear and restrictive, likely to lead to divergences between the parties, while their application is seemingly highly dependent on US consent. In contradiction with the objectives and provisions of the CDCE, states parties to US FTAs are not left with much maneuverability to address eventual cultural concerns as economic globalization and/or the digital revolution unfold. The existence in recent US FTAs with Australia and South Korea of reservations pertaining to digital media arguably indicates some flexibility in the US strategy of cultural liberalization. The scope of this policy shift is very limited, however, as the key US concern, in a sector as sensitive as electronic commerce, remains the free flow of digital prod-

Table 4.1. Main Types of Cultural Regulatory Exceptions across Developed States Parties to US FTAs

Cultural Regulatory Exceptions	States Parties	
	Australia	South Korea
Restrictions re. property/control/management and licensing of cultural enterprises	•	•
Domestic content requirements - Public (free-to-air) radio and/or television	•	•
- Subscription television		•
- Advertising	•	
- Cinema (screen quotas)		•
Audiovisual cooperation agreements	•	•
Digital or new technologies/platforms - Interactive audio and/or video	•	•

ucts. In fact, such e-commerce exceptions are accompanied by a series of conditions so strict as to raise uncertainties regarding their potential use.

The exceptions falling under the so-called traditional instruments of cultural policy, even though significantly greater in number and scope in the US-Australia and US-Korea FTAs, can nonetheless be seen as compatible with the new US trade strategy on cultural products. At the same time, Australia's and South Korea's cultural interests and/or concerns, as well as their status as developed countries, arguably gave them increased leverage to provide for more exceptions with regard to the cultural sector, particularly to digital media. Indeed, unlike other US FTAs, nearly all of which concluded with developing states, Australia has secured certain exceptions with a specific concern for maintaining flexibility toward new media. As for the exceptions in favor of culture in the US-Korea FTA, these are more extensive, compared to those included in the US-Australia FTA. This is also the case with respect to the exceptions pertaining to new media, which seems to indicate a growing awareness of new technologies in states' cultural policies. The relevance of states' leverage as well as of negotiation dynamics, in Australia's and Korea's case, is made all the more evident when we consider the stricter, if not forbidding, conditions under the US-Colombia FTA attached to the exception for culture in the field of new technologies.

The provisions relating to culture in the US-Australia and US-Korea FTAs signal an evolving concern over the years for the impact of the digital revolution on states' cultural policies. Such a crucial issue is timely as it has been debated within the TPP, TiSA, and TTIP negotiations. It is also bound to lead to divergences of views and interests, particularly as a result of the historical US and EU perspectives on the trade and culture debate.

NOTES

1. For more on the US-Australia FTA negotiations and key provisions, see Mitchell and Voon (2009) and vis-à-vis Australia's cultural policies more specifically, see Breen (2010).

2. On the background and key issues in the US-Korea FTA negotiations, see Lee (2015).

3. Subscription-based video services are understood as being supplied to end-users over dedicated transmission capacity that the supplier owns or controls (including by leasing) and includes Internet protocol-based television (IPTV) and interactive broadcasting.

4. In this entry, a digital audio or video service means a service that provides streaming audio content, films or other video downloads or streaming video content, regardless of the type of transmission (including through the Internet), but does not include broadcasting services or subscription-based video services.

FIVE

Recent and Ongoing US Trade Negotiations

The United States, within the past few years, has been taking part in three major sets of preferential trade negotiations. In chronological order, the first are those of the TPP. These were conducted from 2010 and 2015, and, together with the United States, came to include twelve countries of the Pacific Rim. The second set of negotiations is known as the TiSA. It has grouped twenty-three WTO members (the EU counted as one) that belong to the "Really Good Friends of Services." The third is the TTIP negotiations between the United States and the European Union. With currently fifty countries from all continents representing over 70% of world trade in services, the TiSA corresponds to the usual understanding of plurilateral negotiations. On the other hand, the TPP and TTIP negotiations are those of two large-scale PTAs. They are indeed the most high-profile PTA negotiations, either recent or under way. Both are also known as mega-regionals and each covers nearly one-third of world trade.

Although the 2002 TPA expired in 2007, US trade negotiations had not stopped. Yet, without the TPA, the chances to see them come to fruition were slim. Shortly before the TPP negotiations were scheduled to conclude, the Obama administration secured in June 2015 the renewal of the TPA. With the TPA now effective, more US FTA negotiations, including bilateral ones, may be launched or revived, alongside the TPP, TiSA, and TTIP. Similarly to the 2002 TPA, which set the parameters within which the United States concluded a series of eleven FTAs with sixteen countries, the 2015 TPA is indicative of the evolution of US trade objectives and priorities, particularly with respect to digital trade.

In this regard, it will be seen that the 2015 TPA, like its 2002 version, is in line with the new or revised American strategy on cultural products.

The three PTA negotiations until now conducted under the 2015 TPA comprise, however, not only a great variety of countries with which the US government has sought to strike a deal, but also different and sometimes opposing positions among parties on the treatment of cultural products. On this note, given its setting and parties' stances, the TTIP is undoubtedly to be the main test for the US resolve to secure its views and interests on the trade and culture debate.

Following the highlights of the 2015 TPA as they relate to cultural products, the chapter discusses the outcomes of the recently signed TPP agreement, then turns to the continuing TiSA and TTIP talks, before concluding on the recent and ongoing US plurilateral trade negotiations.

THE US TRADE PROMOTION AUTHORITY OF 2015

The fast-track trade negotiating authority, or now TPA, was created pursuant to the Trade Act of 1974. After being restored by the Trade Act of 2002, which lasted until June 30, 2007, the Trade Act of 2015 represents the third enactment of the TPA, to be effective until July 1, 2018, and, if extended, to July 1, 2021.

The Bipartisan Congressional Trade Priorities and Accountability Act of 2015 reiterates the nine US overall trade negotiating objectives that figured in the 2002 TPA, but adds four, among which are "10) to ensure that trade agreements reflect and facilitate the increasingly interrelated, multi-sectoral nature of trade and investment activity" and "11) to recognize the growing significance of the Internet as a trading platform in international commerce" (2015 TPA, section 102(a)). As regards the principal trade negotiating objectives, the 2015 TPA further mentions that the expansion of trade in services "should be pursued through all means, including through a plurilateral agreement with those countries willing and able to undertake high standard services commitments for both existing and new services" (section 102(b)(2)(B)). Concerning foreign investment, intellectual property, and electronic commerce, the latter now titled "Digital Trade in Goods and Services and Cross-Border Data Flows," the description that accompanies the last two of these fields adds further specifications meant to strengthen the US digital trade agenda (section 102(b)(4)(5)(6)). Hence, the revised US trade strategy on cultural products, that oriented the negotiations of US FTAs under the 2002 TPA, remains in place, apparently with a further emphasis on a free, open, and global digital marketplace.

The 2015 TPA also increases Congressional oversight and contains more extensive provisions on consultations with members of Congress and on public access to information and participation (transparency). The committees of Congress primarily involved in trade negotiations remain the House Ways and Means Committee and the Senate Finance Committee, while, with the same membership, the Congressional Oversight Group under the 2002 TPA gives place to two distinct House and Senate Advisory Groups on Negotiations (section 104). As was the case in the 2002 TPA, trade agreements for which negotiations have been under way, among which the TPP, the TTIP, and TiSA, can nonetheless benefit from the fast-track procedures (section 107). As made clear by the 2015 TPA, the terms, conditions, and procedures under which Congress allows the Administration to enter into trade agreements are ever more specific and, as a result, constraining on US authorities in charge of trade negotiations.[1] In fact, the USTR can hardly do otherwise than insist on wide-ranging liberalization for cultural products and the absence of restrictions in digital media. In turn, this might lead to serious difficulties for PTA negotiations, especially the TTIP, where the views and interests of the United States are to collide with those of some other parties.

THE TRANS-PACIFIC PARTNERSHIP

The TPP initiative follows on the Trans-Pacific Strategic Economic Partnership Agreement between Brunei, Chile, New Zealand, and Singapore, in place since 2006, which encouraged accession by other states. Then led by the United States, the TPP has been the cornerstone of the economic policy of the Obama administration in Asia and the economic arm of the "Asian Pivot" (Kim 2015, 140). The negotiations started on March 15, 2010, between eight countries: Australia, Brunei, Chile, New Zealand, Peru, Singapore, the United States, and Vietnam. They were joined by Malaysia later in 2010, Canada and Mexico in 2012, and Japan in 2013, to encompass twelve countries of the Pacific Rim. The TPP negotiations concluded on October 4, 2015, while the Trans-Pacific Partnership (TPP) Agreement was signed on February 4, 2016, in Auckland, New Zealand. The TPP is expected to enter into force within two years of its signature or after being ratified by at least six states, accounting for more than 85% of all signatories' GDPs (TPP, article 30.5). Although the TPP parties all belong to the APEC forum, the TPP is not an APEC initiative.[2]

Arguably, the TPP comprises an almost equal number of developed (Australia, Brunei, Canada, Japan, New Zealand, Singapore, United States) and developing (Chile, Malaysia, Mexico, Peru, Vietnam) countries. Among the TPP parties, seven (Japan, Malaysia, Mexico, New Zealand, Singapore, the United States, and Vietnam) have undertaken commitments in the audiovisual sector within the WTO. Six states (Australia, Canada, Chile, Mexico, Peru, and Singapore) already count among US FTA partners, while five (Brunei, Japan, Malaysia, Singapore, and the United States) are not parties to the CDCE. On the basis of a leaked document on countries' positions prepared by the US government in late 2013, a slight majority, namely Australia, Brunei, Canada, Chile, Malaysia, New Zealand, and Vietnam, was reportedly favorable to a "cultural exception," whereas Japan, Mexico, Peru, Singapore, as well as the United States were opposed (WikiLeaks 2013). Interestingly, not all CDCE parties were supportive of provisions for cultural exception in the TPP. Likewise, some non-parties to the Convention were nonetheless in favor of a trade agreement more sensitive to cultural policy concerns.

The TPP is unquestionably the largest and most diverse FTA ever negotiated by the United States. Despite its plurilateral setting, the TPP essentially corresponds to the US FTA template as it emerged from the 2002 TPA and later updated by the 2015 TPA, reflecting the leading role of the United States in this mega-regional initiative. In many cases, the TPP broadens countries' commitments, especially for those not already parties to US FTAs. As for each successive US FTA, apart from updating known approaches to issues covered by previous agreements, the TPP includes new and emerging trade and cross-cutting issues. The TPP notably includes chapters on "Cooperation and Capacity Building" as well as "Development," to provide technical assistance and trade capacity-building to enable developing parties to fully implement a high-standard agreement. In particular, the US government stressed the importance of upgrading the NAFTA, including setting standards to protect "digital freedom." The TPP also takes additional steps for promoting legitimate digital trade, including the delivery of movies, music, and books online.

As regards the relationship between the TPP and existing trade agreements, notably previous US FTAs, the TPP is to coexist with them. This is similar to existing US FTAs, whose provisions normally prevail over WTO agreements, to the extent that the provisions of such FTAs are more recent, more specific, more liberalizing, and between a smaller group of countries. Yet, since the TPP is the first instance of "double PTAs" for the United States, it is no so clear which rules are to prevail. The TPP (article 1.2.2) provides for consultation in case of deemed inconsistency with another agreement to which some of its parties belong, while explicitly excluding more favorable treatment of goods, services, investments, or persons under another agreement. Hence, it appears that the rules of earlier US FTAs are to prevail when these are more specific and more liberalizing.[3]

In this section, some key developments in the TPP text and chapters, most relevant for cultural products, are first pointed out. As was the case of the CAFTA-DR, the exceptions secured by different states concerning cultural products are later described, beginning with the United States and countries already parties to US FTAs, before turning to new US FTA partners. As in previous chapters, this is to be followed by a summary and an analysis of these exceptions.

In the preamble of the TPP, it is stipulated that parties are resolved to "recognize the importance of cultural identity and diversity among and within the Parties, and that trade and investment can expand opportunities to enrich cultural identity and diversity at home and abroad." Although a PTA to which the United States is a party now specifically refers to cultural identity and cultural diversity, the second part of the entry ensures that such recognition could not involve trade restrictions and, thus, much leeway for the pursuit of cultural policies. This is evident in light of another entry recognizing parties' inherent right to regulate and resolve to preserve their flexibility, but with references limited to public health, safety, the environment, the financial system, and public morals. As in the US FTAs negotiated under the 2002 TPA, subsidies or grants provided by parties are specifically exempted from the TPP's investment and services chapters (TPP, articles 9.12.6(b) and 10.2.3(d)) and, as in the case of the US-Australia and US-Korea FTAs, from the e-commerce chapter (TPP, article 14.4.3). Unlike most existing US FTAs, the TPP includes a chapter on temporary entry for business persons. Yet, despite specific commitments from parties on access for each other's business people, the latter could still only travel to the United States through the present US visa system (TPP, ITAC–10 Report, 8).

The e-commerce chapter notably strives to ensure both the free flow of data and the security and privacy of Internet users (see TPP, ITAC–8 Report, 10–11). It does not apply to government procurement (article 14.2.3(a)) and broadcasting, in the latter case, exempted from the chapter's national treatment obligation (article 14.4.4). Unlike the US FTAs with Singapore and Korea, broadcasting is here explicitly mentioned, but left undefined. Such exclusion seems reflective of the concerns for broadcasting shared by a number of Asian countries. The telecommunications chapter, for the first time, extends pro-competitive principles to mobile services, the fastest-growing sector of the industry. The TPP is also the first US FTA to comprise a chapter on "Regulatory Coherence," which, together with the one on "Transparency and Anti-Corruption," seek to ensure ready access to information about laws and regulations, due process, as well as effective consultation and coordination, in addition to "good regulatory practices," across parties' agencies. As for the intellectual property chapter, reminiscent of the post-NAFTA investment chapters of US FTAs,[4] it aims to better balance copyright protections and exceptions/limitations, notably in the case of news reporting and Internet service providers (ISPs).[5]

United States

The US government essentially repeats the exceptions it has taken in its existing FTAs. Yet, under the TPP, the United States has also reserved the right to prohibit a person from offering DTH and DBS television and digital audio services into US territory unless the TPP party to which that person belongs: a) allows US persons to obtain a license for such services in that party in similar circumstances; and b) treats the supply of audio or video content originating in its territory no more favorably than the supply of such content originating in a non-party or any other party (TPP, annex II-US, 1). The US exception pertaining to cable television systems, included in the NAFTA and five of the FTAs negotiated under the 2002 TPA, is broadened in the TPP. It now provides that the United States may forbid a person of a party from owning or operating a cable television system in US territory unless that person establishes that the party: a) permits US persons to own or operate such systems in its territory under similar circumstances; and b) treats the supply of video content originating in the party no more favorably than the supply of any other party or non-party's content (TPP, annex II-US, 2).

Australia

When compared to the US-Australia FTA, the threshold for the screening of investments in telecommunications has been raised, from A$ 50 million to A$ 252 million, while the provisions regarding Telstra have been maintained. Australian authorities continue to screen proposed (this time, either direct or portfolio) investments by foreign persons of 5% or more in the media sector, regardless of size (TPP, annex I-AU, 3–6, 13). Further restrictions in broadcasting and newspapers were dropped, as a result of new media rules from 2007 or Australia's subsequent unilateral liberalization (Bosworth and Trewin 2008, 641).

Australia has reserved the right to adopt or maintain any measure with respect to: a) transmission quotas for national content on free-to-air commercial television broadcasting; b) non-discriminatory expenditure requirements for Australian production on subscription television broadcasting; c) transmission quotas for national content on free-to-air radio broadcasting; d) other audiovisual services transmitted electronically, in order to make Australian content reasonably available to Australian consumers; e) spectrum management and licensing of broadcasting services (applies only to market access); and f) subsidies or grants for investment in Australian cultural activity (TPP, annex II-AU, 9–10). The Australian government has also preserved leeway with regard to preferential co-production arrangements for film and television productions, as well as creative arts, indigenous traditional cultural expressions, and other cultural heritage (TPP, annex II-AU, 11–12). Australia has also made further positive-list commitments than those under the GATS with respect to telecommunications (TPP, annex II-AU, 23).

The exceptions secured by Australia essentially involve the same cultural sub-sectors under both the US-Australia FTA and the TPP. Except for the higher threshold for investment in telecommunications, the trade commitments under the latter are below those under the former and, therefore, leave a much greater margin of maneuver for the Australian government to pursue cultural policies. Since such TPP commitments are less liberalizing, they are not to affect the trade relations with the United States, which should continue to be governed by the relevant provisions of the US-Australia FTA.

Canada

Instead of a cultural exemption clause applying to the whole trade agreement, as in the US-Canada FTA and NAFTA, Canada opted for a more targeted, chapter-by-chapter exemption, as it had done in the CETA.[6] Thus, Canada has secured a cultural exemption for the goods chapter, which stipulates that national treatment shall not apply to a measure affecting the production, publication, exhibition, or sale of goods (i.e., books, magazines, and media carrying video or music recordings) that supports the creation, development, or accessibility of Canadian artistic expression or content (TPP, chapter 2, annex 2A, Measures of Canada). Acquisition or establishment of a new business relating to cultural heritage or national identity continues to be subject to review (TPP, annex I-CA, 2–4). Nationality restrictions apply in the case of examination services for the export and import of cultural property, as well as of foreign investment in telecommunications (TPP, annex I-CA, 13, 34–35). Public cultural enterprises, namely the Canadian Broadcasting Corporation, Telefilm Canada, as well as any new, reorganized, or transferee enterprise related to cultural industries, are excluded from the chapter dealing with state-owned enterprises (TPP, annex IV-CA, 4–7).

More importantly, the Canadian (main) cultural exemption clause, which pertains to investment and services, now reads:

> Canada reserves the right to adopt or maintain any measure that affects cultural industries and that has the objective of supporting, directly or indirectly, the creation, development, or accessibility of Canadian artistic expression or content, except: a) discriminatory requirements on service suppliers or investors to make financial contributions for Canadian content development; and b) measures restricting the access to online foreign audio-visual content. (TPP, annex II-CA, 16–17)

The two exceptions or conditions now attached to Canada's main cultural exemption have been subject to highly contrasting appreciations. For some, they would prevent Canada from adopting almost any tax and/or regulation in regard to digital media (Geist 2016a, 2016b; Maltais 2016, 15–17; Guèvremont 2016). Another concern has to do with whether the definition of cultural industries, which has not changed from the NAFTA, is neutral from a technological standpoint so as to encompass digital platforms and notably the Internet. In this regard, if the websites of broadcasters and newspapers could be covered by the definition, it might be different for Internet-only services, which would then fall outside the cultural exemption (Geist 2016c). Long opposed to Canada's broad cultural exemption under the NAFTA, the United States would have brought the vanguard of cultural exception/diversity to surrender to its views and interests on digital freedom, and that to an even greater degree than other US FTA partners, such as Australia and South Korea, also known for their cultural policies.

For others, on the other hand, the new language accompanying the Canadian cultural exemption would not much affect Canada's latitude for pursuing cultural policies, including with respect to digital media. Financial contributions or expenditure rules could still be imposed, as long as these are non-discriminatory, i.e., apply to both domestic and foreign suppliers or investors. Canada could also regulate, and notably adopt content requirements for, online foreign suppliers, to the extent that exceptions for investment and services in the TPP apply to the e-commerce chapter (article 14.2.4). The latter also includes an exception for broadcasting, which would be broad enough to embrace electronically delivered services, and, in Canada's case, its specific exceptions for investment and services include cultural industries (Grant 2016; Vallerand 2016). If accurate, this second set of interpretations, however, would render superfluous the conditions in the TPP accompanying the Canadian cultural exemption.

Such "constructive ambiguity," to quote a Canadian negotiator, is attributable to the old fundamental disagreement between the United States and Canada on the treatment of cultural products in trade agreements. In turn, these convoluted provisions might well lead to differing interpretations from their two negotiating parties, at the same time, allowing both sides to save face and better sale the TPP to their constituencies.

Chile

As for Australia, Chile essentially restates the exceptions under Annexes I and II of its FTA with the United States, notably in the form of restrictions regarding the property, control, and/or management of media, broadcasting licenses, and a 40% domestic quota on public television (TPP, annex I-CL, 4–5, 21). One exception pertains to cross-border trade and investment in one-way satellite broadcasting of digital telecommunications services, and another to an MFN exemption in favor of arts and cultural industries,[7] such as audiovisual cooperation agreements (TPP, annex II-CL, 4–5, 11). As in its FTA with the United States, Chile has reserved the right to adopt or maintain any measure relating to market access, except for certain sectors and sub-sectors, including advertising, printing and publishing, only subject to restrictions concerning mode 4, i.e., the supply of a service by a national of a party in the territory of another party (TPP, annex II-CL, 18–24). Lastly, the *Televisión Nacional de*

Chile or its successor, its subsidiaries and affiliates, are excluded from the state-owned enterprises chapter (TPP, annex IV-CL, 5).

Under the TPP, Chile, like Australia, has made less commitments and kept a larger margin of maneuver with respect to the regulation of cultural products. Again, to the extent that such provisions are more restrictive than those contained in its FTA with the United States, the latter will continue to preside over Chilean-US trade relations.

Mexico

The exceptions secured by the Mexican government are generally reminiscent of similar ones under the NAFTA. In particular, for radio and free-to-air television broadcasting, frequency band and sole concessions are to be granted only to Mexican nationals or enterprises constituted under Mexican laws and regulations. TPP investors or investments may participate up to 49% in broadcasting enterprises, such maximum being subject to the reciprocity existent with the country in which the investor or trader is constituted. A favorable opinion of the Mexican Foreign Investment Commission is also required before a sole concession for providing broadcasting services with foreign investment participation may be granted. The Mexican state should guarantee that the broadcasting promotes the values of national identity, while broadcasting concessions should use and stimulate local and national artistic values and expressions of Mexican culture. Daily programs starring actors must include a larger time covered by Mexicans (TPP, annex I-MX, 11–12).

As under the NAFTA, Mexico has reserved that TPP investors or investments may only own, directly or indirectly, up to 49% of the ownership interest in daily newspapers written primarily for a Mexican audience and distributed in the territory of Mexico (TPP, annex I-MX, 28). The total screen time to the projection of Mexican films is set at 10%, as against 30% under the NAFTA (TPP, annex I-MX, 65). As for Chile, Mexico has preserved latitude with regard to market access, except for some sectors and sub-sectors, including advertising, printing and publishing, recreational and cultural services, only subject to restrictions on mode 4, and, in the case of audiovisual services, also often subject to restrictions pertaining to mode 3, i.e., foreign investment (TPP, annex II-MX, 12–42).

As for Canada, inasmuch as some exceptions taken by Mexico under the TPP are more liberalizing than those under the NAFTA, as in the case of the cinematographic screen quota, the former are to apply.

Peru

Only Peruvian nationals or juridical persons organized under national law and domiciled in the country may be authorized or licensed to offer radio or television broadcasting services, while no foreign national may hold an authorization or a license directly or through a sole proprietorship (TPP, annex I-PE, 5). At least 30%, on average, of the total weekly programs by free-to-air television broadcasters between 5:00am and midnight must be produced in Peru (TPP, annex I-PE, 6). Any domestic artistic audiovisual production, live performance, and commercial advertising must include at least 80% of national artists and technical personnel, who should receive no less than 60% of the total payroll for wages and salaries paid to artists and staff involved in such activities (TPP, annex I-PE, 16, 18). A foreign circus may stay in Peru with its original cast for a maximum of ninety days. This period may be extended for another ninety-day period, in which case, the foreign circus should include Peruvian nationals, to a minimum of 30% as artists, and 15% as technicians, the same percentages applying to the payroll of salaries and wages (TPP, annex I-PE, 17). Free-to-air radio and television broadcasting enterprises must dedicate at least 10% of their daily programming to folklore, national music, and series or programs produced in Peru on the national history, literature, culture, or current issues. This must be ensured with the hiring of a minimum of 80% of national artists and technical personnel receiving no less than 60% of the total payroll (TPP, annex I-PE, 20).

As in its FTA with the United States, Peru has an MFN exemption for international agreements concerning cultural industries (the latter defined as in the US-Peru FTA), including audiovisual cooperation arrangements (TPP, annex II-PE, 6–7). The Peruvian government has also kept its reservations regarding: handicraft industries; a domestic cinematographic 20% screen quota; conditional support for jewelry design, theater and visual arts, music and publishing; and reciprocal treatment to persons of another party in the audiovisual, publishing, and music sectors (TPP, annex II-PE, 8–11). Finally, like Chile and Mexico, Peru has maintained latitude regarding market access, including for cultural services. In the case of printing and publishing, jewelry and handicraft design, advertising, and entertainment, such restrictions are limited to mode 4 and, for the latter two, also to those under Annex I (TPP, annex II-PE, 21–29).

Hence, under the TPP, Peruvian reservations for the benefit of the cultural sector are either similar or, for many under Annex I, less liberalizing than those under the US-Peru FTA. In such conditions, the terms of the latter agreement will continue to regulate cultural trade exchanges between Peru and the United States.

Singapore

Singapore has restated its two broad exceptions related to broadcasting and newspapers, while the first one is further clarified in comparison with the US-Singapore FTA. Thus, Singapore has reserved the right to adopt or maintain any measure with regard to broadcasting[8] services receivable by Singapore's domestic audience or originating from Singapore, including but not limited to: a) transmission quotas for content on television broadcasting; b) non-discriminatory expenditure requirements for Singapore production on television broadcasting; c) transmission quotas for content on radio; d) spectrum management and licensing of broadcasting services; or e) subsidies or grants for investment involving Singapore subjects, persons, and services.

This entry does not apply to: a) a service supplier, an investor, or a covered investment of another party in respect of non-scheduled broadcasting services, in case of an agreement to provide national treatment between Singapore and that party notified under the GATS prior to the TPP's coming into force; b) the sole activity of transmitting licensed broadcasting services to a final consumer; c) the production, distribution, and public display of motion pictures, video and sound recordings, although such mention should not encompass all the broadcasting and audiovisual services and materials that are broadcasting-related, and examples of reserved services include: free-to-air broadcasting, as well as cable and pay television; and d) value-added network services, such as electronic-mail, voice-mail, online information and data-base retrieval, electronic data interchange, and online information and/or data processing (TPP, annex II-SG, 8–9).

Singapore has also taken an exception with respect to the distribution, publishing, and printing of newspapers, including, but not limited to, shareholding limits and management control (TPP, annex II-SG, 18).

Brunei

Brunei has maintained all latitude with respect to any licensable free-to-air or subscription broadcasting services offered on a scheduled programming basis. Measures that could be adopted or maintained include, but are not limited to, ownership, control, and funding of an enterprise providing such services (TPP, annex II-BN, 17). The Bruneian government has also ensured a broad exception related to the printing, publishing, and reproduction of newspapers, including matters regarding the collection and publication of news, as well as the distribution of newspapers (TPP, annex II-BN, 19). These two exceptions are reminiscent of Singapore's, in the first case, applying only to scheduled broadcasting services.

Japan

A prior notification requirement and screening procedures apply to foreign investors in telecommunications and Internet-based services, on grounds of either national security or public order/safety, at the end of which the investor may have to alter the content of, or discontinue, the investment (TPP, annex I-JP, 16). Japan has secured a market access exception for all unrecognized or technically unfeasible services at the time of the TPP's entry into force (TPP, annex II-JP, 5). Japanese authorities have also reserved the right to adopt or maintain any measure relating to the broadcasting[9] industry (TPP, annex II-JP, 8).

Malaysia

Malaysia has maintained restrictions for foreign individuals and companies concerning licenses for the supply of telecommunications services, including broadcasting (TPP, annex I-MY, 12–13). The Malaysian government has taken an MFN exception with respect to broadcasting (TPP, annex II-MY, 7). Cultural products (i.e., books, magazines, periodicals or newspapers, works of art and films, as well as programs licensed for broadcast on television, cable and satellite stations) imported and distributed in Malaysia may be reviewed to ensure consistency with decency standards. Prior approval is required for any arts, filming, and performances by foreign artists, such activities also having to comply with government guidelines. Such review and pre-approval must be administered in an objective, transparent, and impartial manner, in addition to being consistent with national treatment (TPP, annex II-MY, 11).

New Zealand

Government approval is required for the shareholding of any single overseas entity to exceed 49.9% in Chorus Limited, a public company providing telecommunications infrastructure, while at least half of the Board directors must be New Zealand citizens (TPP, annex I-NZ, 7). The acquisition of, or any interest in, licenses or management rights to use the radio frequency spectrum on the part of foreign governments or agents on their behalf is subject to the written approval of the relevant government authority (TPP, annex I-NZ, 8). New Zealand has kept restrictions for foreign investment over NZ$ 200 million by non-government sources and NZ$ 100 million by government sources (TPP, annex I-NZ, 12–13), coupled with a reservation for future measures regarding the approval criteria for such investments (TPP, annex II-NZ, 7–8).

The government of New Zealand has taken an MFN exemption in favor of film and television co-production arrangements (TPP, annex II-NZ, 20). The right to adopt or maintain any measure has been reserved for the promotion of film and television production, as well as of national content on public radio and television, and in films (TPP, annex II-NZ, 21). New Zealand has also ensured latitude with respect to cultural heritage, public archives, library and museum services (TPP, annex II-NZ, 28).

Vietnam

Vietnam has maintained foreign investment restrictions with respect to: the supply of telecommunications services, although some are to be phased out five years after the TPP's entry into force; the production, distribution, and projection of motion pictures; entertainment services, including theater, live bands, and circuses; electronic games services (although some are to be phased out five years after the TPP's entry into force); building and managing theme or amusement parks below US$ 1 billion (TPP, annex I-VN, 9–10, 11, 15, 16, 29). Cinemas must feature Vietnamese films during major national anniversaries and at least one Vietnamese film between 6:00pm and 10:00pm, while the ratio of domestic to total films should be no less than 20% on an annual basis (TPP, annex I-VN, 12).

The Vietnamese government has reserved sound recording, except that foreign ownership of up to 51% is to be permitted in enterprises engaged in such services (TPP, annex II-VN, 14). Vietnam may grant preferential treatment to domestic artists and companies in the performing arts, fine arts, and other cultural activities[10] (TPP, annex II-VN, 17). Vietnam has also kept the right to adopt or maintain any measure concerning: tangible and intangible cultural heritages; press and news-gathering agencies, publishing, radio and television broadcasting, *in any form;* the production and distribution of video records *on whatever medium* (emphasis added) (TPP, annex II-VN, 18–20). In addition, the Vietnamese government has preserved latitude regarding subsidies inconsistent with the obligation on performance requirements for audiovisual services, as well as preferential treatment to television programs and cinematographic works produced under co-production agreements (TPP, annex II-VN, 21). Finally, in the mass-communication, printing, and publishing sectors, state-owned enterprises are excluded (TPP, annex IV-VN, 14).

Summary and Analysis

As in previous US FTAs, the scope of cultural commitments varies, sometimes significantly, among the states parties to the TPP, and, by consequence, their ability to pursue cultural policies. Despite such variations, nearly all have taken exceptions reserving, to different degrees, the ownership, control, and/or management of cultural enterprises, as well as licenses for radio and television broadcasting, while also securing reservations in favor of domestic content in public radio and/or television. TPP parties have also secured such provisions regardless of whether they have cultural commitments under the GATS or belong to the WTO Friends of Audiovisuals or the CDCE. In particular, exceptions for broadcasting, as taken by Brunei, Japan, Singapore, and Vietnam, not to forget those for newspapers, are common among Asian countries, many of which are not CDCE parties. On the other hand, Malaysia's remaining ability to regulate the cultural sector is mostly limited to censorship, the latter apparently not applying to digital media. Ironically, Brunei and Malaysia, reportedly in favor of cultural exception in the TPP, ended up with less cultural policy leeway, while Japan and Singapore, opposed to such exception, secured more extensive reservations regarding cultural products.

For countries that were not already parties to a US FTA, significant commitments, including in the cultural sector, had to be made to satisfy the ambitious American agenda, especially relating to digital trade. With respect to partners to existing US FTAs, it was seen that the exceptions in their respective agreements are essentially repeated in the TPP. Yet, as regards NAFTA partners, a lesser latitude for cultural policy regulation ensues, in view notably of Mexico's reduced domestic screen quota and Canada's exemption of cultural industries now with limitations pertaining to digital trade. Conversely, in the case of US FTAs negotiated under the 2002 TPA, this is accompanied by a (sometimes much) greater margin of maneuver regarding cultural regulation, including new media. In Australia's case, measures in favor of domestic content in subscription television and digital media are not assorted with conditions, as in its FTA with the United States. However, inasmuch as these TPP provisions are more trade restrictive than those of previous US FTAs, the latter rules are to prevail as far as US trade is concerned. In turn, this might well explain why the US government consented to such provisions in the TPP.

For the US Advisory Committee on Services and Finance Industries, while the TPP does not address all of the barriers confronting the US audiovisual sector in the Asia-Pacific region, its achievements in expanding access to the increasingly important online marketplace and in establishing a solid level of intellectual property protection for US business are substantial (TPP, ITAC-10 Report, 12). With regard to states' restrictions affecting the "historical" platforms for content distribution—cinemas, broadcast and cable television and radio—the TPP does not involve much change. Existing US FTA partners have largely reiterated their reservations, the latter mainly pertaining to domestic ownership and content requirements in broadcast and cable television. With no prior US FTA commitments and otherwise a promising market for audiovisual content, the Committee deplores, notably, that Vietnam has locked in its existing cinematographic screen quotas and reserved a broad array of rights and measures to control all audiovisual and other recorded contents (TPP, ITAC-10 Report, 11).

Yet, the Committee underlines that progress has been made with each of the TPP parties to avoid the application to the emerging online market of discriminatory provisions impacting cultural services (TPP, ITAC-10 Report, 12). In particular, the Committee notes that the broad exemption in favor of cultural industries secured by Canada under the NAFTA now explicitly excludes "measures restricting the access to on-line foreign audio-visual content." Although in Singapore's broad reservation concerning broadcasting services, the latter are defined more expansively as any "transmission . . . via any technology for the reception [of] program signals," earlier commitments under the US-Singapore FTA prevail, so that US suppliers will continue to enjoy national treatment for non-scheduled broadcasting, thus allowing non-discriminatory access for video streaming. As for Japan's broadcasting reservation, since on-demand and online services are not included, a digital exception only applies in the case of new services not yet technically feasible (TPP, ITAC-10 Report, 11).

On the whole, the outcome of the TPP negotiations is consistent with the revised US strategy on cultural products. The essential of the reservations either secured or reiterated by states parties relate to so-called traditional instruments of cultural policy. Some countries, mainly Australia, Singapore, and Vietnam, have nonetheless obtained exceptions with possible digital ramifications. In the case of the first two, however, more liberalizing rules under previous FTAs concluded with the United States are to continue to regulate their exchanges with that country. As for the "upgrading" of the NAFTA, the US government notably sought to ensure that Canada's cultural exemption be reformulated so as to limit, if not to prevent, its applicability to the digital marketplace.

THE TRADE IN SERVICES AGREEMENT

The TiSA aims at improving and expanding international trade in services. Initiated by the United States, since April 2013, the TiSA has been negotiated in Geneva, Switzerland, with twenty-three WTO members representing fifty countries, which account for more than 70% of world services trade. The twenty-three participants in the TiSA include: Australia, Canada, Chile, Colombia, Costa Rica, the European Union, Hong Kong, Iceland, Israel, Japan, Liechtenstein, Mauritius, Mexico, New Zealand, Norway, Pakistan, Panama, Peru, South Korea, Switzerland, Taiwan, Turkey, and the United States. Although not totally disconnected from the WTO, a plurilateral setting offers more autonomy and flexibility to negotiators compared with the Doha Round negotiating modalities, notably the positive-list approach and the single undertaking (see Deblock 2010, 152–70).

The TiSA negotiations, as of February 2016, were reportedly progressing well (EU 2016a; see also Hufbauer et al. 2015). The negotiation modalities somehow depart from those of the GATS. Under the latter, market access and national treatment obligations only apply if and to the extent that specific commitments are entered into. On the other hand, under the TiSA negotiations, market access is subject to specific "positive" commitments, as in the GATS, while national treatment applies on a horizontal basis to all services sectors and modes of supply, save for some limitations explicitly stipulated in a party's schedule, as has been the case for MFN treatment under the GATS. Since the United States proposed the negative-list approach, while the European Union preferred the positive-list approach, it seems that a compromise was struck. Besides, the single undertaking approach adopted under both the Uruguay and Doha Rounds entails that nothing is agreed until everything is agreed. This makes an agreement on services dependent on agreement in other, difficult sectors, such as agriculture. Inasmuch as the TiSA negotiations are limited to services and their "Really Good Friends," this increases the likelihood of a successful outcome.[11]

Among the twenty-three parties involved in the TiSA negotiations, ten already have an FTA with the United States, namely Australia, Canada, Chile, Colombia, Costa Rica, Israel, Mexico, Panama, Peru, and South Korea. Seven, i.e., Australia, Canada, Chile, Japan, Mexico, New Zealand, and Peru are also, with the United States, parties to the TPP. Concurrently, nine of the TiSA parties have contracted obligations regarding the audiovisual sector under the GATS, namely Hong Kong, Israel, Japan, Mexico, New Zealand, Panama, South Korea, Taiwan, and the United States. At the same time, fifteen of the twenty-three "Really Good Friends of Services" are parties to the CDCE, namely Australia, Canada, Chile, Colombia, Costa Rica, the European Union, Iceland, Mauritius, Mexico, New Zealand, Norway, Panama, Peru, South Korea, and Switzerland.

Alongside the United States, two of the main proponents of cultural exception/diversity, Canada and the European Union, are involved in the TiSA negotiations (see *Inside US Trade* 2013a). None of these is expected to significantly modify its stance on cultural products in trade agreements. While Canada keeps insisting on "the maximum flexibility to pursue its domestic cultural policy objectives" (Canada 2016), the European Union published on July 22, 2014, its initial negotiating offer. Among limitations on national treatment, it reads: "The EU reserves the right to adopt or maintain any measures with respect to the provision of audiovisual services" (EU 2013c, 13). The EU negotiating offer contains some proposed commitments regarding other cultural sub-sectors, such as entertainment (theater, live bands, circus, and discotheque), printing and publishing, advertising, news and press agency services, as well as libraries, archives, museums, and other cultural services, assorted with a series of various limitations, often by countries. The offer also features a series of requests for MFN exemptions in favor of audiovisual services (EU 2013c). Furthermore, the negotiating mandate of the European Commission was made public on March 10, 2015. Although the European Union seeks an ambitious, far-reaching agreement, it specifies that "[a]s in the GATS, the EU shall not take commitments on audiovisual" (EU 2013a, 3). Together with Norway, South Korea, and Switzerland, the European Union has sought notably to exempt future services from the national treatment obligation. For the United States, this contradicts the negative-list approach used under the TiSA for national treatment, which normally provides for such obligation to apply to services not yet existing (*Chronique commerciale américaine* 2016, 3).

Lack of agreement between the main protagonists of the trade and culture debate is not necessarily to prevent the successful conclusion of such plurilateral negotiations as the TiSA. As within the GATS, Canada and the European Union may maintain their positions and refrain from making commitments on cultural services and on audiovisual services, respectively. At the same time, other countries may liberalize cultural services, if they so wish, subject to varying conditions. In the eyes of the United States, commitments from a certain number of countries under the TiSA may compensate for the lack of audiovisual commitments from others such as the European Union.

THE TRANSATLANTIC TRADE AND INVESTMENT PARTNERSHIP

Proposals for a trade agreement between the United States and (Western) Europe are not new. Already in the 1960s the idea of a North Atlantic Free Trade Area was considered and, in the 1990s, of a Transatlantic Free Trade Area. In early 2013, the United States and the European Union agreed to strengthen their economic relations by launching negotiations for a comprehensive bilateral agreement on trade and investment.[12] Yet, significant tensions were already noticeable before the onset of the talks in July 2013. While the European Commission would have preferred not to exclude *a priori* any sector, notably to strengthen its negotiating position, France obtained that audiovisual services be excluded from the negotiating mandate of the Commission. For its part, the United States seeks, in particular, the inclusion of new or non-linear audiovisual services and threatened France of economic sanctions if no openings were made with regard to the cultural sector (*Inside US Trade* 2013b; *Le Devoir* 2013; Akhtar and Jones 2014, 16).

Some EU member states, such as the Netherlands and the United Kingdom, are closer to the US position and would be willing to make concessions on audiovisual services. The TTIP negotiations, however, are conducted at the Union level by the Commission. In accordance with the present terms of negotiations, unanimity among EU member states is required to modify the negotiating mandate and permit commitments on audiovisual services. In this respect, together with France, some EU members, such as Italy and Spain, as well as the European Parliament insist not only on excluding audiovisual services, but also on retaining flexibility in the cultural sector to respond to the challenges of the digital revolution. Any trade agreement concluded by the European Commission needs to be ratified by the European Parliament in order to come into force.

On October 9, 2014, the European Union released the negotiating mandate for the TTIP. The EU wishes the "preamble and general principles" of the TTIP to stress the right of the parties to take measures that they deem appropriate for the promotion of cultural diversity, as laid down in the UNESCO Convention (EU 2013b, para 6). Within the "objectives" sought by the EU, one reads:

> The Agreement shall not contain provisions that would risk prejudicing the Union's or its Member States' cultural and linguistic diversity, namely in the cultural sector nor limit the Union and its Member States from maintaining existing policies and measures in support of the cultural sector given its special status within the EU and its Member States. The Agreement will not affect the capacity of the Union and its Member States to implement policies and measures to take account of developments in this sector in particular *in the digital environment.* (emphasis added) (EU 2013b, para 9)

As in the TiSA, the TTIP negotiation modalities consist of positive listing for market access and negative listing for national treatment. Hence, the compromise on negotiation modalities reached within the TiSA between the United States and the European Union has been adopted in the TTIP context, thereby ensuring greater compatibility between the offers made in both settings. The European Union made public on July 31, 2015, its TTIP proposal for services, investment, and e-commerce, submitted during the tenth round of negotiations in July 2015. It is stipulated that "[t]he provisions [relating to investment and the cross-border supply of services] shall not apply to audio-visual services" (EU 2015a, articles 2–1 and 3–1). This is accompanied by a series of proposed exceptions for existing and future measures under Annexes I and II, similar to those in existing US FTAs. As in the TiSA, the EU seeks notably to keep full leeway as regards "new services" that may emerge as a result of technological developments (EU 2015b, reservation no. 26). There are also some market access commitments in cultural sectors other than audiovisual, assorted with a series of limitations, often by countries (EU 2015b, annex III).

Both sides are trying to conclude the TTIP negotiations by the end of 2016 (US 2016b; EU 2016b, 8; see also CAE 2015). In view of the US and EU current positions on audiovisual and new services, one could be surprised that the TTIP negotiations have at all proceeded. Moreover, as it depends on unanimous agreement among member states, a change in the EU position is ruled out. Given the importance of the European Union as a trading partner and its leverage, the US government might have come to terms with the absence of trade commitments for the audiovisual sector and even the EU's desire to regulate the new media. If the TTIP negotiations are successfully concluded on such basis, however, the outcome would fall short of US trade objectives, as stipulated in the 2015 TPA, particularly as concerns the US digital trade agenda.

SUMMARY AND CONCLUSIONS

The 2015 TPA, particularly in view of its emphasis on digital freedom, follows on the new or revised US strategy on the treatment of cultural products in trade agreements, first implemented under the 2002 TPA. While the FTAs concluded under the latter TPA were mostly bilateral and with developing countries, the three US FTA negotiations in recent years have taken place either in a plurilateral setting or with a regional grouping. Under the recently concluded TPP, as in the US FTAs negotiated between late 2000 and 2007, nearly all parties have taken exceptions reserving, to different degrees, the ownership, control, and/or management of cultural enterprises, as well as licenses for radio and television broadcasting. Nearly all TPP parties have also secured reservations in favor of domestic content in public radio and/or television, as against just over one-third of states parties to the US FTAs negotiated under the 2002 TPA. If exceptions in favor of cultural policy regulation are widespread in the TPP plurilateral context, and parties have in general secured more leeway for the implementation of cultural policies, such exceptions rarely apply to new or digital media. Thus, the broad exceptions for broadcasting, secured by Brunei, Japan, Singapore, and Vietnam, do not involve non-scheduled and on-demand services, respectively, in the case of the first two countries, therefore excluding services supplied over the Internet, while for Singapore the more limited exception under its FTA with the United States will prevail. An interesting, puzzling case in this respect is Vietnam, whose exceptions extend beyond broadcasting to include nearly all cultural sectors, with implications for digital media. This is hard to explain in view of either the US trade strategy on cultural products or Vietnam's leverage. Because of the country's communist regime, further concessions could have been difficult to obtain by the United States, which may have let go, considering the overall outcome of the TPP plurilateral negotiations.

It is also worth underlining that while the United States secured some further commitments pertaining to cultural products from its NAFTA partners, it got none on the part of the parties to its FTAs negotiated under the 2002 TPA. This is notably the case as regards Singapore's broad exception for broadcasting, as well as Australia's exception to ensure national content in digital media. The US government was seemingly satisfied with the results of its FTAs concluded under the 2002 TPA, which followed its revised strategy on cultural products. Many parties to these US FTAs have even secured more extensive exceptions for the pursuit of cultural policies under the TPP. The United States ensured, however, that, unless otherwise specified, the more liberalizing rules are to prevail, thereby safeguarding the bargains from its FTA negotiations under the 2002 TPA.

The outcome of the TPP negotiations is primarily attributable to the revised US strategy on cultural products. Overall, in accordance with the negative-list approach, the exceptions in the TPP relating to the cultural sector are specified and delimitated. Among cultural policy instruments, while the financial ones are still essentially exempted, a whole series of country-specific "traditional" regulations, of varying scope, have been kept in place, as long as these do not involve the new or digital media.

As for the TiSA and TTIP negotiations, many issues remain to be solved if they are to conclude successfully, including with respect to cultural products and digital trade. In both cases, US cultural and digital liberalization objectives may need to be accommodated with the principles of cultural exception/diversity, as advocated by the European Union and Canada.

NOTES

1. For a summary of the evolution and elements of TPA, including the 2015 version, see Fergusson (2015).

2. On the TPP negotiations and provisions, see *Inside US Trade* (2012); Lim, Elms, and Low (2012); Schott, Kotschwar, and Muir (2013); Voon (2013); Fergusson and Williams (2016).

3. For a general discussion on the relationship between various agreements, and overlapping PTAs in particular, see Pauwelyn and Alschner (2015).

4. While the American government had consistently insisted on strengthening protection for foreign investors or investment, following a series of unanticipated investor-state dispute cases under the NAFTA, the United States, since, has sought a better balance between investor protection and the ability of governments to regulate in the public interest. See Gagné and Morin (2006); Gagné (2011b).

5. The TPP requires parties to establish copyright "safe harbors" for ISPs, so as to allow them to develop their business, while also helping to address Internet copyright infringement in an effective manner. This notably entails that ISPs are not obliged to monitor content on their networks or systems and cannot be held responsible for breaches of copyrights, although they must cooperate with copyright holders to deter such illegal practices (TPP, chapter 18, section J). See TPP, ITAC–15 Report, 5, 26–27; ITAC–8 Report, 14.

6. In the CETA, at EU's request, Canada opted for a more targeted cultural exemption, that applies only to the chapters or sectors for which such an exemption is sought, so as to ensure links with other sectors related to culture, such as intellectual property. Besides a reference to the CDCE in the preamble to the CETA, cultural industries are exempted in Canada's case, and audiovisual services in the EU's case, from the chapters on subsidies, investment, services, domestic regulation, and government procurement. In the chapter on exceptions, both sides recall their reservations applicable to the cultural sector in the relevant CETA chapters (see *Culture, commerce et numérique* 2013; Gagné 2015, 84, 87).

7. In contrast with the US-Chile FTA, "arts and cultural industries" include: e) visual arts, artistic photography, and new media; f) performing arts, including theater,

dance, and circus arts; and g) media services or multimedia. As for the last item in the definition of cultural industries under the US-Chile FTA related to broadcasting, it is subsumed within a broad exception pertaining to "entertainment, audio-visual and broadcasting services." Under the latter, Chile reserves the right to adopt or maintain any measure concerning: a) the organization and presentation in the country of concerts and musical performances; b) the distribution or display of movies or videos; and c) radio broadcasts aimed at the public in general, as well as all radio, television and cable television-related activities, satellite programming services, and broadcasting networks. This exception is subject, however, to a requirement to extend no less favorable treatment to persons and investors of another TPP party and their investments than that accorded by that party to Chilean persons and investors/investments (TPP, annex II-CL, 12).

8. Broadcasting is here defined as the transmission of signs or signals via any technology for the reception and/or display of aural and/or visual program signals by all or part of the domestic public.

9. Under this entry, broadcasting means the transmission of telecommunications with the aim of direct reception by the public and does not include on-demand services including those supplied over the Internet.

10. Other cultural activities refer to photography, art exhibitions, fashion shows, beauty and model contests, karaoke and discotheque business, and festival organization.

11. For more on the TiSA negotiations, see Sauvé and Shingal (2011); Hufbauer, Jensen, and Stephenson (2012); Marchetti and Roy (2013); Sauvé (2013); Broude and Moses (2015, 16–26); Fefer (2016).

12. On the TTIP negotiations, see Akhtar and Jones (2014).

Conclusion

Cultural goods and services, for decades, have been subject to a debate as to their treatment in international trade agreements. Cultural products have both an economic and cultural character and have been at the center of states' policies and measures to foster national identity. Yet, such policies and measures contravene international trade principles. In the context of economic globalization and the digital revolution, while for some countries, and the United States in particular, cultural products should be liberalized, for other countries, such as France and Canada, the same global phenomena make cultural policies all the more essential. The Uruguay Round of multilateral trade negotiations ended in the first half of the 1990s with what amounted to an agreement to disagree. Given the stalemate in the Doha Round within the WTO, the main protagonists of the trade and culture debate have each concluded a series of PTAs, reflecting their policy preferences on the treatment of cultural products.

The debate has evolved in a crucial way through the eleven FTAs concluded by the United States with sixteen countries under the 2002 TPA. This evolution has taken place on the basis of a softened or revised US position on cultural products in trade agreements. The new US strategy follows on the stiff resistance to US requests during the Uruguay Round to remove or at least cap states' existing cultural policy measures and on the efforts of the proponents of cultural exception/diversity to exempt the cultural (particularly audiovisual) sector from trade disciplines.

As it keeps insisting on wide-ranging liberalization, as well as on predictable and clearly defined trade rules, the United States resorts to the top-down or negative-list approach in its FTA negotiations, whereby everything is liberalized save for the sectors and measures specifically exempted. Thus, measures of exception that are agreed upon in US FTAs, here in the case of the cultural sector, tend to be limited and precise in scope. This, however, goes against the efforts in support of cultural diversity, and particularly the UNESCO Convention. These underline the importance for states of keeping flexibility to use a whole set of measures, both financial and regulatory, in order to respond to the challenges of globalization and technological developments.

Table 6.1. Main Types of Cultural Regulatory Exceptions across States Parties to Existing US FTAs

Cultural Regulatory Exceptions	States Parties																		
	US	AU	BH	CA	CL	CO	CR	DR	ES	GU	HO	KR	MO	MX	NI	OM	PA	PE	SG
Restrictions re. property/ control/management and licensing of cultural enterprises	•	•	•	•	•	•	•	•	•		•	•		•	•	•	•	•	•
Domestic content requirements																			
- Public radio and/or television		•		•	•	•	•	•				•		•				•	•
- Subscription television				•		•						•		•					
- Advertising		•		•		•	•	•											
- Cinema (screen quotas)						•						•		•				•	
Audiovisual cooperation agreements		•		•	•	•	•					•	•					•	
Digital or new technologies																			
- Interactive audio and/or video		•		X		•						•		X					

X: Inapplicable, as the NAFTA predates digital developments.

Nevertheless, subsidization measures are not subject to the national treatment and MFN obligations of the services and investment chapters of US FTAs. Such broad exception is particularly important as to states' ability to conduct cultural policies and to favor cultural diversity. Indeed, public subsidies are undoubtedly one of the main forms of support to the cultural development of nations. States parties to US FTAs, thus, preserve a wide margin of maneuver to adopt financial measures as part of national cultural policies. One reason for the US opening on subsidies is that, in contrast with regulatory measures, they are generally less trade-distorting, have a lesser impact on market access and, hence, on the interests of US industries.

It remains that the main consequence of an FTA concluded with the United States is to constrain, often significantly, the ability of governments to carry out public policies benefiting the cultural sector. This is the case as a result of US insistence on limiting measures of regulation of cultural activities and preventing any such measures for digital trade. In this regard, the new US trade strategy in the cultural sector clearly entails that while existing measures may be tolerated in the traditional cultural/audiovisual sectors, as they are bound to decrease with time, no such tolerance may be accepted for digitally delivered contents, which are at the hearth of the new communication economy and must, therefore, remain free of cultural protectionism (Bernier 2003b, 14–15).

Table 6.1 presents the main types of cultural policy regulations kept in place by states parties to US FTAs. The table only includes effective FTAs. The US-Israel FTA, with no coverage of services, and the US-Jordan FTA, with positive-list services commitments, are excluded for lack of comparability.

Nearly all states parties to US FTAs have secured reservations as regards the ownership, control, and/or management of cultural enterprises, as well as licenses for television and radio broadcasting. In addition, half of the parties to the US FTAs negotiated under the 2002 TPA, namely Australia, Chile, Colombia, Costa Rica, the Dominican Republic, Peru, Singapore, and South Korea, not to forget Canada and Mexico under the NAFTA, have obtained exceptions so as to ensure domestic content in public radio and television. An almost equal number of countries have taken MFN exemptions in favor of audiovisual co-production arrangements. With respect to broadcasting (television and radio), the maintenance of a number of restrictions—including foreign equity limitations and content quotas—is the norm rather than the exception, although most often listed under Annexes I and set so as to provide the United States with a predictable level of market access. Such restrictions are more numerous for traditional free-to-air television, and where capacity—or shelf-space—is necessarily limited. Yet, there are less restrictions where the United States has more interests, e.g., satellite television, foreign programming for cable television, and interactive audio/video services (Roy 2008, 367–68). On the other hand, eight parties to existing US FTAs—Bahrain, El Salvador, Guatemala, Honduras, Morocco, Nicaragua, Oman, and Panama—have not secured any significant reservations concerning the audiovisual sector.

There is, in this respect, significant variation in the number and scope of exceptions for the regulation of the cultural sector across states parties to US FTAs. In view of the negative-list approach, a state ought to be prepared to formulate requests for exceptions to the benefit of its cultural sector and to hold on to such requests. Thus, an essential reason why some countries were better able than others at maintaining flexibility to pursue cultural policies has to do with their negotiating capacity. The latter is a function of the importance different states attach to such policies for their cultural identity, often related to the level of mobilization of domestic cultural industries. Beyond, such variations and outcomes are attributable to the revised US trade strategy, which allows for the maintenance of regulatory measures for cultural industries, and makes the United States willing to accommodate specific cultural concerns. It does not appear, as well, to be the result of difficult trade-offs. The United States does not seem to have required anything important in return for such concessions concerning the "traditional" instruments of cultural policy, which the American government does not see as involving major costs. In fact, a relatively greater number of countries' exceptions for the cultural sector in US FTAs is often accompanied by a greater number of exceptions in various sectors. Chase (2015, 236–38) noticed that neither countries' economic size nor trade flows appears to fully explain the varying US ability to secure concessions on audiovisual services from PTA partners. States' leverage is determinant, however, in the case of exceptions relating to new or digital media, obtained by few parties to US FTAs, mainly industrial states.

As Bernier (2004, 19–20) emphasizes, the United States accepts to make concessions, as financial cultural policy instruments are exempted, while a varying array of regulatory measures, notably national content quotas, could be maintained. Yet, such "concessions," through the maintenance of "traditional" instruments of cultural policy, are usually conditioned upon the absence of any restrictions with regard to the electronic commerce of digital products. When state measures of cultural regulation are subject to specific reservations, as in all the FTAs negotiated under the 2002 TPA, it is because US authorities consider that, owing to the digital revolution, they are to become increasingly obsolete. Hence, such FTAs provide the United States with unlimited gains in the future in exchange for well-circumscribed concessions in the present. Australia, Colombia, and South Korea are the only three existing US FTA partners to have obtained exceptions concerning digital cultural content. In these instances, and particularly in Colombia's, these exceptions are assorted with conditions so onerous as to question their applicability. Such e-commerce exceptions, therefore, do not significantly confront the US policy of absence of cultural protectionism in digital networks.

As the TPA was renewed in June 2015, further US PTA negotiations may be initiated or resumed, besides the TPP, TiSA, and TTIP. Unlike most existing US PTAs, concluded bilaterally and with developing countries, the latter three are being negotiated in a plurilateral framework, with the United States and a fair number of developed countries. Thus, if its preferred negotiating approach based on negative listing has nonetheless been used for the TPP, the United States has had to accept a hybrid approach, consisting of positive listing for market access and negative listing for national treatment, for the TiSA and TTIP negotiations. In the TPP, if major advances on the American cultural trade agenda have been made, these essentially involve the new parties to US FTAs and the absence of regulatory exceptions for digital media. The latter has been secured by US authorities notably through the upgrading of the NAFTA and the prevalence of more liberalizing provisions under existing US FTAs. Historical cultural regulatory instruments have largely been maintained, while the United States has not obtained further concessions from the parties to its FTAs concluded under the 2002 TPA. As for the TiSA negotiations, although more than two-thirds of the participants have ratified the CDCE, more than half either already have an FTA with the United States or WTO audiovisual commitments. The United States, therefore, may succeed in securing cultural and digital concessions from a certain number of states. On the other hand, within the TTIP, with the European Union historically committed to cultural exception/diversity and audiovisuals excluded from its negotiating mandate, any liberalization of the cultural sector is bound to remain limited and unsatisfactory from a US perspective.

Undoubtedly, these three recent and ongoing plurilateral negotiations are more challenging for the pursuit of the US trade strategy on cultural products than the series of FTA negotiations conducted under the 2002 TPA. A larger array of traditional cultural policy instruments has been maintained in the TPP and may be so in other negotiations. Even though not all negotiations may significantly advance its cultural/digital trade agenda, the United States has succeeded under the TPP in securing some openings in historical sectors and in largely preventing restrictions affecting its trade in digital products. In fact, the prospects for US PTA negotiations depend on the partners involved, while the likelihood of no openings in audiovisuals and new services under the TTIP remains an exception.

International discussions pertaining to culture within the frameworks of the WTO, PTAs, and the UNESCO Convention could all influence the evolution of the trade and culture debate. However, by 2008, only nine countries had made liberalization offers relating to audiovisual services within the Doha Round. Due to the difficult negotiating climate, the United States has had no high objectives and its proposals have been relatively modest. As for PTAs involving countries other than the United States, the ensuing liberalization of the cultural sector is much more limited. The key directive among the states that have ratified the UNESCO Convention is to refrain from making commitments in favor of cultural liberalization.

In such a context, US initiatives to liberalize the cultural sector, as exercised through the negotiation and implementation of PTAs, are to prove the primary legal constraints on states' ability to pursue effective cultural policies. Some states may have preserved leeway to implement such policies under other PTAs. Yet, it is ineffectual when a PTA concluded with the United States curtails this latitude significantly, since most ensuing changes in states' regulations apply indiscriminately. Hence, the US policy preferences on the treatment of cultural products end up prevailing and being diffused at the international level, with key implications for the trade and culture debate. The evolution of the latter, in turn, will greatly depend on whether the United States holds on to its position on digital freedom, or somehow concedes to countries' concern for maintaining flexibility to regulate the new media, so as to ensure the sustainability of their cultural policies.

Bibliography

Acheson, Keith, and Christopher Maule. 1999. *Much Ado about Culture: North American Trade Disputes*. Ann Arbor: University of Michigan Press.

Aggarwal, Vinod K. 2013. "U.S. Free Trade Agreements and Linkages." *International Negotiation* 18(1): 89–110.

Akhtar, Shayerah I., and Vivian C. Jones. 2014. *Transatlantic Trade and Investment Partnership (TTIP) Negotiations*. Washington, DC: Congressional Research Service. February 4. https://www.fas.org/sgp/crs/row/R43387.pdf.

Armstrong, Sarah. 2000. "Magazines, Cultural Policy and Globalization: The Forced Retreat of the State." *Canadian Public Policy* 26(2): 369–85.

Baker, C. Edwin. 2000. "An Economic Critique of Free Trade in Media Products." *North Carolina Law Review* 78: 1357–435.

Balassa, Carol. 1981. *Trade Issues in the Motion Picture Industry*, unpublished report prepared for the Office of the United States Trade Representative.

———. 2012. "The Impact of the U.S. Position in the Trade and Culture Debate: Negotiation of the Convention on the Diversity of Cultural Expressions." In *The UNESCO Convention on the Diversity of Cultural Expressions: A Tale of Fragmentation of International Law*, edited by Toshiyuki Kono and Steven Van Uystel, 71–93. Cambridge: Intersentia.

Baldwin, Richard E. 2006. "Multilateralising Regionalism: Spaghetti Bowls as Building Blocs on the Path to Global Free Trade." *The World Economy* 29(11): 1451–518.

Bartels, Lorand, and Federico Ortino, eds. 2006. *Regional Trade Agreements and the WTO Legal System*. Oxford: Oxford University Press.

Beaudoin, Louise. 2014. *Convention sur la protection et la promotion de la diversité des expressions culturelles: Impacts et enjeux du numérique*. Report submitted to the Organisation internationale de la Francophonie, April 28. http://www.enap.ca/cerberus/files/nouvelles/documents/Nouvelles%20corpo/L.Beaudoin_Convention%20sur%20la%20diversit%C3%A9%20des%20expressions%20culturelles.pdf.

Bernier, Ivan. 1998. "Cultural Goods and Services in International Trade Law." In *The Culture/Trade Quandary: Canada's Policy Options*, edited by Dennis Browne, 108–48. Ottawa: Centre for Trade Policy and Law.

———. 2003a. "Un nouvel accord international sur la diversité culturelle: objectif, contenu et articulation à l'OMC." Paper presented at the Second International Meeting of Cultural Professional Organizations, Paris, February 2–4. http://www.diversite-culturelle.qc.ca/fileadmin/documents/pdf/disc_yvan_bernier_paris.pdf.

———. 2003b. *A Comparative Analysis of the Chile—U.S. and Singapore—U.S. Free Trade Agreements with Particular Reference to Their Impact in the Cultural Sector*. April. http://www.diversite-culturelle.qc.ca/fileadmin/documents/pdf/update0304.pdf.

———. 2004. *The Recent Free Trade Agreements of the United States as Illustration of Their New Strategy Regarding the Audiovisual Sector*. April-June. http://www.diversite-culturelle.qc.ca/fileadmin/documents/pdf/conf_seoul_ang_2004.pdf.

———. 2005. "La négociation de la convention de l'UNESCO sur la protection et la promotion de la diversité des expressions culturelles." *Canadian Yearbook of International Law* 43: 3–43.

———. 2009. *The Relationship between the UNESCO Convention on the Protection and Promotion of the Diversity of Cultural Expressions and Other International Instruments: The Emergence of a New Balance in the Interface Between Commerce and Culture*. August.

http://www.diversite-culturelle.qc.ca/fileadmin/documents/pdf/FR_Relations_entre_Convention_Unesco_instruments_internationaux.pdf.

Bhagwati, Jagdish. 1995. *Protectionism*. Cambridge, MA: MIT Press.

———. 2000. "Trade and Culture: America's Blind Spot." In *The Wind of the Hundred Days: How Washington Mismanaged Globalization*, edited by Jagdish Bhagwati, 209–13. Cambridge, MA: MIT Press.

———. 2008. *Termites in the Trading System: How Preferential Agreements Undermine Free Trade*. New York: Oxford University Press.

Bosworth, Malcolm, and Ray Trewin. 2008. "The Domestic Dynamics of Preferential Services Liberalization: The Experience of Australia and Thailand." In *Opening Markets for Trade in Services: Countries and Sectors in Bilateral and WTO Negotiations*, edited by Juan A. Marchetti and Martin Roy, 633–66. Cambridge: Cambridge University Press.

Breen, Marcus. 2010. "Digital Determinism: Culture Industries in the USA-Australia Free Trade Agreement." *New Media & Society* 12(4): 657–76.

Brodie, Janine, ed. 1999. *Critical Concepts: An Introduction to Politics*. Scarborough, ON: Prentice-Hall.

Broude, Tomer, and Shai Moses. 2015. *The Behavioral Dynamics of Positive and Negative Listing in Services Trade Liberalization: A Look at the Trade in Services Agreement (TiSA) Negotiations*. Research Paper No. 01–15. Faculty of Law, The Hebrew University of Jerusalem. April. http://papers.ssrn.com/sol3/papers.cfm?abstract_id=2594831.

Bruner, Christopher M. 2008. "Culture, Sovereignty, and Hollywood: UNESCO and the Future of Trade in Cultural Products." *New York University Journal of International Law and Politics* 40: 351–436.

Buckley, Ross, Vai Io Loo, and Laurence Boulle, eds. 2008. *Challenges to Multilateral Trade: The Impact of Bilateral, Preferential and Regional Agreements*. The Hague: Kluwer.

Burri-Nenova, Mira. 2009. "Trade versus Culture in the Digital Environment: An Old Conflict in Need of a New Definition." *Journal of International Economic Law* 12(1): 17–62.

Burri, Mira. 2011. "Reconciling Trade and Culture: A Global Law Perspective." *Journal of Arts Management, Law and Society* 41(2): 138–58.

Burri, Mira, and Thomas Cottier, eds. 2012. *Trade Governance in the Digital Age*. Cambridge: Cambridge University Press.

Cambridge Dictionaries Online. http://dictionary.cambridge.org/us/.

Cameron, Maxwell A., and Brian W. Tomlin. 2000. *The Making of NAFTA: How the Deal Was Done*. Ithaca, NY: Cornell University Press.

Carmody, Chi. 2007. "Creating Shelf Space: NAFTA's Experience with Cultural Protection and its Relevance for the WTO." *Asian Journal of WTO & International Health Law and Policy* 2(2): 287–311.

Caves, Richard E. 2000. *Creative Industries: Contracts Between Art and Commerce*. Cambridge, MA: Harvard University Press.

Chase, Kerry A. 2014a. *Trade, Culture, and Politics in the General Agreement on Trade in Services*. http://people.brandeis.edu/~chase/research/trade-culture.pdf.

———. 2014b. *Commerce and Culture: The Contentious Politics of Filmed Entertainment*. http://people.brandeis.edu/~chase/research/commerce.html.

———. 2015. "Audiovisual Goods and Services in Preferential Trade Agreements." In *Trade Cooperation: The Purpose, Design and Effects of Preferential Trade Agreements*, edited by Andreas Dür and Manfred Elsig, 218–45. Cambridge: Cambridge University Press.

Chronique commerciale américaine. 2016. "Chassé-croisé dans les grandes négociations commerciales internationales," 9(5): 2–6. http://www.ieim.uqam.ca/IMG/pdf/cca_2016–06_ver_1.2.pdf.

Cottier, Thomas, Charlotte Sieber-Gasser, and Gabriela Wermelinger. 2015. "The Dialectical Relationship of Preferential and Multilateral Trade Agreements." In *Trade*

Cooperation: The Purpose, Design and Effects of Preferential Trade Agreements, edited by Andreas Dür and Manfred Elsig, 465–96. Cambridge: Cambridge University Press.
Cowen, Tyler. 2006. *Good and Plenty: The Creative Successes of American Arts Funding*. Princeton: Princeton University Press.
Craufurd Smith, Rachael. 2007. "The UNESCO Convention on the Protection and Promotion of Cultural Expressions: Building a New World Information and Communication Order?" *International Journal of Communication* 1: 24–55.
Culture Action Europe (CAE). 2015. *A Little Guide Through the TTIP Negotiations*. July 31. http://cultureactioneurope.org/news/updates-on-ttip-negotiation-process/.
Culture, commerce et numérique. 2013. "Accord Canada-UE: l'exemption culturelle spécifique et ses implications," 8(9): 2–4. http://www.ieim.uqam.ca/IMG/pdf/oif-volume8-numero9-novembre-2013ceim.pdf.
———. 2015. "Carte mondiale des goûts musicaux: À la découverte des préférences locales," 10(6): 11–12. http://www.ieim.uqam.ca/IMG/pdf/oif-volume10-numero 6juillet-2015ceim_vf.pdf.
Culture Research Education and Training Enterprise (CREATE) Australia. 2004. *Australia United States Free Trade Agreement and the Cultural Industries Sector in Australia*. May 12.
Deblock, Christian. 2010. "Le bilatéralisme commercial des États-Unis." In *Le commerce international entre bi et multilatéralisme*, edited by Bernard Remiche and Hélène Ruiz Fabri, 115–73. Brussels: Larcier.
Destler, I.M. 2005. *American Trade Politics*, 4th ed. Washington, DC: Institute for International Economics.
Doern, G. Bruce, and Brian W. Tomlin. 1991. *Faith and Fear: The Free Trade Story*. Toronto: Stoddart.
Dür, Andreas, and Manfred Elsig, eds. 2015. *Trade Cooperation: The Purpose, Design and Effects of Preferential Trade Agreements*. Cambridge: Cambridge University Press.
Evenett, Simon J. 2014. "The Doha Round Impasse: A Graphical Account." *The Review of International Organizations* 9(2): 143–62.
Evenett, Simon, and Michael Meier. 2008. "An Interim Assessment of the US Trade Policy of 'Competitive Liberalization.'" *The World Economy* 31(1): 31–66.
Fefer, Rachel F. 2016. *Trade in Services Agreement (TiSA) Negotiations: Overview and Issues for Congress*. Washington, DC: Congressional Research Service. January 28. https://www.fas.org/sgp/crs/misc/R44354.pdf.
Fergusson, Ian F. 2015. *Trade Promotion Authority (TPA) and the Role of Congress in Trade Policy*. Washington, DC: Congressional Research Service. June 15. https://www.fas.org/sgp/crs/misc/RL33743.pdf.
Fergusson, Ian F., and Brock R. Williams. 2016. *The Trans-Pacific Partnership (TPP): Key Provisions and Issues for Congress*. Washington, DC: Congressional Research Service. May 4. https://www.fas.org/sgp/crs/row/R44489.pdf.
Footer, Mary E., and Christoph Beat Graber. 2000. "Trade Liberalization and Cultural Policy." *Journal of International Economic Law* 3(1): 115–44.
Formentini, Silvia, and P. Lelio Iapadre. 2007. *Cultural Policies and Regional Trade Agreements: The Case of Audiovisual Services*. Working Paper W-2007/4. Comparative Regional Integration Studies Unit, United Nations University, Bruges, Belgium.
Gagné, Gilbert. 1999. "Libéralisation et exception culturelle: le différend canado-américain sur les périodiques." *Études internationales* 30(3): 571–88.
———. 2003/2004. "Cultural Sovereignty, Identity, and North American Integration: on the Relevance of the U.S.-Canada-Quebec Border." *Québec Studies* 36: 29–49.
———, ed. 2005a. *La diversité culturelle: vers une convention internationale effective?* Montreal: Fides.
———. 2005b. "Une Convention internationale sur la diversité culturelle et le dilemme culture-commerce." In *La diversité culturelle: vers une convention internationale effective?*, edited by Gilbert Gagné, 37–62. Montreal: Fides.

———. 2005c. "La diversité culturelle: vers un traité?" In *Cultural Diversity in Question(s)*, edited by Marie-Françoise Labouz and Mark Wise, 277–302. Brussels: Bruylant.
———. 2008. "La Convention sur la protection et la promotion de la diversité des expressions culturelles et l'interface culture-commerce." In *Diversité culturelle, identités et mondialisation: De la ratification à la mise en œuvre de la convention sur la diversité culturelle*, edited by Guy Lachapelle, 77–89. Quebec City: Les Presses de l'Université Laval.
———. 2011a. "Free Trade and Cultural Policies: Evidence from Three US Agreements." *Journal of World Trade* 45(6): 1267–84.
———. 2011b. "The U.S. Policy on the Protection of Foreign Investment: From the NAFTA to the U.S.-Korea FTA." *The Journal of World Investment & Trade* 12(6): 807–25.
———. 2014. "Free Trade, Cultural Policies, and the Digital Revolution: Evidence from the U.S. FTAs with Australia and South Korea." *Asian Journal of WTO & International Health Law and Policy* 9(1): 257–86.
———. 2015. "The World Trade Organization and Preferential Trade Agreements: The Case of Cultural Goods and Services." In *Governance Facing Structural Changes: New Institutional Trajectories in the Internet Era*, edited by Michèle Rioux and Kim Fontaine-Skronski, 79–90. New York: Palgrave.
Gagné, Gilbert, René Côté, and Christian Deblock. 2004. *Les récents accords de libre-échange conclus par les États-Unis: une menace à la diversité culturelle*, Report submitted to the Agence intergouvernementale de la Francophonie, June 18. http://www.francophonie.org/IMG/pdf/accords_libre-echange_US_-_menace_pour_la_div_cult.pdf.
Gagné, Gilbert, and Jean-Frédéric Morin. 2006. "The Evolving American Policy on Investment Protection: Evidence from Recent FTAs and the 2004 Model BIT." *Journal of International Economic Law* 9(2): 357–82.
Gagné, Raymond. 1972. "French Canada: The Interrelationship Between Culture, Language and Personality." In *Canadian History since Confederation: Essays and Interpretations*, edited by Bruce Hodgins and Robert Page, 521–40. Georgetown, ON: Irwin-Dorsey.
Geist, Michael. 2016a. *The Trouble with the TPP, Day 18: Failure to Protect Canadian Cultural Policy*. January 27. http://www.michaelgeist.ca/2016/01/the-trouble-with-the-tpp-day-18-failure-to-protect-canadian-cultural-policy/.
———. 2016b. *The Trouble with the TPP, Day 26: Why it Limits Canadian Cultural Policies*. February 8. http://www.michaelgeist.ca/2016/02/the-trouble-with-the-tpp-day-26-why-it-limits-canadian-cultural-policies/.
———. 2016c. *The Trouble with the TPP, Day 29: Cultural Policy Innovation Uncertainty*. February 11. http://www.michaelgeist.ca/2016/02/the-trouble-with-the-tpp-day-29-cultural-policy-innovation-uncertainty/.
Germann, Christophe. 2008. *Diversité culturelle et libre-échange à la lumière du cinéma: Réflexions critiques sur le droit naissant de la diversité culturelle sous les angles du droit de l'UNESCO et de l'OMC, de la concurrence et de la propriété intellectuelle*. Basel: Helbing Linchtenhahn.
Goff, Patricia. 2007. *Limits to Liberalization: Local Culture in a Global Marketplace*. Ithaca, NY: Cornell University Press.
Graber, Christoph Beat. 2006. "The New UNESCO Convention on Cultural Diversity: A Counterbalance to the WTO?" *Journal of International Economic Law* 9(3): 553–74.
Graber, Christoph Beat, Michael Girsberger, and Mira Burri-Nenova, eds. 2004. *Free Trade versus Cultural Diversity: WTO Negotiations in the Field of Audiovisual Services*. Zurich: Schulthess.
Grant, Peter S. 2016. *Does the TPP Protect Canadian Cultural Policy?* February 7. http://www.cdc-ccd.org/Est-ce-que-le-PTP-protege-la?lang=en.
Grant, Peter S., and Chris Wood. 2004. *Blockbusters and Trade Wars: Popular Culture in a Globalized World*. Vancouver: Douglas & McIntyre.

Guerrieri, Paolo, P. Lelio Iapadre, and Georg Koopmann, eds. 2005. *Cultural Diversity and International Economic Integration: The Global Governance of the Audio-Visual Sector*. Cheltenham: Edward Elgar.

Guèvremont, Véronique. 2016. *TPP and Culture—A Trojan Horse?* April 7. https://www.cepci.hei.ulaval.ca/en/tpp-and-culture-trojan-horse.

Guèvremont, Véronique, Ivan Bernier, Mira Burri, Marie Cornu, Lilian Richieri Hanania, and Hélène Ruiz Fabri. 2013. *La mise en oeuvre de la Convention sur la protection et la promotion de la diversité des expressions culturelles à l'ère numérique: enjeux, actions prioritaires et recommandations*. Report submitted to the Intergovernmental Committee of the Convention on the Protection and Promotion of the Diversity of Cultural Expressions, Seventh Ordinary Session, Paris. December 10–13. http://www.diversite-culturelle.qc.ca/fileadmin/documents/pdf/Rapport_du_RIJDEC_-_Version_francaise_-_4_decembre_2013.pdf.

Hahn, Michael. 2006. "A Clash of Cultures? The UNESCO Diversity Convention and International Trade Law." *Journal of International Economic Law* 9(3): 515–52.

Hao, Ken. 2013. "E-Commerce and the Global Battle for Internet Economics." *Fortune*, June 21. http://fortune.com/2013/06/21/e-commerce-and-the-global-battle-for-internet-economics/.

Hart, Michael, with Bill Dymond and Colin Robertson. 1994. *Decision at Midnight: Inside the Canada-US Free-Trade Negotiations*. Vancouver: UBC Press.

Heydon, Kenneth, and Stephen Woolcock. 2009. *The Rise of Bilateralism: Comparing American, European and Asian Approaches to Preferential Trade Agreements*. Tokyo: United Nations University Press.

Hoekman, Bernard, ed. 2012. *The WTO and Trade in Services*. Cheltenham: Edward Elgar.

Hoekman, Bernard, and Aaditya Mattoo. 2012. *Liberalizing Trade in Services: Lessons from Regional and WTO Negotiations*. December 13. http://globalgovernanceprogramme.eui.eu/wp-content/uploads/2012/11/Hoekman-Mattoo-Services-Cooperation_International_Negotiation_final.pdf.

Horn, Henrik, Petros C. Mavroidis, and André Sapir. 2010. "Beyond the WTO: An Anatomy of the EU and US Preferential Trade Agreements." *The World Economy* 33(11): 1565–88.

Hufbauer, Gary C., J. Bradford Jensen, and Sherry Stephenson. 2012. *Framework for the International Services Agreement*. Policy Brief PB12–10, April. Washington, DC: Peterson Institute for International Economics. https://piie.com/sites/default/files/publications/pb/pb12–10.pdf.

Hufbauer, Gary, Eujin Jung, Sean Miner, Tyler Moran, and Jeffrey Schott. 2015. *Recovery Program for the WTO*. Report to the International Chamber of Commerce, Peterson Institute for International Economics, June. http://www.iccspain.org/wp-content/uploads/2015/06/4.45-ICC-WTO-Report-080415.pdf.

Ibbitson, John. 2014. *The End of Cultural Protectionism*. Blog Centre for International Governance Innovation, September 24. https://www.cigionline.org/blogs/john-ibbitsons-blog/end-of-cultural-protectionism.

Inside US Trade. 2012. "Kirk Flags Difficult Areas of TPP Talks; Says U.S. Committed to Conclusion," 30(49).

———. 2013a. "USTR Says it Will Seek To Cover New Services in Plurilateral Agreement," 31(3).

———. 2013b. "17 Senators Call For US-EU Negotiations to Cover All Sectors," 31(8).

International Trade Daily. 2006. "Audiovisual 'Friends' Moderate Demands in WTO Plurilateral Requests," March 8.

Kahler, Miles. 2000. "Conclusion: The Causes and Consequences of Legalization." *International Organization* 54(3): 661–83.

Kearns, Jason. 2009. "United States—Morocco Free Trade Agreement." In *Bilateral and Regional Trade Agreements: Case Studies*, edited by Simon Lester and Bryan Mercurio, 144–91. Cambridge: Cambridge University Press.

Kim, Soo Yeon. 2015. "Regionalisation in Search of Regionalism: Production Networks and Deep Integration Commitments in Asia's PTAs." In *Trade Cooperation: The Purpose, Design and Effects of Preferential Trade Agreements*, edited by Andreas Dür and Manfred Elsig, 134–63. Cambridge: Cambridge University Press.

Koh, Tommy, and Li Chin Chang, eds. 2004. *The United States—Singapore Free Trade Agreement: Highlights and Insights*. Singapore: World Scientific.

Kolliopoulos, Alexandros. 2005. "La Convention de l'UNESCO sur la protection et la promotion de la diversité des expressions culturelles." *Annuaire français de droit international* 51: 487–511.

Kono, Toshiyuki, and Steven Van Uystel, eds. 2012a. *The UNESCO Convention on the Diversity of Cultural Expressions: A Tale of Fragmentation of International Law*. Cambridge: Intersentia.

———. 2012b. "The Convention on the Diversity of Cultural Expressions: Beyond a Trade and Culture Convention." In *The UNESCO Convention on the Diversity of Cultural Expressions: A Tale of Fragmentation of International Law*, edited by Toshiyuki Kono and Steven Van Uystel, 3–42. Cambridge: Intersentia.

Krist, William. 2013. *Globalization and America's Trade Agreements*. Washington, DC: Woodrow Wilson Center Press/Johns Hopkins University Press.

Kuper, Adam. 1999. *Culture—The Anthropologists' Account*. Cambridge, MA: Harvard University Press.

Lachapelle, Guy, ed. 2008. *Diversité culturelle, identités et mondialisation: De la ratification à la mise en œuvre de la convention sur la diversité culturelle*. Quebec City: Les Presses de l'Université Laval.

Le Devoir. 2013. "À quoi sert l'Europe?" June 21. http://www.ledevoir.com/international/europe/381376/a-quoi-sert-l-europe.

Lee, Yong-Shik. 2015. "The United States—Korea Free Trade Agreement." In *Bilateral and Regional Trade Agreements: Case Studies, Second Edition*, edited by Simon Lester, Bryan Mercurio, and Lorand Bartels, 1–38. Cambridge: Cambridge University Press.

Leebron, David W. 2002. "Linkages." *American Journal of International Law* 96(1): 5–27.

Lemieux, Pierre, ed. 2006. *La diversité culturelle: Protection de la diversité des contenus culturels et des expressions artistiques*. Quebec City: Les Presses de l'Université Laval.

Lester, Simon, and Bryan Mercurio, eds. 2009. *Bilateral and Regional Trade Agreements: Case Studies*. Cambridge: Cambridge University Press.

Lester, Simon, Bryan Mercurio, and Lorand Bartels, eds. 2015. *Bilateral and Regional Trade Agreements: Case Studies, Second Edition*. Cambridge: Cambridge University Press.

Lim, Aik Hoe, and Bart De Meester, eds. 2014. *WTO Domestic Regulation and Services Trade: Putting Principles into Practice*. Cambridge: Cambridge University Press for the World Trade Organization.

Lim, C.L., Deborah K. Elms, and Patrick Low, eds. 2012. *The Trans-Pacific Partnership: A Quest for a Twenty-First-Century Trade Agreement*. Cambridge: Cambridge University Press.

Loisen, Jan, and Ferdi De Ville. 2011. "The EU-Korea Protocol on Cultural Cooperation: Toward Cultural Diversity or Cultural Deficit?" *International Journal of Communication* 5: 254–71.

Low, Patrick, and Aaditya Mattoo. 2000. "Is There a Better Way? Alternative Approaches to Liberalization Under GATS?" In *GATS 2000: New Directions in Services Trade Liberalization*, edited by Pierre Sauvé and Robert M. Stern, 449–72. Washington, DC: Brookings Institution Press and Center for Business and Government, Harvard University.

Maltais, Alexandre L. 2016. *The TPP and Cultural Diversity*. Canadian Centre for Policy Alternatives. March. https://www.policyalternatives.ca/sites/default/files/uploads/publications/National%20Office/2016/03/TPP_and_Cultural_Diversity.pdf.

Marchetti, Juan A., and Martin Roy, eds. 2008a. *Opening Markets for Trade in Services: Countries and Sectors in Bilateral and WTO Negotiations*. Cambridge: Cambridge University Press for the World Trade Organization.

———. 2008b. "Summary and Overview." In *Opening Markets for Trade in Services: Countries and Sectors in Bilateral and WTO Negotiations*, edited by Juan A. Marchetti and Martin Roy, 1–18. Cambridge: Cambridge University Press.

———. 2013. *The TISA Initiative: An Overview of Market Access Issues*. WTO Staff Working Paper ERSD-2013–11, November 27. https://www.wto.org/english/res_e/reser_e/ersd201311_e.pdf.

Marsh, James H., and Jocelyn Harvey. 2006. "Cultural Policy." *The Canadian Encyclopedia*. http://www.thecanadianencyclopedia.ca/en/article/cultural-policy/.

Mattoo, Aaditya, and Pierre Sauvé. 2011. "Services." In *Preferential Trade Agreement Policies for Development: A Handbook*, edited by Jean-Pierre Chauffour and Jean-Christophe Maur, 235–74. Washington, DC: World Bank.

McCarthy, Daniel R. 2015. *Power, Information Technology, and International Relations Theory: The Power and Politics of US Foreign Policy and the Internet*. Basingstoke: Palgrave Macmillan.

Meisel, John. 1986. "Escaping Extinction: Cultural Defence of an Undefended Border." In *Southern Exposure: Canadian Perspectives on the United States*, edited by David H. Flaherty and William R. McKercher, 152–68. Toronto: McGraw-Hill Ryerson.

Mitchell, Andrew D., and Tania Voon. 2009. "Australia—United States Free Trade Agreement." In *Bilateral and Regional Trade Agreements: Case Studies*, edited by Simon Lester and Bryan Mercurio, 6–43. Cambridge: Cambridge University Press.

Motion Picture Association of America (MPAA). 2001. "Impediments to Digital Trade." Testimony by Bonnie J.K. Richardson, Vice President, Trade & Federal Affairs, Motion Picture Association of America, before the House Commerce Committee Subcommittee on Commerce, Trade & Consumer Protection, May 22.

———. 2014. *Theatrical Market Statistics 2014*. Washington, DC: MPAA. http://www.mpaa.org/wp-content/uploads/2015/03/MPAA-Theatrical-Market-Statistics-2014.pdf.

———. 2015. *The Economic Contribution of the Motion Picture & Television Industry to the United States*. Factsheet, February. http://www.mpaa.org/wp-content/uploads/2015/02/MPAA-Industry-Economic-Contribution-Factsheet.pdf.

Mukherjee, Arpita. 2008. "Services Liberalization in PTAs and the WTO: The Experiences of India and Singapore." In *Opening Markets for Trade in Services: Countries and Sectors in Bilateral and WTO Negotiations*, edited by Juan A. Marchetti and Martin Roy, 600–32. Cambridge: Cambridge University Press.

Mulcahy, Kevin V. 2000. "Cultural Imperialism and Cultural Sovereignty: U.S.-Canadian Cultural Relations." *American Review of Canadian Studies* 30(2): 181–206.

Neuwirth, Rostam J. 2010. "The 'Culture and Trade Debate' Continues: The UNESCO Convention in Light of the WTO Reports in *China-Publications and Audiovisual Products*: Between Amnesia or *Déjà Vu*?" *Journal of World Trade* 44(6): 1333–56.

———. 2012. "The Convention on the Diversity of Cultural Expressions: A Critical Analysis of the Provisions." In *The UNESCO Convention on the Diversity of Cultural Expressions: A Tale of Fragmentation of International Law*, edited by Toshiyuki Kono and Steven Van Uystel, 45–69. Cambridge: Intersentia.

———. 2013. "The Future of the 'Culture and Trade Debate': A Legal Outlook." *Journal of World Trade* 47(2): 391–420.

Nye, Joseph S. 2004. *Soft Power: The Means to Success in World Politics*. New York: Public Affairs.

Nye, Joseph S., and William A. Owens. 1996. "America's Information Edge." *Foreign Affairs* 75(2): 20–36.

Obuljen, Nina, and Joost Smiers, eds. 2006. *UNESCO's Convention on the Protection and Promotion of the Diversity of Cultural Expressions: Making it Work*. Zagreb: Institute for International Relations.

Pang, Eul-Soo. 2011. *The U.S.—Singapore Free Trade Agreement: An American Perspective on Power, Trade, and Security in the Asia Pacific*. Singapore: Institute of Southeast Asian Studies.

Pauwels, Caroline, and Jan Loisen. 2003. "The WTO and the Audiovisual Sector: Economic Free Trade vs Cultural Horse Trading." *European Journal of Communication* 18(3): 291–314.

Pauwelyn, Joost, and Wolfgang Alschner. 2015. "Forget about the WTO: The Network of Relations between PTAs and Double PTAs." In *Trade Cooperation: The Purpose, Design and Effects of Preferential Trade Agreements*, edited by Andreas Dür and Manfred Elsig, 497–532. Cambridge: Cambridge University Press.

Pham, Nam D. 2010. *The Impact of Innovation and the Role of Intellectual Property Rights on U.S. Productivity, Competitiveness, Jobs, Wages, and Exports*. US Chamber of Commerce, Global Intellectual Property Center, April 24. http://www.theglobalipcenter.com/impact-innovation-and-role-ip-rights-us-productivity-competitiveness-jobs-wages-and-exports/.

Poirrier, Philippe, ed. 2011. *Pour une histoire des politiques culturelles dans le monde (1945–2011)*. Paris: La documentation Française.

Richieri Hanania, Lilian. 2009. *Diversité culturelle et droit international du commerce*. Paris: La documentation Française.

———. 2012. "Cultural Diversity and Regional Trade Agreements—The European Union Experience with Cultural Cooperation Frameworks." *Asian Journal of WTO & International Health Law and Policy* 7(2): 423–56.

———, ed. 2014. *Cultural Diversity in International Law: The Effectiveness of the UNESCO Convention on the Protection and Promotion of the Diversity of Cultural Expressions*. London and New York: Routledge.

Richieri Hanania, Lilian, and Hélène Ruiz Fabri. 2014. "Introduction." In *Cultural Diversity in International Law: The Effectiveness of the UNESCO Convention on the Protection and Promotion of the Diversity of Cultural Expressions*, edited by Lilian Richieri Hanania, 1–21. London and New York: Routledge.

Rioux, Michèle, Christian Deblock, Gilbert Gagné, Destiny Tchéhouali, Kim Fontaine-Skronski, and Antonios Vlassis. 2015. *Pour une culture en réseaux diversifiée: Appliquer la Convention sur la protection et la promotion de la diversité des expressions culturelles (CDEC) à l'ère du numérique*. Centre d'études sur l'intégration et la mondialisation, Université du Québec à Montréal, February. http://www.ieim.uqam.ca/IMG/pdf/rapportcdecvfinale.pdf.

Ritchie, Gordon. 1997. *Wresting With the Elephant: The Inside Story of the Canada-US Trade Wars*. Toronto: Macfarlane, Walter & Ross.

Robert, Maryse, and Sherry Stephenson. 2008. "Opening Services Markets at the Regional Level under the CAFTA-DR: The Cases of Costa Rica and the Dominican Republic." In *Opening Markets for Trade in Services: Countries and Sectors in Bilateral and WTO Negotiations*, edited by Juan A. Marchetti and Martin Roy, 537–72. Cambridge: Cambridge University Press.

Roy, Martin. 2005. "Audiovisual Services in the Doha Round: 'Dialogue de Sourds, The Sequel'?" *The Journal of World Investment & Trade* 6(6): 923–52.

———. 2008. "Beyond the Main Screen: Audiovisual Services in PTAs." In *Opening Markets for Trade in Services: Countries and Sectors in Bilateral and WTO Negotiations*, edited by Juan A. Marchetti and Martin Roy, 340–77. Cambridge: Cambridge University Press.

———. 2011. *Services Commitments in Preferential Trade Agreements: An Expanded Dataset*, WTO Staff Working Paper ERSD-2011–18, November 9. https://www.wto.org/english/res_e/reser_e/ersd201118_e.pdf.

Roy, Martin, Juan Marchetti, and Hoe Lim. 2007. "Services Liberalization in the New Generation of Preferential Trade Agreements: How Much Further than the GATS?" *World Trade Review* 6(2): 1455–93.

Ruggie, John Gerard. 1982. "International Regimes, Transactions, and Change: Embedded Liberalism in the Postwar Economic Order." *International Organization* 36(2): 379–415.

———. 2008. "Taking Embedded Liberalism Global: The Corporate Connection." In *Embedding Global Markets: An Enduring Challenge*, edited by John Gerard Ruggie, 231–54. Aldershot,UK and Burlington, VT: Ashgate.

Ruiz Fabri, Hélène. 2014. "Foreword." In *Cultural Diversity in International Law: The Effectiveness of the UNESCO Convention on the Protection and Promotion of the Diversity of Cultural Expressions*, edited by Lilian Richieri Hanania, xvi–xvii. London and New York: Routledge.

Sáez, Sebastián. 2008. "The Chilean Experience in Services Negotiations." In *Opening Markets for Trade in Services: Countries and Sectors in Bilateral and WTO Negotiations*, edited by Juan A. Marchetti and Martin Roy, 667–705. Cambridge: Cambridge University Press.

Salas, Mauricio. 2009. "Central American—Dominican Republic—United States Free Trade Agreement." In *Bilateral and Regional Trade Agreements: Case Studies*, edited by Simon Lester and Bryan Mercurio, 44–58. Cambridge: Cambridge University Press.

Sauvé, Pierre. 2010. "Going Preferential in Services Trade: Lessons from Practice." Presentation at the Conference *Regionalism in an Integrating World Economy*, Utrecht University School of Economics, May 7. http://www.nccr-trade.org/fileadmin/user_upload/nccr-trade.ch/wp2/publications/Sauve_PTAs_Services_Utrecht_7May_REV%20[Read-Only].pdf.

———. 2013. *A Plurilateral Agenda for Services? Assessing the Case for a Trade in Services Agreement (TISA)*, NCCR Trade Regulation, Working Paper No. 2013/29, May. http://www.wti.org/fileadmin/user_upload/nccr-trade.ch/wp2/publications/TISA_P_Sauve.pdf.

Sauvé, Pierre, and Karsten Steinfatt. 2000. "Towards Multilateral Rules on Trade and Culture: Protective Regulation of Efficient Protection?" In *Achieving Better Regulations of Services*, 323–46. Conference Proceedings, Australian National University, Canberra, June 26–27.

Sauvé, Pierre, and Anirudh Shingal. 2011. "Reflections on the Preferential Liberalization of Services Trade." *Journal of World Trade* 45(5): 953–63.

———, eds. 2014. *The Preferential Liberalization of Trade in Services: Comparative Regionalism*. Cheltenham: Edward Elgar.

Schiller, Herbert I. 2000. *Living in the Number One Country: Reflections from a Critique of American Empire*. New York and London: Seven Stories Press.

Schott, Jeffrey J., ed. 2004. *Free Trade Agreements: US Strategies and Priorities*. Washington, DC: Institute for International Economics.

Schott, Jeffrey, Barbara Kotschwar, and Julia Muir. 2013. *Understanding the Trans-Pacific Partnership*. Washington, DC: Peterson Institute for International Economics.

Shi, Jingxia. 2013. *Free Trade and Cultural Diversity in International Law*. Oxford and Portland, OR: Hart.

Singh, J.P. 2008a. *Negotiation and the Global Information Economy*. Cambridge: Cambridge University Press.

———. 2008b. "GATS Plus or Minus? Services Commitments in Comparative Contexts for Colombia and Uruguay." In *Opening Markets for Trade in Services: Countries and Sectors in Bilateral and WTO Negotiations*, edited by Juan A. Marchetti and Martin Roy, 505–36. Cambridge: Cambridge University Press.

———. 2011a. *United Nations Educational, Scientific and Cultural Organization (UNESCO): Creating Norms for a Complex World*. London and New York: Routledge.

———. 2011b. *Globalized Arts: The Entertainment Economy and Cultural Identity*. New York: Columbia University Press.

Siwek, Stephen E. 2014. *Copyright Industries in the US Economy: The 2014 Report*. International Intellectual Property Alliance, December 17. http://www.iipa.com/pdf/2014CpyrtRptFull.PDF.

The Hankyoreh. 2006. "US Makes Proposal on FTA Screen Quota Issue: Sources," October 24. http://english.hani.co.kr/arti/english_edition/e_business/166852.html.
Thiec, Yvon. 2014. "From a Moratorium in the Conflict between Trade and Culture to the Creation of a Digital Deal for Cultural Diversity." In *Cultural Diversity in International Law: The Effectiveness of the UNESCO Convention on the Protection and Promotion of the Diversity of Cultural Expressions*, edited by Lilian Richieri Hanania, 95–106. London and New York: Routledge.
Thompson, John Herd. 1996. "Canada's Quest for Cultural Sovereignty: Protection, Promotion, and Popular Culture." In *NAFTA in Transition*, edited by Stephen J. Randall and Herman W. Konrad, 393–410. Calgary: University of Calgary Press.
Throsby, David. 1995. "Culture, Economics, and Sustainability." *Journal of Cultural Economics* 19(3): 199–206.
———. 1999. "Cultural Capital." *Journal of Cultural Economics* 23(1–2): 3–12.
Vallerand, Charles. 2016. *The Trouble with the TPP—Michael Geist. Analysis from Charles Vallerand*. February 8. http://www.cdc-ccd.org/Le-probleme-avec-le-PTP-Michael?lang=en.
Vlassis, Antonios. 2011. "La mise en œuvre de la Convention sur la diversité des expressions culturelles: Portée et enjeux de l'interface entre le commerce et la culture." *Études internationales* 42(4): 493–510.
———. 2013. "L'UNESCO face à l'enjeu « commerce-culture »: Quelle action politique pour une organisation internationale?" *Politique et Sociétés* 32(3): 81–101.
———. 2015. *Gouvernance mondiale et culture: De l'exception à la diversité*. Liège: Presses Universitaires de Liège.
Vlassis, Antonios, and Lilian Richieri Hanania. 2014. "Effects of the CDCE on Trade Negotiations." In *Cultural Diversity in International Law: The Effectiveness of the UNESCO Convention on the Protection and Promotion of the Diversity of Cultural Expressions*, edited by Lilian Richieri Hanania, 25–39. London and New York: Routledge.
Voon, Tania. 2006. "UNESCO and the WTO: A Clash of Cultures?" *International & Comparative Law Quarterly* 55(3): 635–52.
———. 2007. *Cultural Products and the World Trade Organization*. Cambridge: Cambridge University Press.
———, ed. 2013. *Trade Liberalisation and International Co-operation: A Legal Analysis of the Trans-Pacific Partnership Agreement*. Cheltenham: Edward Elgar.
Watson, K. William. 2015. "United States—Colombia Trade Promotion Agreement." In *Bilateral and Regional Trade Agreements: Case Studies, Second Edition*, edited by Simon Lester, Bryan Mercurio, and Lorand Bartels, 60–76. Cambridge: Cambridge University Press.
WikiLeaks. 2013. *TPP Salt Lake Positions*, Second Release of Secret Trans-Pacific Partnership Agreement Documents, December 9. https://wikileaks.org/IMG/pdf/tpp-salt-lake-positions.pdf.
Williams, Raymond. 1983. *Keywords: A Vocabulary of Culture and Society*. London: Fontana.
Wouters, Jan, and Bart De Meester. 2008. "The UNESCO Convention on Cultural Diversity and WTO Law: A Case Study in Fragmentation of International Law." *Journal of World Trade* 42(1): 205–40.
Wunsch-Vincent, Sacha. 2003. "The Digital Trade Agenda of the U.S.: Parallel Tracks of Bilateral, Regional and Multilateral Liberalization." *Aussenwirtschaft* 58: 7–46.
———. 2006. *The WTO, the Internet and Trade in Digital Products: EC-US Perspectives*. Oxford and Portland, OR: Hart.
Yang, Josh. 2012. *U.S. E-Commerce Landscape & Trends*. Harvard Business School, February. http://www.slideshare.net/joshyang/ecommerce-landscape-2012.

OFFICIAL DOCUMENTS

United States

Free Trade Agreements

United States—Israel Free Trade Agreement (US-Israel FTA), signed April 22, 1985, effective September 1, 1985. http://www.sice.oas.org/Trade/US-Israel/index_e.asp#PDF.

United States—Canada Free Trade Agreement (US-Canada FTA), signed January 2, 1988, effective January 1, 1989. http://www.international.gc.ca/trade-agreements-accords-commerciaux/assets/pdfs/cusfta-e.pdf.

North American Free Trade Agreement (NAFTA), signed December 17, 1992, effective January 1, 1994. https://www.nafta-sec-alena.org/Home/Legal-Texts/North-American-Free-Trade-Agreement.

United States—Jordan Free Trade Agreement (US-Jordan FTA), signed October 24, 2000, effective December 17, 2001. https://ustr.gov/trade-agreements/free-trade-agreements/jordan-fta/final-text.

United States—Singapore Free Trade Agreement (US-Singapore FTA), signed May 6, 2003, effective January 1, 2004. https://ustr.gov/trade-agreements/free-trade-agreements/singapore-fta/final-text.

United States—Chile Free Trade Agreement (US-Chile FTA), signed June 6, 2003, effective January 1, 2004. https://ustr.gov/trade-agreements/free-trade-agreements/chile-fta/final-text.

United States—Australia Free Trade Agreement (US-Australia FTA), signed May 18, 2004, effective January 1, 2005. https://ustr.gov/trade-agreements/free-trade-agreements/australian-fta/final-text.

Dominican Republic—Central America—United States Free Trade Agreement (CAFTA-DR), signed August 5, 2004, effective March 1, 2006. https://ustr.gov/trade-agreements/free-trade-agreements/cafta-dr-dominican-republic-central-america-fta/final-text.

United States—Morocco Free Trade Agreement (US-Morocco FTA), signed June 15, 2004, effective January 1, 2006. https://ustr.gov/trade-agreements/free-trade-agreements/morocco-fta/final-text.

United States—Bahrain Free Trade Agreement (US-Bahrain FTA), signed September 14, 2004, effective August 1, 2006. https://ustr.gov/trade-agreements/free-trade-agreements/bahrain-fta/final-text.

United States—Oman Free Trade Agreement (US-Oman FTA), signed January 19, 2006, effective January 1, 2009. https://ustr.gov/trade-agreements/free-trade-agreements/oman-fta/final-text.

United States—Peru Trade Promotion Agreement (US-Peru FTA), signed April 12, 2006, effective February 1, 2009. https://ustr.gov/trade-agreements/free-trade-agreements/peru-tpa/final-text.

United States—Colombia Trade Promotion Agreement (US-Colombia FTA), signed November 22, 2006, effective May 15, 2012. https://ustr.gov/trade-agreements/free-trade-agreements/colombia-fta/final-text.

United States—Panama Trade Promotion Agreement (US-Panama FTA), signed June 28, 2007, effective October 31, 2012. https://ustr.gov/trade-agreements/free-trade-agreements/panama-tpa/final-text.

United States—Korea Free Trade Agreement (US-Korea FTA), signed June 30, 2007, effective March 15, 2012. https://ustr.gov/trade-agreements/free-trade-agreements/korus-fta/final-text.

Trans-Pacific Partnership (TPP), signed February 4, 2016. https://ustr.gov/trade-agreements/free-trade-agreements/trans-pacific-partnership/tpp-full-text.

Trade Advisory Committee Reports

Industry Sector Advisory Committee on Services for Trade Policy Matters (ISAC-13), *Advisory Committee Report to the President, the Congress and the United States Trade Representative on the U.S.-Singapore Free Trade Agreement* (US-Singapore FTA), February 28, 2003. https://ustr.gov/archive/assets/Trade_Agreements/Bilateral/Singapore_FTA/Reports/asset_upload_file184_3249.pdf.

Industry Sector Advisory Committee on Services for Trade Policy Matters (ISAC-13), *Advisory Committee Report to the President, the Congress and the United States Trade Representative on the U.S.-Chile Free Trade Agreement* (US-Chile FTA), February 28, 2003. https://ustr.gov/archive/assets/Trade_Agreements/Bilateral/Chile_FTA/Reports/asset_upload_file605_4951.pdf.

Industry Functional Advisory Committee on Electronic Commerce (IFAC-4), *Industry Functional Advisory Committee Report to the President, the Congress and the United States Trade Representative on the U.S.-Australia Free Trade Agreement* (US-Australia FTA), March 8, 2004. https://ustr.gov/archive/assets/Trade_Agreements/Bilateral/Australia_FTA/Reports/asset_upload_file705_3399.pdf.

Industry Functional Advisory Committee on Intellectual Property Rights for Trade Policy Matters (IFAC-3), *Advisory Committee Report to the President, the Congress and the United States Trade Representative on the U.S.-Australia Free Trade Agreement* (US-Australia FTA), March 12, 2004. https://ustr.gov/archive/assets/Trade_Agreements/Bilateral/Australia_FTA/Reports/asset_upload_file813_3398.pdf.

Industry Sector Advisory Committee on Services for Trade Policy Matters (ISAC-13), *Report to the President, the Congress and the United States Trade Representative on the U.S.-Australia Free Trade Agreement* (US-Australia FTA), March 12, 2004. https://ustr.gov/archive/assets/Trade_Agreements/Bilateral/Australia_FTA/Reports/asset_upload_file118_3412.pdf.

Industry Sector Advisory Committee on Services for Trade Policy Matters (ISAC-13), *Report to the President, the Congress and the United States Trade Representative on the U.S.-Central America Free Trade Agreement* (CAFTA), March 17, 2004.

Industry Sector Advisory Committee on Services for Trade Policy Matters (ISAC-13), *Report to the President, the Congress and the United States Trade Representative on the U.S.-Morocco Free Trade Agreement* (US-Morocco FTA), April 6, 2004. https://ustr.gov/archive/assets/Trade_Agreements/Bilateral/Morocco_FTA/Reports/asset_upload_file426_3152.pdf.

Industry Sector Advisory Committee on Services for Trade Policy Matters (ISAC-13), *Report to the President, the Congress and the United States Trade Representative on the U.S.-Dominican Republic Free Trade Agreement* (DRFTA), April 22, 2004. https://ustr.gov/archive/assets/Trade_Agreements/Regional/CAFTA/DR_Reports/asset_upload_file418_3346.pdf.

Industry Trade Advisory Committee on Services and Finance Industries (ITAC-10), *Report to the President, the Congress and the United States Trade Representative on the U.S.-Bahrain Free Trade Agreement* (US-Bahrain FTA), July 14, 2004. https://ustr.gov/archive/assets/Trade_Agreements/Bilateral/Bahrain_FTA/Reports/asset_upload_file376_5523.pdf.

Industry Trade Advisory Committee on Services and Finance Industries (ITAC-10), *Report to the President, the Congress and the United States Trade Representative on the U.S.-Oman Free Trade Agreement* (US-Oman FTA), November 15, 2005. https://ustr.gov/archive/assets/Trade_Agreements/Bilateral/Oman_FTA/Reports/asset_upload_file346_8397.pdf.

Industry Trade Advisory Committee on Services and Finance Industries (ITAC-10), *Report to the President, the Congress and the United States Trade Representative on the U.S.-Peru Free Trade Agreement* (US-Peru FTA), February 1, 2006. https://ustr.gov/archive/assets/Trade_Agreements/Bilateral/Peru_TPA/Reports/asset_upload_file209_8983.pdf.

Industry Trade Advisory Committee on Services and Finance Industries (ITAC-10), *Advisory Committee Report to the President, the Congress and the United States Trade Representative on the U.S.-Colombia TPA Agreement* (US-Colombia FTA), September 20, 2006. https://ustr.gov/archive/assets/Trade_Agreements/Bilateral/Colombia_FTA/Reports/asset_upload_file823_9830.pdf.

Industry Trade Advisory Committee for Information and Communications Technologies, Services and Electronic Commerce (ITAC-8), *Report to the President, the Congress and the United States Trade Representative on the U.S.-Panama Trade Promotion Agreement* (US-Panama FTA), April 25, 2007. https://ustr.gov/archive/assets/Trade_Agreements/Bilateral/Panama_FTA/Reports/asset_upload_file118_11244.pdf.

Industry Trade Advisory Committee on Services and Finance Industries (ITAC-10), *Advisory Committee Report to the President, the Congress and the United States Trade Representative on the U.S.-Panama Trade Promotion Agreement* (US-Panama FTA), April 25, 2007. https://ustr.gov/archive/assets/Trade_Agreements/Bilateral/Panama_FTA/Reports/asset_upload_file130_11239.pdf.

Industry Trade Advisory Committee for Information and Communications Technologies, Services and Electronic Commerce (ITAC-8), *Report to the President, the Congress and the United States Trade Representative on the Korea-U.S. Free Trade Agreement* (US-Korea FTA), April 27, 2007. https://ustr.gov/sites/default/files/uploads/Countries%20Regions/africa/agreements/korus/ITAC%208%20-%20Technologies,%20Services%20&%20Electronic%20Commerce.pdf.

Industry Trade Advisory Committee on Services and Finance Industries (ITAC-10), *Advisory Committee Report to the President, the Congress and the United States Trade Representative on the U.S.-Korea FTA Agreement* (US-Korea FTA), April 25, 2007. https://ustr.gov/sites/default/files/uploads/Countries%20Regions/africa/agreements/korus/ITAC%2010%20-%20Services%20and%20Finance%20Industries.pdf.

Industry Trade Advisory Committee for Information and Communications Technologies, Services and Electronic Commerce (ITAC-8), *Advisory Committee Report to the President, the Congress and the United States Trade Representative on the Trans-Pacific Partnership Trade Agreement* (TPP), December 3, 2015. https://ustr.gov/sites/default/files/ITAC-8-Information-and-Communication-Technologies-Services-and-Electronic-Commerce.pdf.

Industry Trade Advisory Committee on Intellectual Property Rights (ITAC-15), *Advisory Committee Report to the President, the Congress and the U.S. Trade Representative on the Trans-Pacific Partnership Trade Agreement* (TPP), December 3, 2015. https://ustr.gov/sites/default/files/ITAC-15-Intellectual-Property.pdf.

Industry Trade Advisory Committee on Services and Finance Industries (ITAC-10), *Advisory Committee Report to the President, the Congress and the United States Trade Representative on the Trans-Pacific Partnership Trade Agreement* (TPP), December 3, 2015. https://ustr.gov/sites/default/files/ITAC-10-Services-and-Finance-Industries.pdf.

Other Documents

Bipartisan Trade Promotion Authority Act of 2002, Public Law 107–210, August 6, 2002.

Bipartisan Congressional Trade Priorities and Accountability Act of 2015, Public Law, June 29, 2015.

(US) Mission—Geneva (2002), *Press Release*, July.

United States, Department of Commerce, Economics & Statistics Administration and United States Patent and Trademark Office. 2012. *Intellectual Property and the U.S. Economy: Industries in Focus*. March. http://www.uspto.gov/news/publications/IP_Report_March_2012.pdf.

United States, Intellectual Property Enforcement Coordinator. 2013. *2013 Joint Strategic Plan on Intellectual Property Enforcement*. June. http://www.whitehouse.gov/sites/default/files/omb/IPEC/2013-us-ipec-joint-strategic-plan.pdf.

United States International Trade Commission (USITC). 2009. "US Trade Policy since 1934." In *The Economic Effects of Significant U.S. Import Restraints: Sixth Update 2009*, Chapter 3, 59–123. Investigation No. 332–325, USITC Publication 4094, September. https://www.usitc.gov/publications/332/us_trade_policy_since1934_ir6_pub4094.pdf.

———. 2013. *Digital Trade in the U.S. and Global Economies, Part 1*, Investigation No. 332–531, USITC Publication 4415, July. http://www.usitc.gov/publications/332/pub4415.pdf.

———. 2014. *Digital Trade in the U.S. and Global Economies, Part 2*, Investigation No. 332–540, USITC Publication 4485, August. http://www.usitc.gov/publications/332/pub4485.pdf.

———. 2015. *Recent Trends in U.S. Services Trade: 2015 Annual Report*, Publication Number: 4526, Investigation Number: 332–345. Washington, DC: USITC, May. http://www.usitc.gov/publications/332/pub4526.pdf.

United States, Office of the United States Trade Representative. 2015. *2015 Special 301 Report*. April. https://ustr.gov/sites/default/files/2015-Special-301-Report-FINAL.pdf.

———. 2016a. *Trans-Pacific Partnership, Intellectual Property, Chapter Summary*. https://ustr.gov/sites/default/files/TPP-Chapter-Summary-Intellectual-Property.pdf.

———. 2016b. *U.S. Press Statement at the Close of the T-TIP Round in Brussels*, February 26. https://ustr.gov/about-us/policy-offices/press-office/speechestranscripts/2016/February/US-Press-Statement-TTIP-Round-Brussels.

Canada

Canada—Chile Free Trade Agreement, signed December 5, 1996, effective July 5, 1997. http://www.international.gc.ca/trade-agreements-accords-commerciaux/agr-acc/chile-chili/menu.aspx?lang=en.

Canada, Department of Foreign Affairs, Trade and Development. 2016. "Trade, Opening New Markets, Trade Topics, Culture." http://www.international.gc.ca/trade-agreements-accords-commerciaux/topics-domaines/ip-pi/culture.aspx?lang=eng.

Cultural Industries Sectoral Advisory Group on International Trade (SAGIT). 1999. *Canadian Culture in a Global World: New Strategies for Culture and Trade*. February. http://www.international.gc.ca/trade-agreements-accords-commerciaux/topics-domaines/ip-pi/canculture.aspx?lang=en.

European Union

EU, Council. 2013a. *Draft Directives for the Negotiation of a Plurilateral Agreement on Trade in Services*. Doc. 6891/13 ADD 1, March 8. http://data.consilium.europa.eu/doc/document/ST-6891–2013-ADD-1-DCL-1/en/pdf.

———. 2013b. *Directives for the Negotiation on the Transatlantic Trade and Investment Partnership between the European Union and the United States of America*. Doc. 11103/13, June 17. http://data.consilium.europa.eu/doc/document/ST-11103–2013-DCL-1/en/pdf.

EU. 2013c. *Trade in Services Agreement: Schedule of Specific Commitments & List of MFN Exemptions*. November. http://trade.ec.europa.eu/doclib/docs/2014/july/tradoc_152689.pdf.

———. 2015a. *Transatlantic Trade and Investment Partnership: Trade in Services, Investment and E-Commerce*. European Union's proposal, July. http://trade.ec.europa.eu/doclib/docs/2015/july/tradoc_153669.pdf.

———. 2015b. *Transatlantic Trade and Investment Partnership: Services and Investment Offer of the European Union*. July. http://trade.ec.europa.eu/doclib/docs/2015/july/tradoc_153670.pdf.

EU, Commission. 2016a. *In Focus: Trade in Services Agreement (TiSA)*. http://ec.europa.eu/trade/policy/in-focus/tisa/.

———. 2016b. *The Transatlantic Trade and Investment Partnership (TTIP)—State of Play*, April 27. http://trade.ec.europa.eu/doclib/docs/2016/april/tradoc_154477.pdf.

United Nations

UN, General Assembly. 2006. *Fragmentation of International Law: Difficulties Arising from the Diversification and Expansion of International Law*, Report of the Study Group of the International Law Commission, finalized by Martti Koskenniemi, Doc. A/CN.4/L.682, April 13. http://legal.un.org/ilc/documentation/english/a_cn4_l682.pdf.

United Nations Educational, Scientific and Cultural Organization

Martin, Robert S. 2005. *Final Statement of the United States Delegation*, Third Session of the Intergovernmental Meeting of Experts. Paris: UNESCO, June 3. http://www.coalitionsuisse.ch/docs/decl_us050603.pdf.

UNESCO. 1995. *Our Creative Diversity: Report of the World Commission on Culture and Development*. Paris: UNESCO. http://unesdoc.unesco.org/images/0010/001016/101651e.pdf.

———. 2005a. *Convention on the Protection and Promotion of the Diversity of Cultural Expressions*, adopted October 20, 2005, effective March 18, 2007. https://en.unesco.org/creativity/convention/what-is/convention-text.

———. 2005b. *Records of the General Conference, 33rd Session, 3–21 October 2005, Volume 1: Resolutions*. http://unesdoc.unesco.org/images/0014/001428/142825E.pdf.

General Agreement on Tariffs and Trade

General Agreement on Tariffs and Trade (GATT), adopted October 20, 1947, effective January 1, 1948. https://www.wto.org/english/docs_e/legal_e/gatt47_e.pdf.

GATT. 1990a. *Draft Multilateral Framework for Trade in Services: Introductory Note by the Chairman of the GNS Negotiations on a Framework Agreement*. Doc. MTN.GNS/35, July 23. https://docs.wto.org/gattdocs/q/.%5CUR%5CGNS%5C35.PDF.

———. 1990b. *Matters Relating to Trade in Audiovisual Services, Note by the Secretariat*. Doc. MTN.GNS/AUD/W/1. October 4. https://www.wto.org/gatt_docs/English/SULPDF/92110148.pdf.

General Agreement on Trade in Services (GATS), adopted April 15, 1994, effective January 1, 1995. https://www.wto.org/english/docs_e/legal_e/26-gats.pdf.

World Trade Organization

WTO, Council for Trade in Services. 1998a. *Audiovisual Services, Background Note by the Secretariat*. Doc. S/C/W/40, June 15.

———. 1998b. *Communication from the United States, Audiovisual Services*, Doc. S/C/W/78, December 8.

———, Special Session. 2000. *Communication from the United States, Audiovisual and Related Services*. Doc. S/CSS/W/21, December 18.

———. 2005. *Communication from Hong Kong China, Japan, Mexico, the Separate Customs Territory of Taiwan, Penghu, Kinmen and Matsu, and United States: Joint Statement on the Negotiations on Audiovisual Services*. Doc. TN/S/W/49, June 30.

———. 2010. *Audiovisual Services: Background Note by the Secretariat*. Doc. S/C/W/310, January 12.

WTO. 2011. *World Trade Report 2011. The WTO and Preferential Trade Agreements: From Co-existence to Coherence*. Geneva: WTO. http://www.wto.org/english/res_e/booksp_e/anrep_e/world_trade_report11_e.pdf.

———. 2015. *Annual Report 2015*. Geneva: WTO. https://www.wto.org/english/res_e/booksp_e/anrep_e/anrep15_e.pdf.

Index

About the Author

Gilbert Gagné is professor of international relations in the Department of Politics and International Studies at Bishop's University. He holds a Bachelor's and a Master's Degree in Political Science from the University of Ottawa, and a Doctorate in International Relations from the University of Oxford. His research interests mainly pertain to international economic regimes, subsidies and trade dispute settlement, the protection of foreign investment and investor-state arbitration, and the trade and culture debate. Much of his research is at the intersection of international trade agreements and states' regulatory autonomy, with a particular focus on cultural policies.